The World and His Wife

A True Story Told by Two Unreliable Narrators

Written by

Stephen Wyatt

OAK TREE BOOKS

Published in 2023 by
Oak Tree Books
oaktreebooks.uk

an imprint of
Andrews UK Limited
andrewsuk.com

Contents

Prologue: June 1858

From the diary of Rosina, Lady Lytton

So, Sir Liar, you've finally succeeded. Out of that festering home of dark secrets, hidden vices and execrable novels which is your brain, you have devised a plot to deceive me and lock me away where I can no longer speak the truth about your vile nature. No doubt you think you've silenced me forever, but you are wrong. One day the truth about you will emerge for all your clever scheming and your comrades in vice in high places. Oh yes, I don't doubt that and neither should you, Sir Elegant Tight-fisted Bullying Liar.

What a relief to pen those words. But, in the meantime, I struggle to remain sane. I have always been contemptuous of the sad souls who chronicle their every moment in some dreary leather-bound volume as if it meant anything to anyone except them. I have been of the opinion that only madmen – and, of course, madwomen – talk to themselves because they have no one else to talk to. It gives some significance to the pathetic insignificance of all that they do and dream of doing. But it seems Rosina must change her views if she is to survive.

No, I will not be cowed. I must record the truth and if the truth is known then surely my release ought – must – follow.

And yet, to begin at the very beginning of it all just now would unhinge me entirely. That task is for later. So many disappointed hopes, so many deceptions, so many betrayals between first love and the death of love. Years of persecution and intimidation. My children torn from me, my daughter dead, my friends bribed or else too frightened to assert the truth of my case. Too much pain, too much confusion.

So let me begin with the election in Hertford, which took place on June the eighth. Less than two weeks ago and already that seems an age. I can understand how the confined lose all sense of time.

I left Taunton the day before with my Taunton landlady, Mrs. Clarke, a good soul, of limited understanding, but loyal and staunch in my defence. The journey was terrific because I would not go by London, the direct way, for fear of meeting Sir Liar or some of his set of sycophants bound for the same place.

So we went by Oxford, on which line all the trains were twenty minutes behind their time (so much for Bradshaw), with the result we reached Bedford at eleven at night. The last train to Hertford had been gone a quarter of an hour, so we had to post the remaining thirty-five miles. It was five in the morning before we got to Hertford and knocked the people up at the Dimsdale Arms. However, by seven, all my placards, which I had brought ready printed, inviting the electors and yeomen to meet me at noon, not indeed for their votes, but for their interest, were pasted all over the town and produced the greatest excitement. Unfortunately, the nomination was to take place at eleven, and just as we were setting off for the hustings, Mrs. Clarke, God bless her, discovered that she had blue ribbons in her bonnet, vowed she would not wear his colours and went to buy another. This lost hour was fatal to us, for when we arrived on the ground, Sir Liar had made his speech and been nominated.

Nevertheless, the moment I drove into the field the mob began to cheer. Even Sir Liar's two powdered flunkeys and both his postillions, who took off their hats and caps, joined in. I instantly alighted and walked calmly and deliberately to the hustings, gently putting the crowd aside with my fan and saying, 'My good people, make way for your member's wife.' They then began to cheer again and cry, 'Silence for Lady Lytton!' Sir Liar's head fell literally as if he had been shot. Mrs. Clarke said she never saw such a thing in her life. He staggered and seemed not to have strength to move. I then ascended the platform and spoke to him in a loud, calm and stern voice: 'Sir Edward George Earle Bulwer-Lytton, as I am not in the habit of stabbing in the back, it is to you, in the first instance that I address myself. In the step your cruelty and your meanness have driven me into taking this day, I wish you to hear every word I have to say; refute them if you can; deny them if you dare'. Then, turning to the crowd, I said, 'Men of Herts! If you have the hearts of men, hear me!'

'We will. God bless you! Speak out.'

Here, Sir Liar, with his hands before his face, made a rush from the hustings. The mob began to hiss and cry, 'Ah, coward! He's guilty. He dare not face her,' which he must have had the pleasure of hearing, for instead of attending the public breakfast in the Corn Exchange, he bolted from the town and left them all in the lurch.

The stage was mine. I apologised first by saying that unaccustomed as I really was to public speaking, I was unable to favour them with any of those oratorical gymnastics they were accustomed to receiving from the right honourable baronet, the new Colonial Secretary. The peals of laughter confirmed my opinion of the crowd's basic decency and perspicacity.

I then put on a graver face and warned the people that one of two things would happen: either that not one syllable of the scene that had just taken place, or of what I was about to say, would be reported in the *Times* and the rest of the press, or that the most barefaced falsehoods would be propagated as to my having rushed on to the ground like a mad woman. Cries of 'Only let them try!' I thanked them but said I did rather think the silent suppression system would be adopted on this occasion. Further cries to the effect that he couldn't silence the whole county and the next time he wanted their votes, he may seek them in a horse-pond. His colours were accordingly pulled from the hustings and trampled under foot.

I then gave a brief résumé of his infamies to me, assuring them it was a farce to look for political probity in England so long as private vice was made the high-road to public honours. I continued that, though the gentlemen in England have a perfect right to brutalise their wives as they please, our elastic conventionalities have not yet quite extended that autocratic power to the usage of their daughters. I then described the manner in which my poor child's young heart had been broken, how she had been slaved to death over her quack of a father's German translations (he not knowing one word of German!), her scanty wardrobe and the wretched house in which she died. The poor boors gave me their tears, which I was more grateful to them for than all their cheers.

But then I turned more directly to my own situation. I told them that I was tired of having the most insulting calumnies publicly disseminated of me by Sir Edward and his emissaries, the latest of which, I understood, was that I was mad. At this the voices of protest became tumultuous. It was then that I revealed the sad truth of my economic circumstances as the wife, still the wife, of a man of vast financial resources. I told them that I won't be a peeress upon an income of £180 a year, which is what Sir Sodomitic Liar's original swindle of £400 has dwindled down to. And, as it appeared that the right honourable baronet who had just been re-elected could not afford the legal encumbrance of a wife, then I supposed I would have to go on living, as I had been living for the last eighteen months, on charity. There were cries of 'Shame!' and voices calling Sir Liar a blackguard, a term which I have to confess was very gratifying to me as it coincided entirely with my own view of Lord Little Truth.

I then moved to my peroration. 'My good people,' I said, 'Do not suppose that I have lightly or without first trying everything else made a show of myself here today. Friends and foes alike have for the last year warned Sir Edward Bulwer-Lytton not to drive me to this public exposure, but he preferred parting with his character rather than his money. Well, everyone knows that he has plenty of money and scarcely a shred of character, so that it was all the more generous of him to part today unreservedly with something of which he has so small a supply.'

The cheering became uproarious as the crowd followed me to the Mayor's house. Mrs. Woodhouse, the Mayor's wife, told me, as I drove up, that a poor old woman, a tenant of Sir Liar's who had been a tenant of his father's and his grandfather's, and who had brought Mrs. Woodhouse some eggs and chickens in from Knebworth, fell upon her knees when she heard it was I and said, 'Now I don't care how soon I die, for Heaven has sent her here today to unmask that villain, who so cruelly broke the heart of his poor young daughter, and has behaved so inhumanly to her, poor lady.'

All the way to the station the crowd was dense, every window full, and at the tops of the houses people were waving their caps and handkerchiefs and crying, 'God bless you! God prosper you, brave noble woman! You'll defeat the wretch yet. He could never buy what you have won today.'

Again I thanked them all from my heart and they continued to wave and cheer even as the train moved out. I grasped Mrs. Clarke's hand but I could not speak. My heart was so full.

Of course, the London press, almost without exception, ignored the whole proceedings as I had predicted. But quite enough sensation had been created to make Sir Edward Barefaced Liar's position exceedingly uncomfortable. Far from responding to my modest financial suggestions for a settlement, however, he set in motion proceedings to get me branded insane. I could never have imagined in my worst of nightmares that he would succeed. Until I look round the drab walls of my prison and realise that for the moment at least I have no hope of escape.

But I must not give in to despair.

He did not wait long to put his nefarious plans into action. Last Saturday, the 12th if I can still record rightly, at two p.m., I was still in bed, not having recovered from the dreadful fatigue of body of two consecutive nights' travelling and the terrible prostration of mind from the overwrought excitement at Hertford. Mrs. Clarke brought me up a card from a Mr. Hale Thomson, in Piccadilly, saying he wanted to see me on particular business. I sent word I was in bed and could not see him, and either to write or tell his business to Mrs. Clarke. Still he persisted, saying he was an old medical man of sixty and that I need not mind seeing him in my room. I was very indignant at this unwarrantable and vulgar perseverance in an utter stranger when I was ill in bed, and wrote upon a piece of paper, 'Any communication for Lady Bulwer Lytton's advantage or for her injury can be made to her solicitor, Mr Charles Hyde, 33, Ely Place, London.' At this, according to Mrs. Clarke, he flew into a great rage and flung out of the house, but soon returned with that ruffian, Loaden, Sir Liar's attorney, and the willing second to all his perfidy, little Dr. Woodford, and a great tall but very respectable-looking woman – as I discovered later, a keeper from Gillet's madhouse there in Taunton.

At this, poor good Mrs. Clarke was furious, rushed upstairs, locked both my doors and put the keys in her pocket, vowing that they should not enter my room but by first cutting her down. Upon this, the ruffian Loaden grinned in her face, said he'd break open the door, and told her to make the most of me, as they were going to carry me off to a madhouse and she should never see me more. Here, she said, Mr. Thomson interposed and said, 'No, I will not have any violence or outrage offered to Lady Lytton. I have come down to make a medical enquiry and it shall be done strictly and conscientiously.'

Hearing this dreadful uproar at my door, I called out to Mrs. Clarke to unlock it and let Mr. Thomson in, but to come with him as I would not be left alone with anyone capable of such an outrage as to force themselves into my bedroom. She did so, and he entered followed by the tall keeper. They both looked at me and then at each other in evident surprise, for upon all these occasions of dastardly outrage and moral earthquakes I have always sufficient command over myself to remain, on the exterior at least, deadly calm and cool. They knew at once they were not looking at a mad woman.

Mr. Thomson opened the session with a deliberate lie that he had *not* been sent by Sir Liar, which I nipped in the bud with an, 'Of course not; he never by any accident does his own dirty work. But as the amiable, creditable and manly impeachment against me is, apparently, lunacy, confine yourself to that count, Dr. Thomson, and don't presume to presuppose me an idiot by telling me such clumsy lies. Who else but my Lord Derby's new Colonial Secretary could have authority to send anyone to offer me this crowning outrage?'

He hung his head and said, 'Lady Lytton, no one can or shall kidnap you – but did you write these letters?' He produced some old letters of mine from years ago, directed to Sir Liar Coward Bulwer-Lytton, and, with the same truths, to the ruffian Loaden.

'I certainly did,' I replied, 'and they contain truths I will write again and again, however shocking they may seem to those who do not know Sir Edward's true nature. But if these are the grounds upon which he and his cohorts found my insanity, pray why have they bottled them up all these years and never acted upon them till now?'

Not a word. Mr. Thomson next produced a placard printed on blue paper (as all Sir Liar's were at Hertford) which hit off his pompous, inflated, stilted style to a T, but was a vicious lampoon upon his hypocrisy, claiming his wife would be accompanying him to the hustings and that the pride he felt in their suffrages that day was from their heartfelt tribute to the purity of his private character. It was admirably done, but almost reluctantly, I had to deny authorship. I offered to swear upon the Bible to that effect but Mr. Thomson refused, saying my simple negation was quite enough.

He then got me into a long argument over all that had ever happened, feeling my pulse and looking into my eyes and mouth the while as if I were a horse. After this pretty little *scena,* he turned to the keeper and said, 'Well, I must say I never found a clearer head or a more logical mind or sounder flesh and blood than Lady Lytton. What do you think?'

'I think, sir,' said the woman, wiping tears from her eyes, 'that this is one of the cruellest outrages I ever witnessed in my life to a person so pre-eminently in her senses, as this lady appears. Only half of what she has told you about her treatment would certainly have been enough to have driven most ladies quite raving mad.'

This forced Mr. Thomson, a gentleman not yet entirely in Sir Liar's pocket, to offer to explain that it was my going to Hertford which had made Sir Liar question my sanity. Sir Liar himself, of course, does not think me mad, Mr. Thomson assured me with all earnestness. Maybe Mr. Thomson himself believed that, but it is undoubtedly another lie, for Lady Glamis warned me months ago that my husband was trying to hatch some such diabolical plot. I laughed the notion to scorn then because there would be publicity and investigation and I would have nothing and the cowardly brute everything, to fear. But now I know better.

Mr. Thomson and the women withdrew. He then took Mrs. Clarke into the drawing-room and asked if I was not occasionally very violent and very cruel to her? She laughed in his face. Meantime, the ruffian Loaden had all the servants up in another room to ask them the same question, when it appears that Anne and Frizzledom particularly distinguished themselves, Anne by piously hoping that they might all drop down dead if they injured a hair of mine, and Frizzledom by modestly admitting that, though he not much of a man to signify, he thought he 'should be quite equal to putting the fellers who accused me into the horse-pond.'

Poor little provincial Dr. Woodford was now brought in to look at the maniac. This cruel yet farcical outrage lasted from 2 p.m. till nine at night. I heard Loaden was like a rampaging madman when he heard the result of the medical enquiry was not the result he had sought. When I thought the wretches were at length gone, Mr. Thomson came sneaking back and asked me with some hesitation as a favour, if I would write down, in a note addressed to him, what terms I would accept from Sir Edward not again to publicly expose him? The very lenient and moderate terms I required for such life-long villainy, crowned by such a fiendish outrage, were that he should be bound stringently, that is *legally* (his oath not being worth the breath that went to form it), never again to malign or molest me directly or indirectly. Also that I should be henceforth free to live where I liked and go where I pleased and that he must instantly pay into Coutts's the sum of £4,500, the amount of legal and other expenses his eighteen years of persecution have hampered me with. Finally, that he would allow me the very small sum of £500 a year for the duration of my life, not his. This modest amount, without deduction of income tax, made payable to my sole order, quarterly by £125 at Coutts's, for I never would receive again through Loaden, nor did I want to be put to the expense of employing an attorney to receive this pittance, or be insulted by a demand for clergymen's certificates. I refrained from speculating about how many thousand, nay thousands upon thousands, that Sir Epicure Mammon receives each year from his estates, from his politics and from the immense sales of his unreadable and ponderous literary masterpieces.

Apropos of which, I must record one more small triumph for my self-esteem. Ordinarily, Sir Edward Littletalent ensures that newspaper editors and their lackeys ignore my own humble literary efforts. Indeed, he would deter publishers too if he could. So it was a source of surprise and pleasure to me when, in this week of wonders, the *Constitutional Press,* Derbyshire's leading paper, published a review of my recently published novel, *The World and His Wife, or a Person of Consequence,* full of unqualified praise. I will be honest and admit I savoured every syllable of its description of the wit and vivacity of my writing. Even though the reviewer refused to accept what was staring him in the face. The book is subtitled *A Photographic Novel* but the reviewer chose to see it as an engaging satire upon the political class in general rather than an all too accurate depiction of the life and mores of a certain Sir E.B.L. But at least, the novel was not ignored nor was it vilified.

But to return to Mr. Thomson, who at least had the decency to be a troubled rogue. I assured him that if Sir Bully acceded to my mild and merciful terms, I would promise never to mention again his wretched name, which I should be too happy to forget. I gave him until the next Saturday, the 19th that was, to consider this, after which, if he did not agree, he might rely upon my being in London on Monday next and making Downing Street not only too hot for him but for his whole set.

After I had given Mr. Thomson the note he required, I remember saying, 'But, pray, what guarantee have I that when they find your report on my sanity is not amenable to their diabolical conspiracy, that they will not employ other emissaries to repeat this disgraceful outrage?'

'Mine, Lady Lytton', came the instant reply, 'for it would indeed be an outrage. I only hope that you will have no cause to regret my having forced my way into your room today but that you will henceforth be happier than you have ever been.' I still believe that elderly conspirator believed what he said. He had not been long enough in the noxious company of Sir Liar and his cronies to have totally abandoned his belief in a gentleman's word.

Why am I bothering to be fair to this person? Because I do not want to believe that the whole world dances without question to Sir Blackguard's tune or else that I am confined in here forever and will go mad in earnest.

The week duly passed and, of course, there was no answer. I lost whatever patience I had nor, in the circumstances, did I deem patience much of a virtue. I determined to endeavour to bring matters to a crisis. So, accompanied by the good Mrs. Clarke, on Monday June 21st, I set out for London. We arrived there at eight o'clock the following morning, took rooms at the Hyde Park Hotel opposite the Marble Arch. Why set all this down? Because it attests to my grasp of the truth of what happened to me.

At twelve o'clock we went to Mr. Hale Thomson's house in Clarges Street, Piccadilly. We were shown into the drawing-room and presently the fellow came to us, saying he was delighted to see me and hoped I had come to dine with him. I said, 'Mr. Thomson, I have neither come to dine with you nor to be fooled by you. You had better communicate with Sir Edward Bulwer-Lytton, and tell him I must have a definite answer one way or the other, for which I shall call at six o'clock this evening.' I then went to call on Miss Rebecca Ryves, a young friend of mine of stout Irish stock, and she asked to be present when I returned to Thomson's. Fortunately, I had also the foresight to give her two important letters of Sir Edward's, in case I should, in my agitation, drop or mislay them.

At six she, Mrs. Clarke and I again drove to the corner of Clarges Street, and there got out. As we did so, I observed an impudent-looking snub-nosed man, who was walking up and down. He stared at me as if he had been watching for us, as afterwards turned out to be the case. We were again shown into the drawing-room at Thomson's but this time the folding- doors were closed between the two rooms and we heard the low murmuring of voices in the back room. After we had been kept waiting for more than half an hour, Thomson made his appearance, saying he had been detained by patients. Soon after him stalked into the room a tall raw-boned Scotchman with hay-coloured hair, who, I subsequently learned, was an apothecary of the name of Ross, keeping a druggist's shop in Fenchurch Street (another friend of Loaden's) and the second signatory with Thomson on the certificate of my insanity. He had never seen me before or I him and we never exchanged a single word directly.

Finding I was to get no answer about the letter from Thomson, I said to Miss Ryves and Mrs. Clarke, 'Come, don't let us waste any more time in being fooled and insulted here. We'll go.'

Easier said than done, for on reaching the hall we found it literally filled with two mad doctors, the infamous Mr. Hill, in whose property I am now incarcerated, Hill's assistant, the impudent snub-nosed man who had stared so when I got out of the brougham, two women-keepers, one a great thing of six feet high, the other a moderate and nice-looking woman, and a very idiotic footman of Thomson's, who had his back against the hall door to bar egress. Seeing this blockade, I exclaimed, 'What a set of blackguards!'

Mr. Hill, wagging his head, replied, 'I beg you speak like a lady, Lady Lytton.'

'If I was being treated like one then I certainly would,' I replied, refusing to be intimidated either by his impertinent tone or the threatening mob massed against me. Then, hearing loud talk in the dining-room, into which Mrs. Clarke had been summoned by Thomson, I walked into it in time to hear her very energetically saying, 'I won't!', to some proposition they were making. And then, seeing a side door ajar that led into a back room, I looked in, and there saw those two precious scoundrels, Loaden, the attorney, and Sir Coward Bulwer Liar himself, dyed and dandified as is his wont.

He froze when he saw me there. All the years of bitter conflict condensed into one intense look of sheer hatred between us. That I could ever have liked, let alone trusted, this man seemed beyond comprehension. He could not sustain my gaze and his eyes dropped to the floor. 'You cowardly villain,' I said, 'Why do you always do your dirty work by deputy?' At this he rushed as he had done from the Hertford hustings, but not this time into a flower-garden but down Mr. Hale Thomson's kitchen stairs and up his area steps into the street. I doubt if I shall ever see him again. I turned to Miss Ryves, who had followed me and said, 'See, the contemptible wretch has again taken to his heels.' Though I wish I had something grander and more fitting as my final sight of the man I once loved who has blighted my entire life.

Meanwhile, returning to the hall, Miss Ryves pushed the idiotic footman aside and said, 'Whatever villainy you may be paid to practise towards Lady Lytton, you have no right to detain me.' Thomson then ordered the hall door to be unchained and unlocked and she rushed out into the street. I, on the contrary, seated myself there in the hall and told Thomson that nothing he could threaten would move me from that place at his bidding. Whereupon the hall door opened again and two policemen entered. I rose to my feet knowing that the game was up and said, to the policemen, 'Don't presume to touch me! I'll go with these vile men but the very stones of London will rise up against them and their infamous employer.'

Following the arrival of the police, I really had no recourse but to get into Hill's carriage, which was in waiting. He, the two keepers, Mrs. Clarke and myself were inside, while the impudent-looking snub-nosed assistant perched on the box. Mr. Thomson attempted to make his peace with me for the cruel deception he had been party to by mouthing treacly sentiments about it all being in my best interests. I did not deign to reply and left him stewing in his own unhappy skin. The creatures took me all through the Park and, as there had been a breakfast at Chiswick that day, it was crowded. Many whom I knew kissed their hands in great surprise to see me. I acknowledged them but in reality I was a helpless prisoner.

After a journey conducted almost entirely in silence, apart from suppressed sobbing from Mrs. Clarke, we arrived at the infamous Mr. Hill's stronghold in Brentford. He handed me down and I felt like the fairy-tale princess arriving at the castle of the ogre, though it has to be admitted, since I am committed to the truth, that Inverness Lodge is a very fine house in fine grounds, which had formerly belonged to the Duke of Cumberland. I fortunately had the presence of mind to enquire the name and locale of my prison and write it down on one of my cards for Mrs. Clarke, that she might bring me my things from the Hyde Park Hotel. The good soul promised that before she left me truly alone in the company of my paid persecutors.

I was then shown upstairs into a large bedroom by the two keepers. It is here that I sit writing these words. The windows are nailed down and only open about three inches from the top. The furnishings are not of the best nor of the worst either, all of a uniform dull grey, lest colour should ignite the prisoner's imagination to rebellion. But I will also acknowledge my bed is tolerably comfortable if I was ever able to sleep.

But let me finish the story of my arrival here. After kneeling down and praying to God in a perfect agony, I bathed my face in cold water. The little keeper was very kind and feeling and she said to me, 'Oh, pray, my lady, try and keep calm under this severe trial. It does seem to me to be something very monstrous, and, depend upon it, God will never let it go on.'

'I know He will not', said I, speaking out of hope rather than confidence. And then, looking through the nailed-up window, I saw between thirty and forty women walking in the grounds. 'Are all these unfortunate incarcerated here?' I asked of the little keeper. 'Those,' she said, rather evasively, 'are our ladies. They are out gathering strawberries.'

From the Uncollected Correspondence of Lord Lytton

My dear Dickens,

I write to tell you that the sadly inevitable has now become an even sadder reality and my unfortunate wife has been confined to an asylum. There can be no doubt that it is the kindest thing that could be done. As you know all too well, I have endured cruel humiliations and groundless accusations with as much Christian forbearance as I could manage. But her behaviour in Hertford finally revealed to the world what I had previously hoped would remain a matter of my private grief and suffering. Her pathetic delusions and unbalanced mind were all too apparent to the large crowd assembled for my election. They heard her in silence with pity in their hearts but unease in their minds that somebody of such fragile sanity should be allowed abroad.

Thankfully, Inverness Lodge, the asylum she has been taken to is humane and liberal in its treatment of its female inmates. There is no bodily restraint and there are no cruel punishments. So long as they remain within its confines and do not attempt to leave them, the fair prisoners are allowed every freedom to walk in the garden or to read or to sew as the mood takes them.

I itemise the institution's merits not just to reassure myself. Should Mrs. Dickens continue to be reluctant to accede to your very reasonable demand for a separation, you might do well to inform her that such institutions do exist.

Yours affectionately and faithfully,

Edward Bulwer-Lytton

Chapter One: 1825

From an Unpublished Autobiography by Lord Lytton

When I was twenty-one, I went one day for a walk down a country lane. The sun was shining and for once I felt at peace with the world. I was stopped by a gypsy fortune-teller, who offered to tell my fortune for a few pence. She was young and good-looking so, out of curiosity, I crossed her palm with the requested silver. She stared deeply at the palm of my upheld hand. There was the usual mixture of shrewd guesses and possible surmises in what she said. She prophesied much success for me, as has indeed proved true, but then her thoughts took a more sombre tone. She told me I would always hunger for love and, though I would have much of it, there would be less satisfaction than sorrow. And then she said words I have never forgotten, 'Your best friends and your worst enemies will be women.'

To my wife and her clique of supporters, I am a perjured blackguard, fleeing from her just demands. In the World, though there are many who envy me, I am acknowledged as a man of probity, a successful statesman and a not inconsiderable man of letters, who is pursued by a vengeful harpy of a wife. How to explain the discrepancy? In attempting to account for this in writing, I believe I must be as honest about my own failings as about my wife's. I need to reveal painful truths about the upbringing that made me the man I am and made me the way with women that I am. I have also to offer some insight into my painful state of mind at the time when I first encountered Rosina Wheeler. I do not expect to be fully exonerated on every score by my description of what happened but I do hope to be understood a little better and perhaps even forgiven.

To understand, it is necessary to go back to the very beginning. My first memory is of a fierce face, moustachioed and heavily veined, purpling with rage, close to mine. He may well have been screaming at me and I may well have been screaming back in terror but in the memory there is no sound. There is also no smell, though the fumes of alcohol would have been heavy on his breath. This was my father, General William Earle Bulwer of Heydon Hall and

Wooddalling. He had a self-willed nature wholly uncultivated by literature. Ask him to read aloud, he would do so as if he had been at the head of his regiment. He once turned down an heiress because he objected to the shape of her nose. He then eloped with a schoolmistress and lived with her until her death. It was only then he married my mother, Elizabeth Barbara, heiress of the families of Robinson and Lytton of Knebworth in the county of Hertford.

This memory records the fact that my father took an unaccountable aversion to me when I was but an infant of three months and unfortunately found no occasion to revise that judgement before he died, when I was four. I still struggle not to take it personally. Because, let me be frank, I was born just at the time when my parents' married life was saddest. For in unions, however ill-assorted, so long as there are good qualities on either side, the partners do not lose hope completely. My father's temper was of the roughest, though at the start he was very much in love. But gradually the temper rose superior to the love, exacerbated by the gout that suddenly fixed on him prematurely and took up habitual residence. My eldest brother was less of a tie between both parents than children usually are. My father considered William, the heir to his name, as his special property. He regarded my mother's right as a privilege of temporary sufferance and the nursery was not her empire. My second brother, Henry, became my maternal grandmother's particular care even before he left the nursery. Therefore, when a child was born to my mother in her darkest hour – a child all her own – a child weakly and delicate, who claimed all her affection – a child not destined to the heritage of Heydon Hall, and therefore left undisputed to her care – perhaps it is not so surprising that the dreams that had deserted her own life gathered round the cradle of her youngest child.

There was another aspect to the conflict which raged over my infant head. The lands of Lytton, when they devolved upon my mother on the death of her father, would be at her own disposal and my father must have known enough of my mother's family pride to suspect that she would want to keep the representation of her own line distinct from that of the Bulwers. William would inherit my father's Heydon Hall and the estates attached; Henry, my second brother, in all probability the separate fortune of his maternal grandmother, who doted upon him. The merest hint that my mother's Lytton estates, including Knebworth, might pass to me would have been galling to my father, who had huge ambitions for his own inheritance and would gladly have seen every acre in Knebworth under the hammer of the auctioneer if the proceeds might enable him to add to his hereditary domains in Norfolk.

All this is speculation. He bought largely, and bought dearly, whatever lands were to be sold in the neighbourhood of his estates. But in the midst of all these dreams and acquisitions, Death smote the aspiring man. He died after being kicked by a horse, an end I suspect he would have chosen for himself if given the choice.

It was a shock to my mother to discover the parlous state of my father's affairs, though fortunately her own emerged unscathed. After his death, my mother did as others in similar circumstances. She consulted the male members of her family, and, acting on their advice, obtained from the Court of Chancery an order assigning to her the guardianship of her children, with an adequate allowance for their education. William went to a famous preparatory school, Henry remained with the ever-doting Mrs Lytton, and I was left alone with my mother.

My maternal grandfather, Richard Lytton, it must be added, was so totally immersed in the world of books that he had likewise muddled away much of a large inheritance. For his wife, perversely, he had chosen a girl of sixteen, many years younger than himself, with no interest in literature at all. Not surprisingly, they were separated long before my birth and my maternal grandmother lived a busy social life in London, far removed from my grandfather's book-lined home in Ramsgate.

Since I am recording the sad rejections of my childhood, I have to record that my maternal grandmother also took an aversion to me from an early age. I have no recollection of anything untoward I did as a child to provoke this. Perhaps it was out of jealousy of her daughter's devotion to me. Perhaps it was because she had already chosen my brother Henry as the apple of her eye. I can only speculate. The aversion was unsoftened till her dying day. But then a woman who had once put three highwaymen to flight on Hounslow Heath single-handed with a riding whip was never one for changing her mind.

My mother took a house in London, to the purchase of which her father made a generous contribution. This re-established an affectionate understanding between father and daughter and so we went to visit him at his house at St. Lawrence, near Ramsgate. I had encountered my grandfather rarely before this and had high hopes that he would welcome and pet me as the first of his grandsons he had been in close contact with. But, alas, when we arrived, there was no sign of a caress or a kind word. He stared at me unsmilingly like a bibliophile assessing the provenance of a rare first edition. This intense study continued over supper that evening and into the next day. Finally, when I had been barely twenty-four hours in the house, he solemnly assured my mother in my presence that 'I should break her heart and (what was worse) that I should never know my A.B.C.' He maintained this ill opinion of my disposition and talents with the obstinacy which he carried into most of his articles of belief.

I do not wish to linger longer on these painful truths. I am all too aware that to the unsympathetic they may reek of self-pity. But if I am sometimes a mistrustful, sometimes a melancholic man, some of the roots of my nature may well be found in the cruel rejections of my childhood, judged unlovable as I was by those who should have cherished me. So, in essence, the only bond of love was between me and my mother.

And then a new love came unexpectedly into my life. When I was seven, my maternal grandfather died suddenly of an apoplectic seizure. My mother inherited all he had but, while she struggled yet again with the chaos of an estate poorly managed, I was left free in his library. I had been familiar with books before, but they had been given me one by one at a time, from mahogany cases under lock and key, with cautions not to dog-ear them and an infinity of troublesome restrictions. Now I was a chartered libertine. I was Solomon in all his glory surrounded by his seraglio. I was not married to a single volume. I could take down any book that I wished, bend its spine, open its pages, devour its contents, and then, if bored or sated, move on to another book. I am all too aware of the promiscuity this implies and its possible application to my later life.

My grandfather's library was sold to help my mother settle the many debts he had left. She chose at this juncture in her life to reassume her maiden name of Lytton and was known henceforth as Mrs. Bulwer Lytton, which gives a very clear indication of her family loyalties. However, the sad truth is that all that remained of her inheritance was the estate at Knebworth. I can recall only dimly the moment when I saw for the first time the house which is now my home and will be the home of my son, however much my wife rails against it. She talks about justice but where is her justice to our boy, who suffers deep humiliation from her absurdities? But I must not anticipate. If there is a difference between my lamented wife's view of the world and my own, it is that I understand chronology and consequence, she sees only the moment. So let me set down in sequence my first impressions of Knebworth when I was eight. I have broken reminiscences of a deep, gloomy archway, of a long gallery covered with portraits, and chambers in which the tapestry seemed rotting on the walls. As part of her plans to regain some control over her family estate, having now experienced a second great lesson in male improvidence, my mother resolved to pull down three sides of the great quadrangle and confine the house to the fourth side. When I next saw Knebworth, the work of demolition had begun.

I allot only a few paragraphs to my education, despite my obstinate belief that to understand a human being fully you must understand every aspect of what he has undergone. My first school when I was nine was at a 'Preparatory

Institution' in Fulham. My mind was filled with books and the protected world in which I had grown up. The boys there seemed to me like fiends. Infants though they were, their language was filthily obscene and my ignorance of its meaning excited their contempt, which they vented in mocking jeers and vague threats. This was not the happiest introduction to the pleasures of the flesh I was later to explore. Oh, that first night, when my mother was gone, the last kiss given, the door closed and I alone with the little mocking fiends to whom my anguish was such glee. Not having been brought up with other boys, I was a great source of amusement to them, while my utter ignorance of their low, gross slang and the disgust with which their language, their habits, their very looks inspired me was all excellent sport to them.

I did not remain in that school above a fortnight, but I had learned lessons for life. I must not let others be in a position to take advantage of my weakness. If attacked, I must always retaliate. These notions I converted into practice at the numerous other schools I attended. Then came the suggestion from the headmaster of the last and most congenial of my schools that I should transfer to Eton. My mother thought this an excellent idea. I did not. To be honest, being older in mind and appearance than my fifteen years, I considered myself too much of a man to go to any school whatever. This sounds childish arrogance but I think I had begun to grasp the peculiarity of my own character. I am very sensible of the advantages which follow in life, especially in public life, from a probation at one of our great National Schools. I have often felt a certain distaste for discipline and co-operation with others, and a kind of shyness, when thrown into company with contemporaries of very familiar social manners, or addicted to the sports of the field, which is seldom the defect of one reared at a public school. Always, throughout my career, I have been too thin-skinned and sensitive – faults which Eton might have cured. But I continue to think otherwise. I had never been flogged, and, after my first two or three years of school, I had never submitted to a blow from any of my companions. In every schoolboy fight I had come off victorious and I am certain that if I had been flogged by a master or fagged by a boy, it would have produced an injurious consequence on my future health and character.

Private tutors, of greater or lesser ability, came and went in my life, sometimes assisting my journey towards greater knowledge and insight, sometimes impeding it. When I was eighteen, I proceeded to Cambridge University for the completion of my academical career. Here I at last found congenial companions and, impelled by curiosity, perhaps a sense of destiny, I joined the Union Debating Society. It was a long while before I could be called a good speaker. I wanted the management of voice and I was hurried away into imperfect articulation by the tumultuous impetuosity of my thoughts. But I learned by example and application and came in time to be a very respectable orator. But reminiscences of university days are ten a penny from the likes of William Makepeace Thackeray and his crew and I have more important matters to write of, namely the development of my young heart and the sad shocks it received, shocks that were to reverberate forward through my relations with women. For, when I was twenty-one, I became involved with Lady Caroline Lamb.

In truth, my acquaintance with this singular woman had commenced in childhood. Some poor man had got injured in a crowd at a race meeting and, with the impulsive benevolence which naturally belonged to her, Lady Caroline had placed him in her carriage and taken him to her home. My family home was but a few short miles distant from hers and so I heard the story. With the impetuousness of fifteen years, I wrote some childish lines on her benevolent deed and sent them to her without thought that this was a woman who knew the great Lord Byron intimately. I transcribe some of them here for my own mortification.

> 'The guardian angel hov'ring near,
> Soar'd upwards with that deed of thine,
> And as he dropt the applauding tear,
> Wrote down the name of C...'

She was pleased with this adolescent offering and wrote to my mother, begging to bring me over to Brocket Hall. She took a fancy to me and even painted my portrait as a child seated on a rock in the midst of the sea, with the motto under it, *Seul sur la terre*, which was thrillingly romantic, though I have never been entirely sure what Lady Caroline had in mind. But then it's very possible neither did she.

It was some years before our acquaintance was renewed when I had accepted an engagement to pass a week or so with Lady Caroline at Brocket before returning to Cambridge. I was twenty-one, she was, well, to be honest, somewhere between thirty and forty and certainly closer to forty, though she looked younger than she was. A creature of caprice, and impulse and whim, her manner, her talk and her character shifted their colours as rapidly as those of a chameleon. She confided in me graphic descriptions of her intimacy with Byron, who had written to her that she was the only woman who had never bored him. But then they had fiercely quarrelled and she depicted him in a wild romance called *Glenarvon* as a beautiful monster – half-demon and yet demigod. He never forgave her, although I believe he should have been flattered by this addition to his mythical status.

Slowly and delicately, drawn in by her hushed intimacy, I had enquired about what it had been like to go to bed with this demon / demigod. Lady Caroline, by her standards, was coy, even evasive, but somehow the conversation turned to a younger poet who might possibly be able to experience directly the charms that Lord Byron had enjoyed but somehow failed to fully appreciate. I was not slow to follow up the hint. This truly was the time of my maturing. Of course, I had had carnal knowledge of several prostitutes because that was what was expected of me by my peers and if, as a young man, you had strong carnal desires, where else could you relieve them? But those encounters had been crude physical acts accompanied by coins thrown on to a less than spotless mattress. With Lady Caroline I had found a woman who required a gentleness and skill in love-making. I realised that I had already a certain expertise and virility in these matters. Maybe her breasts were too boyish for my taste, maybe I was sometimes aware that Lady Caroline's skin lacked the smoothness and elasticity of younger women, maybe I even balked secretly at the thought she was twice my age, but she was a woman of the world, she had been loved by Lord Byron and when she stroked my dark curls and neatly trimmed whiskers or praised the proportions of my tall, slim but manly figure, I felt truly loved for the first time. When my male member was taken into the mouth that had also supped upon the male member of the great Lord Byron himself, I confess I was in ecstasy.

And she knew how to flatter and reassure an insecure young man too. She told me I had a genius potentially near to Byron's and accepted my unforgivable moments of rage and insecurity as indications of that greatness. I was even allowed to wear a ring which Lord Byron had given to Lady Caroline, a ring she insisted could only be worn by those she loved. At one point, she had been so besotted with me that she proposed to give it to me forever but, with a resolve I was proud of at the time and continue to be proud of, I recognised its value and returned the gift. Light-headed with her praise and her sophistication in the bedroom, I had no comparison to tell me the flattery was empty and would all too soon come to an end.

We corresponded regularly after my return to Cambridge and in our correspondence there was a great deal of sentiment and romance which seemed like love. In retrospect, she was a clever woman with time on her hands, but for me it was my soul that I was pouring on to the pages of my letters. I believed with all the innocence of first love that I had found the soul mate I had been searching for, the one who understood all my feelings and all my pain.

Then came an invitation to a party assembled at Brocket for the purpose of going to a ball given at Panshangar nearby. I arrived, full of love and hope, but Lady Caroline seemed captivated with a singularly handsome man in the prime of life, Mr. Russell, a natural son of the Duke of Bedford. She spent the entire evening upon his arm. At first I consoled myself with the fact that I was superior to Mr. Russell in everything but good looks. I fondly imagined that Lady Caroline, a natural coquette, had chosen this way to arouse my jealousy and retain my devotion but I gradually realised with growing dismay that I had been supplanted. She ignored me until the end of evening and, when she did finally speak to me, I felt myself becoming very angry and sarcastic in my response. Finally, the only way to escape my humiliation was to gasp out the words, 'I go tomorrow before you are up. Goodbye.' Would I had stopped there. But then I had one of the stormy paroxysms of rage which seize upon me in moments of distress, paroxysms that frighten me – and others – by their intensity.

Shocked, she entreated me to forgive her, threw her arms about me and cried. She said that she had known Mr. Russell for a very long time and had once felt a love for him but not the sort of love she felt for me. I was almost inclined to believe her because it was clear to me in all honesty that I was in all respects more worthy of her affections. But when we returned to the main room, arm in arm, Mr. Russell was seated, handsome profile illuminated by the chandeliers, talking to an acquaintance. The orchestra was playing a melancholy air by Rossini. Mr. Russell raised his hand and my jealous eye immediately saw that he was wearing a ring. The ring that Lord Byron had given to Lady Caroline.

I turned away in mortification. How could she have humiliated me in this way? No longer able to keep any control over my emotions, I pulled away from the traitoress and threw myself upon a sofa. Lady Caroline came towards me. 'Are you mad?' she asked. I was unable to reply. Tears were starting in my eyes. Suddenly my whole universe had crashed into pieces.

All might still have been well if Lady Caroline had said something to console, to remind me that the nature of human beings, particularly of poets, was to suffer. But instead she observed my tears and, turning to the assembled company, who were, despite their pretence of indifference, riveted by the spectacle being played out in front of them, said, addressing the orchestra, 'Pray, don't play this melancholy air any more. It affects Mr. Bulwer so much that he is actually weeping.'

The company laughed knowingly, impressed that Lady Caroline had found so elegant a way to explain what was transpiring, albeit a way entirely untrue. Mr. Russell rose from his seat and led her on to the dance floor. The couples began to dance around them, closing them from my view. My tears, my softness, my love were over in a moment. I had learned a bitter lesson at the start of my romantic life, which probably scarred its course for ever. I felt I could never trust, never love again.

At the earliest opportunity, I left for Paris. There, I drained with an unsparing lip whatever enjoyment that enchanting Metropolis could offer. The courtesans, who had a style and hauteur quite beyond their English counterparts, were welcoming and accommodating to every need a gentleman might indicate. I set out to explore the depths of my sexual nature. I experienced the swish of a cane across my buttocks, only to discover that it was no more alluring than when I had rejected the disciplinary regime of Eton. There was no doubt that I preferred a more conventional but hearty rogering of these elegant demoiselles. Their squeals of delight were, of course, partially fabricated but they reassured me that I was more than adequately equipped to give sexual pleasure to the fair sex, something I had begun to doubt after Lady Caroline's desertion. Meanwhile, the houses of the very best French families were also available to me, places where wit and style abounded, and it was not considered bad taste to talk about art and philosophy as if such subjects mattered.

And then there was Mrs. Cunningham, an accomplished and intelligent woman of the world resident in Paris, who proved herself a wise and affectionate friend in my hours of need. She was some thirty years older than me and the difference in our age gave a freedom to our intercourse without the least hint of scandal or amorous intent. Yes, I insist upon that, though my enemies have seen fit to doubt it. She was that rarity, a happily married woman, whose husband was not a fool, and she understood me as few had before, and not that many since. We discussed books and politics and I confided in her the story of my family. The things that you have read here I first understood looking into Mrs. Cunningham's kind unshockable grey eyes. I told her about my unloving father and my two brothers, who patronised me if they noticed me at all. I even told her of my rejection by Lady Caroline, though of course I told her nothing of our physical intimacy. But I certainly explained to her that it had destroyed all my romantic hopes for the future and turned all my literary plans to dust. To be dropped by the woman who had been abandoned by Lord Byron gave you a very distinct idea of what your place in the literary canon was.

Above all, I spoke about my mother, who had selected me as her favoured son because of all that had happened and who intended to leave me all that she had to leave, whatever my brothers might think. And it was then I faced a truth I had never faced before. I realised that my mother planned a worldly match for me. I was financially dependent upon her, as well as grateful for her kindness, so I could never make a match which she would condemn. There was no escape. I believed that Lady Caroline had dealt a death blow to my hope of a true marriage of the heart. And my mother, with all her love for me, would only tolerate a union where money played a greater part than love.

All this Mrs. Cunningham helped me to understand. She listened closely and she questioned with sympathy and without judgement. Yet despite my doubts about my literary future, half teasingly, she called me Childe Harold. Like Byron's hero, I had adopted opinions and a style of dress and manner different to that of other people and, if I'm honest, I liked to be noted for it. It gave me pleasure to be different and I did not take amiss Mrs. Cunningham's teasing and references to my 'beautiful curls' because they included admiration and perhaps flirtation along with the mockery. And, yes, more perhaps like Lord Byron himself, I was that disillusioned wanderer around the European continent, contemplating its splendour, its sadness and its corruption, with my own soul exhausted by the *tristesse* of life. Understand, I was young and the description was flattering but also, I felt, accurate. So here, with the exception of my mother, was the first of those women whom I count among my best friends.

Forgive this necessary prologue. I now proceed to the events of the day that blighted the rest of my life. And in that connection I have to start with some lines of my own, which for all their juvenile faults, I do not entirely wish to disown.

> 'For darkly, like a withered tree
> Which hangs along the ebbing tide,
> That blighted Spirit droops to see
> The waves of life so vaguely glide.'

I was sitting in the library of my mother's London home, studying the copy of my collected poetry entitled *Weeds and Wildflowers* which lay on the desk. There was talk of a second edition and, though I doubted the truth of the talk, I felt it incumbent upon me to see if there were any lines I would alter in what would undoubtedly be the work by which the world would judge me as a writer. The reviews had been respectful, often laudatory, and I had ensured the binding and decorations were of the highest quality money could afford. But I felt deeply disappointed at the reception. It sounds pompous now but at the time I believed this might well be my final testament; a young man of twenty-four with so much to give the world, who was not destined ever to write again. So I judged it best to make a second edition, if there ever was one, as definitive as it could be. Was 'vaguely' really the *mot juste*? 'So aimless glide?' 'So hopeless glide?'

I stopped myself. There was to be no second edition. I would never be a true man of letters. The triumph of the Cambridge Poetry Prize was but a meteor that lit up the sky briefly before falling to earth like a spent firework. Yes, I had the gift, but no, my career was over. It was, after all, a sign of his retirement from the profession when an author begins to collect his works. It is a tacit avowal that he feels that the time has come when he must chiefly rest his hopes of reputation upon the labours he has already performed. Or so I thought at the time. To capture the melancholy mood of that fateful day as honestly as I can is, in my belief, the best way to understand the catastrophe that happened.

I had intended to stay only briefly at my mother's house in Upper Seymour Street before proceeding to my hotel and then back to Knebworth. I meant to enquire after her health and give her a brief (and necessarily expurgated) version of my time in Paris. The truth was that, in my letters to her while abroad, I had told her everything I was prepared to tell her about my trip. And yet there I was, despite my intentions, already back in her thrall, sitting in an all too familiar armchair gazing at the volume of poetry my mother had all too obviously left there. There would never be direct approval of my poetic achievements. Nor indeed of all my later achievements. That was not my mother's style. But she left clues to show that what I had done had been registered and not disapproved of. She loved me, I knew, and loved me above her other sons and anybody else in her life, but still it was with a distance that often, in my childhood and adolescence, left me feeling uncertain and sometimes unloved. I remember thinking that I should get back to the hotel. Yet something held me back – with fatal results.

My mother had mentioned an evening engagement for which she must prepare and had doubtless left me in the library on purpose so that I might discover the copy of *Weeds and Wildflowers* I had dedicated to her. 'From your devoted son, Edward Bulwer,' I had written and I meant it in all honesty. Although I planned when she came back to make my excuses.

There was a knock upon the door and before I could answer the door was opened. It was, of course, my mother, dressed for her evening out. I record as best I can remember.

'You're looking very elegant, mother.'

'One does one's best and one tries not to let standards drop.' My mother showed no obvious signs of pleasure at my compliment but I knew her well enough to know she was pleased. Indeed, though she clung to the styles of yesteryear, they suited her very well. I have always loved clothes and embraced new fashions. Superficial though this may seem to some, my mother included, I have always believed one should embrace the spirit of the age. And on that occasion as on many, her look gave an indication that she was not going to return the compliment.

'I'm sure it's all very *à la mode*, particularly in Paris, but I've never seen a shirt-front of such elaboration or sleeve links like that. Gentleman in my youth

11

went for something much more sober, even Mr. Brummell the one occasion I had a glimpse of him. But I'm doubtless very old-fashioned.'

'We must agree to differ, mother.' I rose and planted a kiss on her cheek. Again there was no obvious response but a slight flush of pleasure across her pale severe face.

'Are you sure I can't persuade you?' She took my hand in hers, a rare enough gesture to suggest an appeal to my better feelings was on the way.

'Persuade me about what, mother?' The possibilities ranged from changing my waistcoat to considering some well-connected heiress for marriage, so I decided to continue to wait. Particularly if a potential bride was in view.

'It really doesn't seem a great deal to ask since you have been on the Continent so long. But you were so adamant when you first arrived that you did not wish to come.'

'Adamant about what?'

'About not accompanying me to Miss Benger's.'

'But I am very tired, mother.' I saw the way the wind was blowing but realised I was becoming powerless to resist.

'Surely not too tired for a short visit. We had much greater stamina for socialising when I was young.' She removed her hand from mine. 'But no, you are tired. You must return to your hotel and then to Knebworth. I quite understand.'

Actually, I remember thinking, she didn't understand at all. The infinite possibilities of Paris had contracted into a dull evening in an over-heated room stuffed with plain English spinsters who consider themselves literary *aficionados* and even authoresses. It was too cruel a contrast but then my mother could have requested something so much more demanding and I had been spared another evening with a buck-toothed, cross-eyed heiress who was clearly all too willing to be yoked to me and my handsome curls. Besides, without my mother's generosity, I could never have afforded the infinite possibilities of Paris. With all my heart, I wish I had resisted. Where was my gypsy fortune-teller when I needed her most? But at the time I felt full of affection and gratitude to my mother and knew it was time to be gracious.

I took hold of the hand which had been withdrawn so firmly. 'If you wish, of course I will accompany you to Miss Benger's.' At least, I remember thinking, at Miss Benger's there would be no chance of encountering Lady Caroline Lamb. They hated each other.

The gathering proved to be as tedious as I had expected. The air was stifling, the spinsters of both sexes not much less oppressive than the air. There were knowing whispers and even admiring looks when I entered, for I was a minor literary lion in a salon desperate for novelty. I was in my best Childe Harold unsociable manner when I was aware of my mother's insistent voice close by.

'Look, Edward! What a beautiful face!'

I did not at first realise whom my mother was talking about. She could hardly openly point out the location of this beautiful face, so I stared into the throng without any sense of where to look. It was so unlike my mother to make comments of this sort, particularly about somebody whose dowry and eligibility for marriage had not been fully checked, that I confess to being intrigued. And if she was the promised heiress, then let her be beautiful. But, restrained by propriety from staring too much, I kept looking in vain.

'No, really, she is a real beauty of a type you rarely see.'

It took me another moment to finally locate a dark-haired girl seated on a sofa by the fire. Our eyes met for a moment and then I turned away. She was indeed a good-looking young woman but why should that concern me? I was Childe Harold, the wandering outlaw of my own dark mind. My fingers had been burned. There was no fire left in me to be lit by love and I would not risk disappointment again. I felt irritated by my mother's untimely persistence.

But then I decided to look again. Her eyes were of the most glorious Irish green.

From the Memoirs of Rosina, Lady Lytton

As I recall, the fatal day which was to blight the rest of my life began dully enough. I was nursing an unpleasant cold and lay on the sofa in the drawing-room of my uncle, General Sir John Doyle, all morning, gazing out of the window at the rain pouring down on a near-empty Somerset Street below. My melancholy was such that I started thinking about my mother, an occupation always bound to increase my gloom. Images flashed before my eyes of that self-proclaimed Goddess of Reason in her ridiculous turban holding forth in Caen to a group of French male sycophants, who listened endlessly to her inaccurate summaries of Mary Wollstonecraft's tedious diatribes about the Rights of Women. She and her drunken rants were on the other side of the Channel, thank God, and my sickly sweet sister Henrietta with her, but that could not rid my thoughts of my mother and her pathetic pronouncements, pronouncements only the French could take seriously.

So to divert my thoughts, I attempted to absorb myself in a recently published volume of poetry entitled *Weeds and Wildflowers*. I had been told great things of its young author and since I did my best to *au courant* with all that was discussed in the literary salons I attended, I had made sure to obtain a copy. It was certainly a handsomely-bound volume with a woodcut depicting a brave little ship negotiating its way through perilous rocks. But, alas, a poetic tale of a doomed romance between the poet and a village virgin dwelling in Ealing meandered to its all too predictable close in heartbreak and relocation abroad. Even less promising was a poem upon the art of sculpture apparently awarded a prize by the University of Cambridge, hymning at length the marble triumphs of Canova and Michelangelo. If it had not been a paradox to describe a poem about statuary as 'wooden', then that would have undoubtedly been the *mot juste*.

But one passage in this work took my attention in all its self-pitying glory.

> '*For darkly, like a withered tree*
> *Which hangs along the ebbing tide,*
> *That blighted Spirit droops to see*
> *The waves of life so vaguely glide.*'

Never, even in the gloomiest moments of my childhood, had I ever been swamped personally by such Byronic gloom but all the same these lines struck a chord and I found myself contemplating my prospects. Although the waves in my life were not so vaguely gliding as to abandon all hope for the future, I certainly currently lacked a guiding purpose. For the moment, to be free from my mother and in London gave me a great deal to be grateful for. My good old uncle was a generous and indulgent host and I had the use of his carriage to attend gatherings where I was welcomed by intelligent women and handsome men. I was twenty-four, generally acknowledged as good-looking in a raven-haired green-eyed Irish way. I was certainly intelligent and quick enough to hold my place in most conversations, perhaps the only useful talent I had inherited from my mother. But there was still the question of the ways the waves of life were gliding, vaguely or not.

Only the week before, Lady Caroline Lamb has been very definite upon the subject, as indeed she was on most subjects. One evening, we had sat in her drawing-room long after the other guests had departed. 'We must get you married,' she had announced, 'You are a beauty and you have wit and intelligence.'

I had protested but to no avail.

'After all, your uncle used to be the Governor of Jersey. He has a title and good standing, even if he is a harmless old bumbler and bit of an old maid.'

Again I had attempted to protest that my background was not of the highest, despite that. My drunken father had consumed most of my inheritance before dying untimely by falling off his horse and my mother, well, she was my mother.

Lady Caroline had brushed my objections aside yet again. Her button bright eyes had burned with enthusiasm in the fire light. 'Let me take you under my wing. Let me take you places. Let us go fishing on your behalf.' And her low, seductive, drawling voice, full of the confidence of an aristocratic background beyond my then understanding, had spoken of a world of romance and intrigue both cynical and joyous.

Oh, how I still longed for that knowledge of the world as I sat there, poetry book in hand, nursing my cold and contemplating my uncertain future.

I had had no chaperone since my mother gracelessly abjured that role and I had attended ball rooms where officers in glamorous uniforms and dandies forced into tight breeches would happily take an attractive young woman on to the dance floor for a waltz, although I already knew it was still best to be wary when epauletted officers whispered obscenities in my ear and paunchy dandies talked of visits to certain establishments in Brighton. The King, it was indicated, was not the only one who took of these exquisite pleasures.

Ah, the waltz, that recent sensation. I still remembered the confusion it caused me at first. I had adored dancing with a man's arm around my waist until I was told that Lord Byron had written a poem about how disgusting it was that a man and a woman should dance together so closely. Fortunately, Lady Caroline had dismissed my concerns. Byron, she explained, was jealous because, with his club foot, he was no dancer. And Lady Caroline after all should know. Lady Caroline was at the time the closest I had ever come to contact with a major literary figure. Perhaps it would have been better if it had stayed that way.

We all savoured the scent of Lord Byron's heady mixture of cynicism, danger and romance in those days and, since he was conveniently recently dead, anyone could try and claim his laurels. The as yet unknown to me author of *Weeds and Wildflowers* had attached a series of world-weary maxims in the French mode to his collection of poems to give credibility to his pose as a thoroughly modern bard. As I recall, my suspicion at the time was that the writer knew far less of the vices of the world than he protested. Probably a mother's boy from a sheltered upbringing. Everybody wanted to be a Lord Byron then.

I feared the Byronic gloom was becoming infectious so, after a cursory glance at the maxims, I put the volume down again. The rain showed no sign of letting up. My uncle's furnishings were good but very much in the style of the last century, ornate, gilded and weighty. I recall that I finally acknowledged the principal source of my unhappiness. Fortuneless as I was, I was at twenty-four, already becoming too old for somebody who wished to make a 'good' marriage, whatever Lady Caroline said or hoped. I knew gentlemen enjoyed flirting with me but I was not sure any of them would go further. And the more gentlemen I flirted with, the less likely that any of them would see me as a marriage prospect. Innocent and comparatively young as I was, I felt I was destined for a life of moneyed happiness and content but, alas, as I sat there, I knew the prospect of achieving that goal was already starting to fade.

There. I set it down. I am committed to being as honest about myself as I can.

It was at this point that Lady Caroline Lamb burst into the room carrying a small dog.

This sudden unannounced arrival of my proclaimed patroness would have been more startling from somebody else, but Lady Caroline had long ago abandoned the niceties of paying a social visit to follow her own instincts and whims. In fact, her unpredictability had become totally predictable.

'Dearest Rosina,' my mentor cooed as she rushed towards me all smiles. As I rose to meet her, she kissed my cheeks and deposited the small damp dog in my arms. 'It's a poodle,' she added in her low drawling voice as if no further explanation was needed.

Normally, I would have been delighted. The one thing I missed from my rackety upbringing in Ireland was living in a household of dogs, from shepherd dogs to hunters, and the one regret I had in London was that I had no dog. I had often talked of my love of dogs to anyone who would listen and the thing with Lady Caroline was that you never knew when she was listening and when she wasn't. And clearly this time she had heard and looked on triumphantly as the toy poodle continued to yap in my arms and try to scrabble down on to the floor. I struggled to hold it and patted it reassuringly. But the truth was that it was not the dog I would have chosen. It was a whiny London lap dog, not a dog with a purpose. Instinctively, I disliked it and it disliked me. The small dog gave a series of ear-splitting high-pitched yelps as if to establish its poodle credentials. It was only a puppy and might well grow larger but there was no mistaking a runt of the litter when I saw it. Drowning at birth might have been best.

On top of which, I wanted to sneeze.

Unfortunately, my dismay must have shown in my face for Lady Caroline, who had never been called stupid by anyone, not even Lord Byron, immediately interjected, 'Oh dear, I do believe you don't like Miss Lamb. Well, I call her Miss Lamb but then Lamb is my name to give and I did feel so sorry for her. Still, you can call it whatever name you like, my dear. If you want to keep her. But perhaps you and Miss Lamb are not a marriage made in heaven. Few, of course, are.'

Lady Caroline gave her one of her distinctive high-pitched laughs, half way between a shriek and a neighing horse. Lady Caroline's husband had been remarkably tolerant in the circumstances of her frenzied pursuit of Lord Byron and her ostentatious suicide attempts when he abandoned her. 'The trouble with Lord Byron,' she had confided to me (and probably countless other intimate acquaintances), 'is that he didn't really like intelligent women, certainly not women with slim boyish figures. For boyish figures, he preferred actual boys. For women, he liked them dumb and implausibly big-breasted.' But through all the separations and the quarrels and family pressure, Sir William had heroically (or possibly stupidly) refused to disown her and even now allowed her use of the family home at Brocket Hall. But no, made in heaven was not the *mot juste*. He seemed blind to all her true qualities and simply tolerant of her weaknesses.

But that is by the bye on this day, which started in gloom and then piled absurdity upon absurdity. Lady Caroline, after all, had been a good friend to me and the last thing I wanted to do was seem ungracious. I started stroking the dog with far greater concern than I felt. Fortunately, Miss Lamb decided to accept my arms and not try to reach the floor. 'Of course, if you don't like this puppy, I can always get you a different one from my brother, Duncannon.'

'Miss Lamb is adorable,' I insisted.

'Or you shall have one of those pretty spaniels of the Duke of Devonshire's that you admire so much.' Lady Caroline was in placatory mood now but there was always the danger she might suddenly burst into tears. Since she had learned of Lord Byron's death in Greece, some eighteen months earlier, it took very little to send her over the edge into sobbing. I recall that, for me at least, her fragility was part of her appeal. If somebody who had had an affair with the greatest poet of their generation, who was on first name terms with half the aristocracy of England (the half who were still talking to her) often felt sad and inadequate, this was somehow comforting, particularly when I was feeling insecure and alone in the great social world of London.

But just now I didn't want the tears, so I promptly added to her previous declaration: 'I like the puppy you have brought me very much.' I stroked the small bundle with as much conviction as I could manage. 'And I would not change her name for the world. She will always be Miss Lamb whatever happens. Unless of course, in the course of time, she has puppies of her own and we shall have to consider whether she becomes Mrs. Lamb. But then her domestic arrangements may not be respectable enough to justify the change.'

Lady Caroline gave another of her high-pitched laughs. This slightly near the knuckle banter between us was one of our links. Lady Caroline must have had her bellyful of disapproving prudes in her time and I had no intention of joining their number. Besides, I enjoyed her airy flirtatiousness, so without the drunken pomposity of my own mother's view of what women should and should not be. Yes, maybe that was it. Lady Caroline, bizarrely or not, had become a second mother to me, although ultimately she served me no better than my own.

At least it was safe now to deposit Miss Lamb upon the floor and the puppy snuffled off to explore whatever smells lingered in my uncle's carpets and furnishings. So all was well. Except that Lady Caroline had clearly seen her gift as the prelude to something else.

'Will you come with us tonight to the opera? Duncannon's box is free. It's something by Signor Rossini but don't ask me to recall its name. The main thing is that Malibran is singing, so I know you will enjoy it.'

Here was a true dilemma and one which required an immediate solution. To sit in a box at Her Majesty's was, I knew, to be fully accepted in society, despite Lady Caroline's dubious reputation. I had been there on several occasions and had relished the opera glasses turned in my direction, the whispered comments and the admiring glances from the gentlemen. Even the less than approving glances from some of the women were gratifying. But not tonight.

'Alas, I have a previous engagement.' There was no way round the fact. I also had a streaming cold but Lady Caroline would despise such an excuse.

'You can send your apologies.' Lady Caroline's comment was more of an order than a suggestion.

'I wish I could. But—'

'But?' Always difficult to tell with Lady Caroline whether she was about to burst into tears or hysterical laughter.

'It's a long term engagement.' Here came the danger. 'I'm promised to Miss Benger's.'

'Miss Benger? That superannuated old blue stocking who thinks Alexander Pope is *à la mode?*' Lady Caroline was working her way into her vindictive mode. I had seen it before directed at others and had no desire to see it directed at myself. But there was a calculation to be made. Lady Caroline would probably forget and forgive. Miss Benger would not. Both were crucial to the fragile social network I had established in London.

Lady Caroline gave me cachet but also a certain reputation that was not necessarily conducive to my future prospects. It might be possible for Lady Caroline to do outrageous things and have open amours with younger men but she was still a wife, a mother, and, above all, an aristocrat. I could simply not afford to take the risks she did, although God knows I had sometimes been tempted. In my darker moments, I sometimes wondered if I merely acted as a bait to draw men towards my older companion. Lady Caroline looked younger than her years, aided by a slight, rounded figure and a childlike mode of wearing her pale golden hair in close curls. She had large expressive hazel eyes, exceedingly good teeth and a musical intonation of voice, despite a certain artificial drawl. Apart from these gift she might be considered plain. Which may be where my usefulness as a companion came in.

Miss Benger, meanwhile, might be a mousy bluestocking with a taste for the duller works of Anna Letitia Barbauld, but she oozed respectability and her gatherings attracted people who were coated in that eminently desirable product. I would not encounter any glamorous young rakes there but I would always be sure that if I was accepted by Miss Benger and her set, my good reputation would never desert me. So Miss Benger was not to be offended, particularly on one of her long-planned literary evenings. And possibly neither should my uncle be. Not usually the most social of beings, he had agreed to accompany me. To be on the arm of my uncle was always a sign of continuing respectability to be cherished, even if it meant a certain tedium and lack of opportunities for flirtation.

Lady Caroline appeared to be in a sulk.

'Of course, I would much rather be there at the opera with you. And Malibran has a voice to die for. But a promise is a promise. It's a principle of mine. Particularly as I have promised to take some people home for her in my uncle's coach.'

'First come, first served,' snapped Lady Caroline. 'Very admirable principle but somewhat dreary in its application.'

I knew that my only hope now was to make Lady Caroline laugh. 'Everything about Miss Benger is dreary in its application but I was always taught that I needed to do acts of charity in order to lay up treasure in heaven. And treasure in heaven has always been deemed a good investment.'

There was a pause and then Lady Caroline laughed. Not a full-blooded laugh but enough. She had realised it would be beneath her dignity to insist upon cancellation and to put herself into any sort of contest with her decidedly virgin opponent would simply be bad form. I inwardly gave a sigh of relief. And promptly sneezed.

'But there is one thing you must promise me,' Lady Caroline suddenly announced, sensing a victory to be achieved from defeat. 'This is to come to me next Thursday. It'll be just the sort of party you like. And I will not take no for an answer. Besides, it will be from eleven to four in the morning. You can surely find time to come to me. And if not, tell me where you're going and I'll send the coach for you. Do promise you'll come.'

I looked into Lady Caroline's hazel eyes. And I realised that she was pleading with me. Whatever the reason, good or bad, she wanted Rosina Wheeler there.

Whether it was because I made her laugh or acted as a honey pot for young men or whether I reminded her of her lost youth, Lady Caroline wanted me.

'Of course, I shall be delighted,' I said with total sincerity. The poodle puppy runt had finished her snuffling and had decided to relieve herself over one of my uncle's most expensive Turkish carpets. I averted my eyes and smiled winningly. 'And thank you so much for the gift of Miss Lamb. I'll take good care of her.'

'That's what all of us Lambs need,' Lady Caroline said, her vulnerability written all across her pale face and her large speaking eyes.

I remember gasping at the realisation that this woman, who had slept with the poet of a generation, truly needed me. I recall that I inwardly congratulated myself upon having made in every way the right decision. In retrospect, I wish I could blame my mood or my cold or the wretched lap dog, but it is inconceivable that I could have made a worse decision.

Later that day, the rain was still pouring down as my uncle handed me into his coach – somewhat nervously it must be confessed – as if he feared he might catch my cold himself. But I told him not to worry. 'My furs – or rather yours – will defy both fog and frost.' To emphasise my point, I pulled the Turkish pelisses about me. They had once been part of Sir John's uniform as a distinguished officer in the Napoleonic Wars but now they had been put to a more domestic use and Sir John seemed to approve rather than otherwise.

The coach rattled on and Sir John protested no more. I should explain that my uncle had always been quietly-spoken and mild-mannered for a military man. A few years earlier, his life had been severely disrupted when his sister had suddenly descended upon him, having left her husband, with two grown-up daughters, a belly full of anger and very distinct views on the rights of women. Sir John had conceived his future as quiet, peaceful and without event. Suddenly he found himself longing for a battlefield or at least the legal feuds of Guernsey instead of drunken diatribes from his sister and an obligation to display his newly acquired nieces across the floors of a fashionable London he neither liked nor understood. A shy man, unused to polite society, he hated every moment. When told that we all decamping to France, his relief was tangible.

When I had returned alone, it was a different matter. He was too gentle and polite to register his dismay or indeed to enquire too deeply into the circumstances of my return but I made every effort to reassure him that I was not my mother. And the effort had paid off. I had done my best not to disrupt his quiet existence with its rituals of water-colour painting, a game of chess with an old military friend and desultory work upon a chronicle of his achievements in Guernsey, which nobody, least of all Sir John, expected to be finished, let alone published.

We had come to quite enjoy each other's company on the occasions we went out together. And, let me repeat, I had no doubts whatever about the social cachet Sir John gave me as a young woman without mother or chaperone. However, I was also genuinely very fond of my bachelor uncle and sometimes contemplated planting a kiss upon his balding brow if I had not believed that it would have embarrassed him beyond measure.

The carriage now rattled to a halt. 'I believe we have arrived,' he announced peremptorily as if I could not have guessed that without his assistance.

I knew that he had agreed to come to Miss Benger's because it was much the least threatening of the social engagements I undertook. Anything involving Lady Caroline Lamb would be altogether a different matter. But here was a drawing-room which would be filled with old maids and, in some hidden way, General Sir John Doyle was also an old maid.

'Darling Rosina, how brave of you to come.' Miss Benger, birdlike and always alert, was all kindness when she saw my delicate state. 'If you have a cold, you must have the place of honour on the sofa by the fire.' I had sneezed delicately as I came through the door and, let me be honest, was delighted to be conducted to a seat which gave me the perfect place to observe all that was going on and to be observed as I elegantly reclined. My uncle, deterred by Miss Benger's effusiveness, withdrew, probably in the vain hope of discovering some old military acquaintance. Or at least a glass of his favourite Tokay. For all her literary airs, Miss Benger knew what gentlemen needed on such an occasion.

'Dearest Rosina, it's been an age since we've been able to talk.' Miss Benger was full of flattering attention and I realised another reason why I had been determined to come. It was rare to find somebody so totally besotted with one's own person and looks as she was. Miss Benger could have been an attractive woman. She had a sweetly-pretty blush-rose complexion. Her forehead, eyebrows and eyes were beautiful, the mouth not bad but the defaulter was her nose, which was one of the most ignoble and ill-formed snubs ever to do duty for that feature. Miss Benger had published what was generally reckoned to be a poetical portrait of my good self in her collection of antique lays, *The Golden Violet*. I blush to affirm that I featured as a dark-haired beauty called Lolotte, the heroine of a somewhat implausible Irish minstrel's legend called *The Haunted Lake*. Londoners had the vaguest idea of how grim the real Ireland was and still do. But given the lusciousness of my portrait, I did sometimes wonder if there might be something Sapphic in Miss Benger's feelings towards me, although she was undoubtedly too much of an innocent to be aware of such things.

'How heroic of you to come when you are far from well,' she murmured, 'You know how much I appreciate it. Mr. Jerdan of *The Literary Gazette* is here and I know he wants to meet you. He is fortunate enough to have met Mary Wollstonecraft in his youth and confirms everything that you wish to believe about her radiant and insightful genius.'

This is not a turn of conversation I had looked for. The mention of the author of *The Rights of Women* immediately raised the spectre of my own mother, the *soi-disante* Goddess of Reason, intoxicated, wagging a finger at my poor well-meaning uncle as she lectured him upon the subject. So despite my best intentions to be obliging, I confess I was only half paying attention. But before I was in danger of being found out, there was a slight commotion at the other end of the room followed by a sudden cessation of voices. Some new arrivals had entered the room.

Miss Benger stopped in the middle of her paean to her feminist goddess and registered who had arrived. But instead of rising to meet them immediately, she whispered to me *sotto voce*: 'Oh here is that odd, rich old woman, Mrs. Bulwer-Lytton, and Mr. Edward Bulwer, her son – her favourite. He is very clever, they say. His was the prize poem this year at Cambridge. He's just returned from Paris, I believe. I must introduce you to them.'

'O, pray don't, on any account,' I urged as Miss Benger hurried away to meet the new arrivals.

I remember that even then I was not sure that I wanted to make the acquaintance of the author of *Weeds and Wildflowers*. I would have to lie so much about how much I had enjoyed his verses. And just then I was feeling relaxed and elegantly ill on my fireside sofa.

The crowds parted slightly for Miss Benger as she rushed to shake the hands of the new arrivals and I had the opportunity to take an inventory of them. How to be true to my first impressions? I was certainly intrigued by what I saw but on no account was I immediately attracted.

They made the oddest contrast. The old lady, straight-backed and sharp-eyed, was dressed in a dark blue robe which, with its flounces and ruffles, would have been *démodé* before the Battle of Waterloo, topped by a turban which would have been dated any time these last thirty years. But if the lady was the incarnation of the dowdy and out of fashion, her son was in advance of his age or perhaps any age. His cobweb cambric shirt-front was a triumph of lace and embroidery. He had three inches of cambric encircling his coat cuffs, fastened with jewelled sleeve links. In his gloved and glittering right hand a gorgeous jewel-headed ebony cane, an item rarely brandished by a gentleman in any drawing-room I had ever visited, but maybe it was *à la mode* in Paris if Mr. Bulwer was fresh from there. His figure was tall and slim and he was certainly striking looking, but the effeminacy of the garb was matched by his hair, gold and abundant, which he wore in long ringlets that almost reached his shoulders. A line from Pope's *The Rape of the Lock* struck me and made me giggle. I longed to share it with Miss Benger.

> *'Sir Plume, of amber snuff-box justly vain,*
> *And the nice conduct of a clouded cane.'*

But I suppressed my giggle when I noticed the old lady had registered my study of them, rather longer than polite society would ordinarily tolerate. The lady gave me a searching look and then turned and made a remark to her son. A disparaging comment, I assumed. Many of those lay in the future. But on this occasion, apparently, it was a complimentary remark about my appearance.

Would that she had never made it.

Chapter Two: 1825–1827

From the Memoirs of Rosina, Lady Lytton

There's a king, I fancy, somewhere in Shakespeare who makes a long mournful speech about the Book of Fate. Retrospectively, the Book is not cheerful reading and he wishes he knew then what he knows now. The happiest youth, he says, who could view his progress through and what lies ahead would shut the book and sit him down and die. Or words to a similar effect. But little good it did the King knowing that, because the past was past, there was little he could do about it and it was too late then to sit himself and die as a perfectly healthy young man instead of living on, a disease-ridden old monarch.

Likewise, seeing Mrs. Bulwer Lytton approaching me inexorably like a stately galleon of an antique type with her lanky eager son in tow, I should have turned tail and run from the room. But, of course, I did not. Miss Benger had come up to where I was seated, bent down, and told me with some excitement that I must let her introduce me to Mrs. Bulwer Lytton and her son. Mrs. Bulwer Lytton had asked Miss Benger twice most particularly already as she had a party on the next evening and wished to invite me.

I pleaded my cold but Miss Benger persisted because it was written in the Book of Fate. She lowered her voice and added, 'Besides, you have made a desperate conquest of the young man. And he is so very clever and though a younger son, he is, they say, the old lady's favourite. So he will not be left without means.' I started to protest to Miss Benger that this was more information than I wished to hear. I was not in the business of fortune-hunting and spinsterhood, her own blessed state, was one I would happily aspire to. But I was fighting Fate and it was all too apparent they were both looking in my direction. 'I'm sure they know that I am speaking to you on the subject, Rosina,' pleaded Miss Benger. 'You cannot refuse without being markedly rude, which I know you would never wish to be.'

I made one last attempt at side-stepping Destiny. I sighed and looked piteously into Miss Benger's eyes. 'But I really feel so ill and so stupid and there doesn't appear to be much inspiration in them. What on earth can I talk to them about?'

'Why, taste, Shakespeare, the opera and all the rest of it. Besides, you who are fond of poetry will be quite at home, as the young man's was the prize poem at Cambridge this year and is really very good, I hear. You can ask him about that and it will be a very good opening.'

I could hardly point out that I had perused these deathless verses early that day as it would only have made matters worse. So there was nothing more to do but resign myself to my (now literally) approaching doom. I stood to undergo the ordeal of presentation. Mrs. Bulwer Lytton told me she was 'at home' on the following evening and said she would be 'vastly' (or as she always pronounced it, '*vaustly*') happy if I could do her the honour of coming with Miss Benger, adding, as soon as I had conditionally accepted her invitation, if my cold was not worse. She urged me to be seated 'though I'm sure you look so *vaustly* well no one could suppose you were labouring under any sort of indisposition.'

So there you have my future mother-in-law in a nutshell. She urged me to sit, although I could not possibly sit down while she was still standing. And while she was expressing concern about my cold, she was also pouring scorn upon the fact that it actually existed, despite the clear signs in my eyes and nose. And then there was her extraordinary pronunciation, the relic, like her clothes of a bygone era. 'My dear' was 'Meddear', 'Edward' was 'Eddard' and 'literary' was 'litry'. To this day I puzzle over why she invited me. Perhaps it was to bring a little youth and vitality to her withered gathering. Perhaps because she has been misinformed by somebody as to my financial prospects. Perhaps at the urging of her son, who stood by her side, smiling and nodding in agreement like a mechanical doll. Perhaps, and this is not the least likely explanation, she was ruled here as elsewhere in her life by the spirit of perversity.

Her objective achieved, Mrs. Bulwer Lytton passed on in search of other 'Curiosities of Literature' and left her son standing beside me. To be fair, for all the affectation of his dress, he was a slim and attractive figure then, before the corsets and the dye bottle attempted to keep the illusion of attractiveness alive. But he overdid the fulsomeness of his compliments, which were quite in keeping with the foppery of his dress. The effect was so nauseating that I vowed I would not pay him in kind and so never mentioned his prize poem to him. Finding me flattery-proof, he glided into something like rational conversation, so that I began to think there was something to him, but not enough to make me wish to meet him again in order to ascertain the truth. It was a relief to me when a peremptory look from his mother summoned him to her side at the other end of the room. Whereupon Miss Benger came back to me, and asked if I did not think him very clever. 'Well – yes, perhaps so,' I replied, 'only he is too decidedly of your opinion on that point.'

Very soon after this, the carriage, which I had ordered early, was announced. It would return for my uncle who, against the odds, was enjoying himself hugely with the attendant old maids of both sexes. No sooner had I reached the drawing-room door that Mr. Bulwer darted across the room to offer me his arm to take me and packed me up as carefully, as if I really had been something of value. He admired my sable as he helped me into the Persian-green Turkish pelisse I had rescued from my uncle's servants' hall. The night was rainy so I begged him not to come out but he would put me into the carriage and, regardless of the little cataracts that were falling from the servant's umbrella, still stood, hoping that I would honour his mother on the following evening.

When I looked back from the carriage window, he was still there.

So that is how I made Sir Liar's acquaintance. I have been as honest as I can about the first impressions he made on me. To receive the unstinted admiration of a young man not ill-looking or stupid is obviously flattering to any young woman but my head had not been turned nor did I foresee an affair of the heart ensuing. Dear Shakespeare, he has words for every occasion if, in this instance, one substitutes 'happiest maid' for 'happiest youth'.

A little note from Miss Benger the next day, just before dinner, nailing me to my appointment, left me no loophole of escape, so at half-past ten I called for her. On the way she enlightened me a little on the complexities of 'Eddard's' family. 'Well, my dear, Mrs. Bulwer Lytton was a Miss Lytton when she married General Bulwer. Two or three years after General Bulwer's death, her father, Mr Lytton of Knebworth, died and left her his sole heiress. She then re-took the name of Lytton and before that, as she was an heiress, all three sons – there are no daughters – were christened Lytton Bulwer.' She continued for some time in this vein till she lost me completely. I certainly had no inkling that I might one day be married to a man who ended up with the ridiculously vainglorious name of Edward George Earle Lytton Bulwer-Lytton, 1st Baron Lytton. Even Sir Liar thought there were one too many Lyttons in there. (Mr. Thackeray christened him 'Sawedwadgeorgeearllittnbulwig' which amused me *vaustly*.)

Miss Benger was still talking lineage like a continental marriage-broker when we arrived at Mrs. Bulwer Lytton's house in Upper Seymour Street. The hostess was dressed as on the previous evening, only with two diamond necklaces instead of one. Not so her son. His costume was greatly subdued and consequently he seemed much more gentleman-like. From not being so exaggerated to look at, he appeared much more worthy of being listened to. His manner, too, had markedly improved. It was more subdued almost to diffidence. And from the moment I sat down, after speaking to his mother, there was an evident appropriation of me on his part, which had nothing offensive or unmannerly in it. So I took a deep breath and enquired as to the subject of his prize poem.

'Sculpture' came the reply.

'So you've chosen a subject which pays homage to two of the liberal arts in one,' I replied, determined never to reveal I'd read this dreary work. 'A very far-sighted selection.' He made me a low bow. Soon after this he asked me to go down and take some refreshment as the heat of the room was overpowering. I agreed since my companion was not, as he was on the previous evening, trying to shine and therefore was much more interesting and really agreeable. I cannot, of course, record half of what was said on that evening, and only wish I could forget it all. Finding we were the only two persons in the as-yet uninvaded refreshment-room, having admired the flowers and drunk a glass of water apiece, which was all I required, I expressed a wish to return upstairs.

'Oh, for heaven's sake, don't!' pleaded my companion. 'It does seem such sacrilege to see you among those old fossils.' He then held my attention by a series of satirical silhouettes of the human mosaic upstairs. I own he made me laugh more than once, though I felt I could not be so ill bred as to join in ridiculing his mother's guests, however ridiculous they might be. But his portraits were full of a sly humour and shrewd observation I had not previously expected of him and I felt a relaxation between us there had not been before.

But then in the midst of all this persiflage, his mother's not very dulcet tones were heard calling down, 'Eddard! Eddard! You really must not hide the star of the evening down here.' She came downstairs and advanced towards me with a paddle-like wave of her right hand, destroying whatever pleasure her son and I were enjoying in each other's company for the first but not the last time. 'So *vaustly* kind of you to come, dear madam, so I cannot have you wasted down here.' She then laid on her compliments so thickly and so coarsely that I felt considerably abashed as we were determinedly marched back upstairs to her son's evident chagrin.

I was introduced to a number of the old fossils, who may or may not have once been eminent literary figures, but now displayed all the animation of antique painted dolls. I was the only guest under the age of twenty-five, so perhaps that really was the reason why the incomprehensible old lady had invited me. Fresh air was notably lacking in the stifling room both practically and intellectually and never before had I felt I might actually embody 'a breath' of that commodity. Though I say it myself, I was charming as I pressed the aged ringed hands and bent to hear anecdotes which seemed to have neither purpose nor end.

'Eddard' reclaimed me when he could. He found me a chair and flung himself into another beside me. Leaning back, as if quite exhausted, he asked me to lend him my fan. I watched in amusement as he fanned himself for about a minute but now he shared my amusement at his foppery. He handed back my fan and was about to continue our scandalous conversation of downstairs when Mrs. Bulwer Lytton was again advancing towards us out of the next room, where there were two card tables.

'My dear,' she said, advancing towards her son with a pack of cards in her hand. 'I'm *vastly* sorry to interrupt your agreeable tête-à-tête with so much beauty and fascination. Her praise is on everyone's lips. But Lady Winterton is waiting for a fourth to make up her whist party and you must come, Eddard.'

He raised his eyes to heaven and apologised profusely but he went. A lesson for the future.

From the Uncollected Correspondence of Lord Lytton

Mr. E. Lytton Bulwer presents his compliments to Miss Wheeler; he has just returned from the Isle of Thanet, and intends going into Hertfordshire tomorrow or the next day. He would feel so extremely flattered could he be the bearer of any note to our neighbour Lady Caroline, or execute any other commission for Miss Wheeler.

From an Unpublished Autobiography by Lord Lytton

Before the drink got to her, my wife was a remarkably beautiful woman. When I first saw her at Miss Benger's gathering, she was breathtakingly so, a fresh Irish rose blooming amidst the drab weeds of London. She was tall, with an exquisite complexion, dark hair and bright grey-green eyes, which sparkled and changed colour with every emotion. Her nose was finely chiselled, her forehead broad and high, her mouth small, her teeth perfect, though her chin was perhaps somewhat too square and determined, an augury of the stubbornness I came to know all too well. But then she also had a remarkably fine figure with the bust and arms of a statue of Venus. She moved with an innate vivacity and elegance that was captivating and would have stood out in any gathering, let alone one as filled with dowdy spinsters as Miss Benger's. No wonder my mother's sharp eye could not fail to notice her.

I write as one who has long awoken from a dream and now endeavours to recapture its seductive magic in the cold light of day. I had known women, of course, and experienced all the pangs of love but she was, alas, a vision. She was lovely and all the more attractive, it must be owned, because she kept a distance and desired to be wooed rather than being easily won. You will, of course, understand that I am not talking carnally here. The courtesans of Paris were one thing and I was glad to have experienced it. But this, at first at least, was something, I have to admit, very close to love.

Perhaps call it enchantment because, as I discovered, there was something calculating and deliberately intriguing about how Rosina responded to me. But it has to be acknowledged that at first I thought her both extremely beautiful, a matter not really up for dispute if you had seen Rosina in her early twenties, and also a delightful companion, who listened attentively but was not afraid to challenge or to question if it was within the bounds of modesty. Oh yes, she had a quick perception and a charming smile to accompany her *apercus,* which meant that in those early days you did not fully register their shallowness.

I was a man whose very soul had been painfully bruised. At the time I thought it was damaged forever. I did not want fulsome adulation. I could already perceive the falsity of flattery not truly meant from those who chose to laugh at me behind my back. There have been women, usually it has to be said homely in their looks, who have expressed such enthusiasm for my writings that it would have been hyperbolic even if I was Shakespeare, Dante and Lord Byron combined. Men too, particularly as I am now also a man of some political influence and authority, will praise my latest novel or my latest stage play with what they see as manly and discreet compliments and I see as blatant sycophancy. Rosina, whatever her faults (and God knows they were and are many), never resorted to such crude means to find her way into my heart. But then she has never been without intelligence, however ill-trained and ill-applied.

I own that I was delighted that my mother invited her to her own literary evening the next night. But it was her decision not mine, though I will regret that she made it until the day I die. Rosina would have been a lovely vision, glimpsed once and never forgotten, a *houri* out of the world of the Arabian Nights, a consolation to my soul for the sadness it was enduring.

So how did the lovely vision appear the next time I saw her? Again in the context of one of my mother's interminable soirées, she seemed adorable. I discerned already a certain superficiality in her mind but then beautiful women are not created to be blue stockings. That is a role reserved for the unmarried and the unattractive, as Lord Byron has so wittily observed in his poem *The Blues*. Please do not imagine that I do not appreciate intelligence in women. My own mother was often most perceptive, particularly in a domestic context. And Lady Caroline could after all not be designated stupid, however foolish she may have been. I should also mention Mrs. Cunningham, a woman of great innate wisdom who never failed to listen nor, if it was necessary, to challenge.

But to return, as I inevitably must, to Rosina and our second meeting. I had endured hours of praise for my Prize Poem from men and women I knew even then were lying. At that time I thought my writing career was over. To be honest, I thought my life was over but even at the time I sensed that was a trifle too Byronic. A woman who could look you in the eye with her own beautiful grey-green eyes and ask straightforward questions was a woman to be cherished. As I talked to her, I became more and more who I truly was. To be honest, my mother's literary evenings were something to be endured. To spend time there with someone with an Irish directness and (let it be said again) a remarkably attractive face and figure was enough to turn Purgatory into Paradise.

She was balm to my soul at a time when it desperately desired consolation. I would have been grateful to her and probably forgotten her if my busy life as a politician and author had developed in the way that it has. But I was young and I was in pain and she had offered me a mild flirtation and some kind of release.

I am reminded of the lines in the second part of the Immortal Bard's *King Henry the Fourth*. The anxious king, tortured by ingratitude and uncertainty, looks back over his life and the betrayals he has endured and arrives at this undisputable conclusion:

> '*The happiest youth, viewing his progress through,*
> *What perils past, what crosses to ensue,*
> *Would shut the book and sit him down and die.*'

In many ways, I was and still am that unhappy monarch.

My mother, to use an analogy which some will find blasphemous (for which I forgive them), was like Our Lord. The Lord Giveth and the Lord Taketh away. My mother was forever both a generous giver and a carping taker-away. It was my mother who pointed out to me the beautiful vision that was Rosina. It was my mother who practically begged Rosina to visit her house. Her motives? To bring a touch of beauty into her drab soirées or to defer the moment at which I left her house and headed as I had planned back to Knebworth? Who can fathom the thoughts of mankind – or woman kind? But now came the Taking Away.

The morning after I had encountered Rosina for the second time and, for reasons all too apparent, favoured her above my mother's other guests, I found myself facing my mother across the breakfast table.

Once the servants had departed, she began. 'Edward, I am concerned.'

Of course, I enquired why, though I could see the signs of worry etched across her face, even though as a true Stoic she did her best to conceal her feelings. I recognised the signs from a past when I had been expelled from yet another school or run up gambling debts of which she did not approve. To be honest, I dreaded their reappearance.

'It's Miss Wheeler.' 'What about her?'

'She is both attractive and charming but all is not what it seems.'

I was, I recall, extremely startled at this description of someone she had insisted upon inviting. But I knew my mother well enough not to protest immediately.

'I am not implying that the girl herself is in any way an improper person to have in one's house. She is after all the niece of Sir John Doyle, a man of untarnished reputation and good social standing.'

Again I deemed it best to wait. 'But last night I made enquiries.' 'Enquiries of whom?' I ventured.

'Those better acquainted with Miss Wheeler's position than we are.' My mother cleared her throat daintily, an action which usually preceded the delivery of unwelcome information. 'It really does not matter who said what. The facts are apparently common knowledge.' She pulled her morning gown around her as if suddenly disturbed by a blast of cold air.

I owed everything to my mother but at times like this I wished that I did not. I could still only wait.

'The problem is not with her uncle but with her mother and father. The father is dead but was a drunken reprobate who wasted the family estates. Her mother, alas, is still alive but a woman of erratic behaviour and even, it is believed, given to heavy drinking. Moreover, her opinions are dangerously radical and totally unbecoming in a woman of any age. She is at present resident in France, indication enough of her unacceptability in polite society here in England. But it is far from certain she will always remain there.'

I waited for a moment respectfully before replying. 'I am still not sure that I feel that this family background reflects badly upon Miss Wheeler, who has obviously distanced herself from her mother and sought out the protection of her uncle.'

'That is indeed to her credit,' my mother acknowledged. 'I am not saying for a moment that it is not or that she should be in any way excluded from polite society. I was, as you know, much taken with the girl. She is a true beauty with a very amiable manner. However, be that as it may, her uncle is not a rich man.'

I failed for the moment to make the connection. 'He is surely comfortably enough off.'

'Indeed, but he has no fortune to leave to his niece. And due to the profligacy of her parents, who have wasted every scrap of money which might come to her, there is no dowry to talk of. She has a small pittance of eighty pounds a year from a small inheritance her mother has failed to get her clutches upon. And that, I fear, is that.'

Her stern eyes studied my countenance for my reaction. At first, I experienced nothing but puzzlement. The old harpies of last night had clearly been only too glad to impart this information to my mother. But why had she felt the need to impart this information to me? And then as I pondered further, I realised that this could only mean one thing. My mother feared that my pleasant little flirtation with the lovely Miss Wheeler might be something more than that.

I think I said teasingly: 'Really, mother, do you really think I have fallen head over heels in love?'

'I'm glad that I don't need to spend any more time discussing this matter. You have set my doubts to rest.'

And so the breakfast conversation turned elsewhere and my mother seemed positively relieved that I was intent on returning to Knebworth as I had always planned.

There is a certain perversity, I acknowledge, in my nature. I have never responded easily to authority, even to that vested quite rightly in my mother. I was after all a grown man and I had seen the world. Or so I thought, although I had really only experienced the merest taste of the cruelties, betrayals and corruption which lay ahead. I honestly believe I might never have thought more of Miss Wheeler, delightful though she seemed, had it not been for that conversation. Seeing Rosina again had implicitly been banned. Bans were something I defied. From the very first, my mother's actions drove me inexorably into the company of my future wife. I had no intention of marrying her so what was the point of my mother's prohibition except to excite me to challenge it?

Besides, I had not been asked never to see Miss Wheeler again, simply to bear in mind she was not a proper marriage object. So I met her on any number of occasions over the next few months at various literary and social gatherings without much prior arrangement. I continued to enjoy her beauty and her sharp if often malicious wit and to look forward to seeing her again. My heart had been blighted and she brought nourishment to its arid core. But I firmly believe matters would have gone no further than that were it not for the other reasons which I will subsequently unfold.

In writing fiction, particularly Romantic fiction of a type I have now abandoned, there is an artifice which insists that nothing important ever happens in the world of the novel apart from the dramatic encounters between the two central lovers.

Life outside their bubble simply does not exist. In real life, of course, many other commitments force themselves upon a man's attention. There are the social engagements that any gentleman must undertake in keeping track of his affairs and cultivating the acquaintance of other gentlemen of the world. There are the duties attendant on having property or administering property on behalf of others.

However, in my case, there was much more. I had come to a momentous decision. I had finally managed to put aside the many doubts I had entertained about my literary ability. I realised that the demons which possessed me were the result of my hyper-sensitive nature when faced with the world and my persistence in judging myself against the geniuses of the English language. To be honest, I had looked around at those who currently wrote and judged my talents as good as theirs. Indeed, almost certainly better. And, let me be frank, as a younger son with a limited income, the modest addition provided from my pen seemed attractive. Of course, I had no idea then of the heights I would achieve nor of the ghastly fate when the pen (though mightier than the sword as I once wrote) might also control my life. But it has always been my nature to anticipate and I must not do that now. I began work upon a long poem in the romantic vein, full of rebels, banshees and scaffolds, entitled *O'Neill, or the Rebel*. Its subject matter owed more to my fondness for the Scottish balladry of Sir Walter Scott and a fascination with the Emerald Isle, which was *à la mode*, than my growing interest in Miss Wheeler. I cannot disown it because I wrote it but I am content that it has been consigned to bibliographic oblivion.

My second undertaking was altogether a different affair because it pointed the way to the future. I embarked upon a novel, albeit in one volume instead of the three volumes which were the custom then, but a novel nevertheless. At the time I poured my soul into it. In the clearer light of reason, I have declined to let it ever be reprinted, despite its respectable initial sales. Since you are unlikely therefore to have encountered this work, I feel I should offer a brief account of its nature, told (I blush to acknowledge) often in the form of letters, that dated device of fiction now abandoned by all but a few benighted souls. Falkland is a young man of sound if complex background, uncertain of himself and afflicted by a melancholy he cannot altogether explain. He meets a fascinating woman, Lady Emily Mandeville, married to a dullard. They begin a doomed flirtation. They are passionately in love but neither of them can bear to cross the boundaries that lead to flight, adultery and social pariahdom, although Lady Emily's marriage is deeply unhappy. Eventually the stress upon Lady Emily becomes unendurable. A song is sung to the lovers as they sit in her family drawing-room which strikes her to the heart:

'If doomed to grief through life thou art,
'Tis thine at least unstain'd to die!
Oh! better break at once thy heart
Than rend it from its holiest tie!'

She staggers from the room and is found apparently lifeless, having broken a blood vessel. Though she survives long enough to exchange sad epistles full of guilt and foreboding with young Falkland, she expires before a second attempt at elopement can succeed. A devastated Falkland, burdened now with more guilt and remorse than ever before, though with slightly better reason, goes off to Spain to fight the French and perishes there.

You will imagine you understand the reasons why I suppressed such a book, but it is not only because it was a piece of juvenilia. Lady Caroline read the novel when it was published. It was written in such a frenzy of inspiration that I had no opportunity to show it to her earlier, but it turned out that there was no need. In her airy way, she declared it accomplished but too gloomily Byronic even for her taste. She never indicated for a single moment that she might be She, I might be I and her husband could be He. For this I suppose I should give some credit to my skill in transforming what had happened into something she did not recognise – or could choose not to recognise. Meanwhile Mrs. Cunningham, my mentor and a lady of impeccable character, suffered considerably from the insinuations of her husband and friends that she might be the doomed lady. This is the problem with literature. People are free to make of it what they may.

Undoubtedly the book is the book of a posturing young man, who takes his own troubles too seriously. It was the book of a puppy who wallowed in self-pity and the grown-up dog wishes to forget it as if it were a well-chewed bone emptied of savour and buried in the earth. When Goethe published *The Sorrows of Young Werther*, it is recorded that young men all over Germany committed suicide in imitation of the despairing young lover. I had no wish to provoke a similar spate of military suicides among the fashionable young men of my own society. I jest about this now but at the time everybody still carried in their mind Byron's heroic but futile death at Missolonghi fighting for Greek independence and most of us would have liked to make a similar gesture, providing it did not have fatal consequences.

But there were reasons for suppressing the book which had nothing to do with its immaturity or with protecting those who might be directly harmed by implication. If Lady Caroline could not see herself in Lady Emily, why should anyone else? So now to the fundamental reason why you would have to discover an antiquated circulating library with mildewed volumes upon its shelves to find

Falkland. It concerns its final pages. Falkland lies dying and he contemplates what lies beyond:

> 'There is no Oedipus to solve the enigma of life. We are – whence came we? We are *not*, whither do we go? All things *in* our existence have their object; existence has none. We live, move, beget our species, perish – and *for what*? Is it merely to pant beneath this weary load; to sicken of the sun; to grow old; to drop like leaves into the grave; and to bequeath to our heirs the worn garments of toil and labour that we leave behind? Is it to sail for ever on the same sea, ploughing the ocean of time with new furrows, and feeding its billows with new wrecks? Or perhaps…'

And here Falkland loses consciousness.

When my mother read these words, she wrote to me:

> 'My dear Edward, what a different, what a much better, moral you might have given to your book had you only altered the last two pages of it! What sort of moral does it contain now? There can be no purpose in life without faith in death, and no moral worth where there is no moral purpose. You paint your hero as superior to the rest of his species. You wish us to recognise his superiority, for you have no right to interest us so powerfully in his feelings and his fate, if they are not those of a person entitled to our admiration or our sympathy. But what does his superiority consist of? And what does it come to? Presumptuous egotism! Selfish vanity in attachments that do no good to their possessor, and do harm to others. Why write as if you thought power could exist without purpose, or purpose without belief? Child, this is unworthy of you.'

I still have this letter, fading now and with the creases for ever cutting across its yellowish paper. A part of me rebelled. A part of me still rebels because I struggle to believe the religious certainties she took as a matter of course. But the novel invites the reader to sympathise with Falkland and he is in many ways not only a flawed human being but a self-obsessed and deeply selfish human being in a way I hope I am no longer.

Of course, Rosina read the novel. She was full of praise. I wrote to her to explain that I was not Falkland. Or at least he was only a small part of me. Unfortunately, she believed me.

From the Uncollected Correspondence of Lord Lytton

My Dear Adored Angel Poodle,

Many, many thanks for oo darling letter. Me is so happy, me is wagging my tail and putting my ears down, me is to meet oo tomorrow. Oh day of days! I cannot tell you how very, very, very happy you had made me! Oh zoo love of loves, me is ready to leap out of my skin for joy!

Adieu. Twenty million kisses.

Puppy

From the Memoirs of Rosina, Lady Lytton

A few years ago, Edward learned that I had kept all the correspondence he had written to me during the ups and downs of our remarkably protracted courtship. I understand his anxiety because the truth is there in all its undeniable awfulness, full of baby talk, sickly sentimentality and self-delusion. Mine, alas, as well as his. Being Sir Niggardly Liar, he offered me a contemptible hundred pounds for their return. As always, his meanness will prove self-defeating and one day they will be published in all their cringe-worthy glory to his eternal chagrin. In the meantime they remain in my possession.

The letters tell the story of how he wooed me and (unfortunately) won me. He was not fully Sir Liar then and so he probably meant much of what he said, at least at the moment he said it. In a way, it's sad to look through the letters and see that as a young man he had a certain vulnerability and a spontaneity that has totally disappeared behind the mask of the public figure he now is. And to read them is to think again of that unfortunate Shakespearean monarch whose name I can never remember.

In his preliminary letters, he is polite, attentive and shyly shares the 'yearning weakness' of his nature. He has the modesty to fear his love may not be shared. While, in the background, lurks Eddard's *vaustly* important mother. Very early on in our correspondence, he wrote: 'I feel too well that she would not give her consent to a marriage which, while she acknowledges it as most honourable, appears to her imprudent. But that is only UNDER PRESENT CIRCUMSTANCES.' Sir Liar always favoured capital letters upon moments of particular self-importance. I recollect being rather startled by the insinuation that that was where our innocent little flirtation was apparently leading, so I assured him that I'd no intention of coming between him and his mother. No doubt, I said it more elegantly, but it was like water off the proverbial duck's back. He continued to bombard me with paper kisses and shared secrets I had no desire to share.

I had also to endure his agonies over his first-born novel. It had the merit which few of his later works shared of being comparatively short, but then there is so much gloom and self-pity in Mr. Falkland that it would be torture to spend longer in his company. Eddard assured me he was not the same as his hero and I own I was convinced. A man who signs himself Puppy, calls me Poodle and draws me elaborate diagrams of how our love eclipses all else in the world, accompanied by a register of kisses exchanged and kisses owing, was both sillier and more likeable than his hero. What Lady Caroline made of the book I never truly found out. It was obvious to the veriest simpleton that Mr. Pen-wielding Puppy had her in mind with his portrait of a near neighbour married to a dullard (though nobody else has ever described William Lamb or Lord Melbourne as he later became as a nonentity). But Lady Caroline had been immortalised by Byron, so perhaps Eddard's tribute meant very little to her. And Lady Emily was so dull and tortured that only Mr. Falkland could have wanted to elope with her. Presumably so that they could stand on the tops of craggy mountains and be thoroughly miserable about the state of the world and the unhappy wretches who inhabit it in the authentic Byronic style. But I could describe forever how I was wooed and how I responded but how did I come to believe myself to be in love with my attentive Puppy? Attention is always flattering, particularly from a man who is well-connected, not unattractive, with good manners and something approaching literary talent. But to believe I loved him? How did that come about? How to explain the inexplicable?

How did we even come to be Puppy and Poodle? That much can be simply explained. The poodle Lady Caroline had given me, Miss Lamb, had happily gone missing while one of my Jeames was taking it for a walk. This particular Jeames, a well built version of the species, was blamed, but I gave him a sovereign and forgave his negligence. When Edward learned of my loss, he was so full of genuine sympathy that I did not dare to tell him that I hated the dog. Instead, I had to accept becoming his beloved Poodle who was never ever to go missing. In return, I offered to call him Puppy or Pups, because at the time he still had a self-awareness which led him on occasion to describe himself as a self-indulgent puppy of a young man. So there you have it. I felt it all to be quite charming at the time.

Much of what happened between us was indeed charming but what Eddard might describe as the magical, the otherworldly, the fairy, and possibly many more adjectives, element was Brocket Hall, the family seat of the Lambs.

You have first to understand about Ballywire, which is where I was brought up. It had been a castle once, but all that remained to entitle it to that appellation was one solitary turret in which was situated the nursery for my sister and myself. Otherwise, it was a long, straggling pile of white, or rather grey, building, stuck on a cliff in the wildest and most remote part of the Western Irish coast. Please do not imagine this was romantic as so many simpering London bards, my husband included, chose to think. It was freezing cold, the rain fell incessantly and the entrance hall, to give an example, was paved with grey marble, it is true, but broken and indented because my drunken father never had the means to replace it. Hanging around its walls were the colossal horns of Irish elk, shot over the centuries by my father's ancestors, more by luck than skill because they were almost certainly drunk at the time. These horns scared me as a child and their shape recurs more often in my dreams than I care to acknowledge.

So imagine then my feelings on being transported to Brocket Hall, a fine tall red-brick mansion in the neoclassical style set in a glorious landscape with a Palladian bridge. The main staircase was an elegant, inviting, circling curve with a decorative balustrade to match. The Grand Saloon was built on a magnificent scale, far beyond not only poor crumbling Ballywire but also Knebworth, of which Eddard and his mama were so vaustly proud. Chippendale furniture, a ceiling where gods and nymphs frolicked in a way that would be unseemly if it were not so impeccably neoclassical. Mirrors and portraits reflected Italian glass candelabra in a way that was giddying after just one glass of wine.

Please bear with me as I try to explain how I fell in love – for bad or bad – with Sir Fopling Windbag.

In this Saloon, apparently, one year Lady Caroline held a state banquet in honour of her husband. The guests were as distinguished as guests can be. She arranged a special surprise course. A large silver dish was brought in by an army of stalwart male servants. When the lid was raised, there was Lady Caroline inside, completely naked. I do not know what the assembled guests made of this spectacle or indeed whether it is true, since Lady Caroline always denied it with a knowing complicitous smile on her face. All I can record is that if Lady Caroline had served herself naked at the point at which I knew her, the guests would probably have been unable to swallow another mouthful of their supper, however sumptuous it may have been.

The truth is that Lady Caroline was not in as good shape as Brocket Hall. Her husband had, with rare generosity, after their separation allowed her the use of Brocket, to which she was devoted. She cavorted ostentatiously with the mad, bad and dangerous to know Lord Byron (I sometimes think she was the dangerous one, not him) and, with dignity, Lamb, as he then was, extricated himself from further involvement. But he was generous!

Sir Liar, for all his earnings from his execrable fiction, cannot apparently afford one hundred pounds to prevent his shameful mawkish correspondence from being published. William Lamb, I salute you.

Lady Caroline, as I have observed before, needed me by her side at Brocket. Without false vanity, I was engaging, attractive and intelligent. I had only to look round the dreary circles that represented literary and social life for the likes of Miss Benger and Eddard's pompous mamma to see why I might be desirable as a house guest. I do not want to be boastful but the truth is that I felt very sorry for Lady Caroline. The love of her life had died in the arms of a Grecian ephebe to whom he was almost certainly more attracted to than her good self. She had built a funeral pyre in the grounds of Brocket and burned every last memento of Byron to the eternal chagrin of his grovelling admirers. Her husband had behaved throughout with a dignity and generosity which made it impossible to blame him for all her ills. However, to be candid, Lady Caroline was no longer a dish to be served up as a banquet and she desired my company.

Edward was, it so happened, a near neighbour, so he could come across and join the assembled gathering and sometimes stay and sometimes not. He was always attentive and, increasingly, I enjoyed his intelligence and elegant figure. The other guests were meanwhile limited to those who were still prepared to be acquainted with Lady Caroline and risk their local reputation for a fine supper in exquisite surroundings. Most of these people were dull as ditchwater, so solid in their own dullness that they could not conceive a world outside their slug-like existence. She was Lady Caroline and, therefore, they came. The remainder prized themselves on their enlightened views and their admiration for George Gordon Byron, late of this parish.

So, without doubt, Eddard shone.

When the dinner guests were no longer there, Lady Caroline always needed me more than ever. She was – God and her medicine chest knew – in a parlous state. She was taking any number of drugs, of which her favourite was what she called 'the black pill' and the rest of us call laudanum. But then there was the 'blue pill' and the 'red pill' and the 'brown pill', all taken with no great regularity or logic but with increasing recklessness. When her digestion was thoroughly disturbed, she imbibed cascara bark, given to her in a glass of sherry to hide the strong taste of liquorice. And then a medicinal glass of sherry was hardly the beginning and end of her drinking and often she lay across my lap in floods of drunken tears.

Undoubtedly there was a price to be paid for the wonderful experience of staying at Brocket. The difference from when I first knew her in London was startling and, it has to be said, instructive. It gives me no pleasure to record her sad decline but it taught me a lesson. A woman must never give in to despair, however great the provocation and however eminent the man.

Meanwhile, in the magical atmosphere of Brocket, the layers of affectation seemed to drop away from Eddard. His every appearance there was like a breath of fresh air; he was no longer a self-seeking dandy but someone who was interested in me for myself.

Several evenings we walked across the grounds to the Palladian bridge and stood there in the clear air, looking down into the water below. There was a stillness, a relaxation I had never experienced before with a man. Somehow, the mask had dropped. When he whispered soft words into my ears, I heard them in a way I had never heard his words when he boasted about himself and what he had achieved. Most of the men I'd encountered – apart from my spinster uncle – had been brutes, commencing with my own father. In addition, I never had a brother so have missed that sort of easy affection with a man. We were Pups and Poodle and it felt (at the time) quite delightful.

Remember, Eddard was handsome (enough), he was intelligent and charming and he was devoted to me. I should say he 'seemed' these things, but at the time I felt them to be true. He hardly mentioned his mother, which was a sign of how happy our idyll was and how little it had to with the world outside. I could tease him and he actually enjoyed it.

Then one evening everything suddenly became more serious. It began, as things so often did at this time, with Lady Caroline. We had all endured a particularly tedious evening's entertainment in the Grand Saloon and Lady Caroline, having imbibed a great deal more wine than she should have, descended into tantrums and floods of tears.

'I hate them! I hate them all! They laugh at me behind my back. They report on me to William in the hope that he will throw me out of Brocket. Oh, I've heard their whispering and their sneering. It's intolerable. What have I done to deserve this?' She threw a wine glass across the floor of the Grand Saloon, having first ensured that it was thoroughly emptied.

Most of the guests had left. Eddard had remained and now he made an attempt to console her by reassuring her that her guests felt no such thing. They all held her in the greatest esteem. It wasn't true, but I admired him for saying it. After all, she had chosen them.

'Get out!' The remark was addressed to the room rather than Eddard in particular and it was accompanied by sweeping a whole array of wine glasses from the table. As the servants, well used to her moods, hurriedly tried to clear up as many fragments of glass as they could before more followed, the few remaining guests headed sheepishly for the door. Eddard and I were soon the only ones left as she put her head on the table and burst into more self-pitying tears.

It was my turn to try and save the situation. I approached Lady Caroline and put my hands reassuringly upon her semi-naked shoulders (she still favoured a décolleté style which denied the years). I had consoled her on other occasions similarly since I had arrived, but not so publicly. Perhaps that was why she screamed at me not to touch her. Then she looked and saw that, apart from an army of servants trying hard not to look at anything except the floor, only Eddard and myself were left.

'And, as for you pair of turtledoves, don't think I don't know what you're up to. Perhaps I should tell you each what I know about the other. I'm not running a whore-house, though the neighbours think I am. Get out!'

The table was nearly cleared but she found one more glass to smash. The servants doubtless bore her to bed, but we looked at each other and left immediately. I was upset and insulted, and only the fact that she had consumed an unusually vicious combination of black, green and grey pills together with quantities of wine could possibly excuse Lady Caroline's behaviour, if I had wanted to excuse her and, at that point, I did not.

Eddard wished to leave because these were scenes embarrassing and upsetting to both of us. The outburst in her last drunken speech lingered, although neither of us spoke. It was at this point Eddard proved himself both tactful and attentive. He led me out into the grounds. We breathed the fresh air and felt the calm that the landscape of Brocket always brought to us with its happy combination of the skill of the gardener and the beauty of nature. He apologised for Lady Caroline, but there was no need for him to apologise because it genuinely was not his fault. I valued his support because the truth is that I was close to tears myself.

We walked slowly towards the bridge, where we had contemplated the river, the river which flowed through Eddard's early poems, and accepted that there was a flow to life like a flow to water and we were part of it. Recall, we were all Romantics then.

On the way, in the fading light, we passed through the shrubbery. The roses were almost over. There were browning petals on the ground and buds withering in the changing climate. But on one plant, an exquisite deep yellow rose bud still grew. Without hesitation, Eddard reached out and plucked it.

'See,' he said, holding it in his fingers, 'Tomorrow it will be in transition from bloom to flower, but this evening it is perfect.' After all the uproar, suddenly in the tranquillity of the shrubbery, *everything* seemed perfect. Eddard held the rose bud for a moment in his hand. He smelt it and then he looked into my eyes and handed it to me. I was moved. After all, he did not later become a successful dramatist without understanding the tawdry effectiveness of theatrical business.

Enchanted, I held the rose bud to my nose. He planted a chaste kiss upon my cheek. It was a moment of enchantment. Morgan le Fay could not have achieved better.

'Dearest Poodle,' he began, but suddenly all his eloquence was gone from him. Instead of producing a thousand words upon any subject under the sun in his usual verbose manner, he was silent. For once he knew that to say too much would be to destroy everything. Tears filled his eyes. Tears filled mine. I felt for him. I felt sorry for him.

I'm afraid that night in that shrubbery I trusted in my instincts and believed in him. That was where the bond was made. Neither of us knew then that it was a pair of manacles we had created for ourselves.

Once he was sure I felt calmer, he left. I went up to bed with the rose bud in my hand. I knew it would fade, but all the same I was trying to hold on to something perhaps even then I knew would never return. A few weeks later, I sent the bud to him as a pledge of our love. I've never seen or heard of it since.

The next day, Lady Caroline, recovered and apologetic, made me a long speech warning me against Eddard. She explained all the problems with his mother, with his inheritance, with his previous amatory history (she did not specify, thank Heaven) and his self-obsession. She made my head ache with her admonitions and I could not wait to quit the breakfast table.

Rarely has good advice been given so inopportunely. I thought I was in love and her words only pushed me more firmly into the arms of Eddard, Sir Liar in Waiting. How could I credit a drunken unhappy woman who envied my looks and my opportunities?

From the Correspondence of Rosina, Lady Lytton

Darlingest Pups,

Does oo remember that day in the shrubbery, darling, when you said oo was sorry that I was upset by what Lady C said? Oo was ready to put down your tail and trot back to Knebworth but oo stayed because Poodle was in tears. Does oo remember plucking this poor little rosebud the only one in the shrubbery and giving it to Poodle?

Yours own Rosebud.

From an Unpublished Autobiography by Lord Lytton

This is a secret I have kept to myself for many years and which I only entrust to paper because I will be dead before this is read by another person. A year or so before our marriage, Rosina gave herself to me. I do not want to excuse myself or to blame her in the way of libertines through the ages. I simply set down the fact. And, of course, it explains everything. This was no longer a flirtation. As an honourable man, I had to marry her whether I wished to or not. She was not a courtesan and her marriage prospects would have been irrevocably damaged if I withdrew.

There. I have said it. Everything that follows ensues from my belief that I could not abandon Rosina, however unfavourable our marriage prospects were and however much her superficial wit and blowsy beauty began to pall.

I do not wish to go into further details. I have honourably kept this secret for many years to protect Rosina and she would go into paroxysms of denial anyway if ever the subject was aired publicly. Suffice it to say that in a house as large and chaotic as Brocket there were many occasions on which, finding ourselves alone, we could have expressed the strong attraction we felt towards each other in the obvious physical way. Oh yes, I will never deny that I found Rosina attractive. Other men who knew her at that time have written admiringly of her charms. And at that period in Brocket our physical infatuation with each other was at its height. Moralists rightly warn of the dangers of succumbing to the lure of the flesh. The Church correctly preaches against incontinence of all kinds. But we were young and often together and it was not always possible to restrain ourselves as we should. I acknowledge I did not behave as a gentleman should in claiming her virginity, even though she pleaded for me to take it. But I behaved like a gentleman afterwards because I did not abandon her to her Fate and the social ignominy that might well have followed if she was recognised as the fallen woman she had become.

It would be wrong to blame my mother for my behaviour. She could not possibly have ever guessed the truth of what had happened at Brocket. Worldlier wise persons than she have never perceived the truth, so my mother with her limited experience and rigorous morality had no chance, I am thankful to say. I suppose I should be grateful that she tried to persuade me from marrying Rosina, since she was wiser than I in perceiving the storm-tossed ship wreck that lay ahead. But, alas, the way in which she went about her self-appointed task drove me straight into the storm instead of out of it. Consider. I was a man in his twenties who considered himself in love and believed he could make an impression upon the world in any field he chose. *Falkland* had not made a great deal of money but it had made an impression and I was deemed an author of promise, so it was not perhaps entire fantasy to believe I might earn a living by my pen. Always mightier than the sword, as I believe I am credited with first observing. The spirit of contradiction is very strong in the young and my beloved mamma probably could not have chosen a worse way to deter me from marrying Rosina than the way she chose. She hectored. She lectured. She forbade. If only some Deity above had whispered in her ear that she was driving her son into the arms of a woman who would prove his Nemesis, his Albatross, his I cannot think of another metaphor.

From the Uncollected Correspondence of Lord Lytton

Dearest Poodle,

For the last twenty-four hours I have been in such a state of utter and perfect wretchedness, that, if it could continue in the same intensity a day longer, I really do believe that I should not be alive; but I now have made myself better and calmer, and feel at last enabled to control my feelings sufficiently to write to you.

I have been waiting with an impatience you will readily conceive for the post that was to bring me an answer from my mother – I cannot go on. I must take some more laudanum and go into the air first.

Well, I received that answer at last. Oh Rose, such a letter! You were right and I was mistaken when I imagined that my mother felt for me any affection unconnected with vanity, or that she cared a single straw for my happiness, so long as it did not reflect lustre and credit upon herself. There is not in this letter one kind expression to redeem its want of almost human consideration for my feelings; and it ends by saying that if I marry I should have, not her consent, but her curse. I must stop again for some minutes!

Well, Rose, I have nerved myself at last and will proceed without further interruption. To say that I do not feel pain at my mother's disapprobation, even if it were utterly unconnected with worldly considerations, would be absurd. But if we marry without my mother's consent, my allowance from her will, of course, cease. We will have nothing but my father's legacy, utterly insufficient at all times, and the interest of which for some years would be, I fear, entirely consumed by the debts I have had the imprudence to incur. This then is out of the question. Comparative poverty and obscurity I might have been selfish enough to ask you to share, but not absolute want. Even were you less dear to me, you should never link yourself only to privation and distress.

Now for the alternative of a private marriage. You said right, Rose, when you said that it was only in a moment of madness that you could consent to such a measure, and it would be certainly only in a moment of the most thoughtless or the most determined selfishness that I could have urged you to do so. Deceit and doubt and anxiety – the probability of the loss of character, the chance (forgive me for repeating the old story) of my dying with our marriage unacknowledged and yourself unprovided for – all this we might both overlook in the blindness or delirium of the moment; but this, in the calmness of reflection, I never will prepare for your destiny. What if we had children? Should I be base enough to suffer by concealment the ruin of your reputation; or should I ensure you, by a disclosure, the penury which would immediately ensue?

Oh Rosina! What can we do?

From the Memoirs of Rosina, Lady Lytton

I hold this letter in my possession along with many others in a similar vein. If you are in a forgiving mood, you can indeed almost feel sorry for poor Eddard, caught between his infatuation with my humble person and the demands and prejudices of his antique mother. At the time, I confess, his communication upset me deeply both for him and for myself. I had no desire to be seen as a mercenary and deceptive woman by anybody, least of all that stick of ancient rectitude and holder of the purse strings, Mrs Tight-fisted Bulwer Heirloom.

I therefore had no hesitation in writing back to Eddard to say that I thought the only honourable thing was to withdraw from our engagement, in so far as it was an engagement. I said that I feared that both Eddard and his mother would come to hate me if I stood in the way of his career and a more brilliant match. I urged him to forget me as I would endeavour to forget him. The letters went back and forth. Eddard insisting that he wanted nothing more in the world than to be married to my humble self, whom he loved so much that he sent a thousand kisses as a postscript and vowed to defy his insensitive and tyrannical mother. She would not hold his happiness to ransom for a paltry legacy. He would earn for us by the power of his pen (more mighty than the sword, a phrase he never stopped telling people he had first created) and we would be happy as only Puppy and Poodle could be in the darlingest little kennel of our own. And so on interminably.

I meanwhile did my best to maintain that my first reaction had been the correct one. I knew it to be the case, although even in my wildest nightmares, I could not have conceived the hatred and contempt with which first mother and then son were soon treating me. The first great mistake I made in my life was being born at all, although the truth is that I had no choice and little part in the matter. The second great mistake was not holding to my resolution to break irrevocably from Eddard. Oh why was I ever cajoled into retracting the separation I insisted upon on first receipt of that letter?

But nothing in our relationship was ever short or sweet. Eddard wrote and wrote and wrote to me with the same relentlessness he has displayed in churning out his works of fiction. No one has ever accused him of using one word when ten could be employed to say the same thing. I endeavoured to reply in kind, answering every objection, sweeping away any sense of guilt on either side, assuring him that, fragile rose though I appeared to be, I would survive without his all-consuming love. But every day, a new letter, every day a new reply to be found.

It is perhaps not surprising that the stress and strain of all this endless correspondence in the end made me seriously ill.

From the Uncollected Correspondence of Lord Lytton

My dearest love,

Your letter gives me great uneasiness. *How* are you ill, my poor Rose? And why do you not rest? Do take advice, dearest, and adopt it. And don't give way to these low spirits I beg you although these are difficult times for both of us. If there is anything I can do, you know I will do it. You know that I only value existence in order to contribute to your happiness. Do, love, I beseech endeavour to be well for my sake. If you knew how much my Being is centred in yours and what self-reproach as well as sympathy I feel when you tell me you are ill and unhappy, you would be more merciful to me, by being more anxious for yourself.

I hope that your next letter will in some degree diminish my uneasiness for you. I await it with the greatest anxiety. Five hundred kisses to be collected when next we meet.

Puppy

From an Unpublished Autobiography by Lord Lytton

Rosina wrote that she was ill. I believed her. Indeed, I was distraught because it was in part my doing and I felt the marriage noose being tightened around my neck. I sensed her fragility and, as the man who had necessarily to take responsibility for her well-being, I could not do other than feel great concern.

I do not know what I think now. Maybe she was ill, maybe she was not. Maybe it was one of her colds which she chose to make seem more serious. Maybe she had contracted something more serious. She always hinted, she never fully told me in what way and in what degree she was sick. Young women of excessive sensibility had died quite often in my experience. I could not have her death on my hands.

So I went to her bedside, fool that I was. She had returned from Brocket and was once more staying at her uncle's. It was more than a cold but at this distance I remain unsure how much more. In my experience, she has always been ill with ailments real or imagined. She had a cold when I first met her and our shared married life was punctuated by her afflictions. Whatever she had, it was unlikely to have been life-threatening. But the sight of a member of the fair sex, and she at that time was one of the fairest of the fair sex, in grave distress would disturb any red-blooded male, let alone one who carried the burden of responsibility that I felt.

I held her hand and we talked. Her weakness left her without that cheap flirtatiousness which was starting to become her stock in trade. The airs and graces had departed and she seemed (truly or not) loving and wishing to hear what I had to say. In a subdued voice, almost a whisper, she continued to voice her objections to our union but in the circumstances, of course, it only led me to insist all the more. I am an honourable man and that was the only honourable course.

The more vehement I became, moved by honour and pity, the less she offered opposition. In the end she became quieter still and argued no more. I had achieved my object. She had finally agreed to marry me at my insistence.

But shall I confide in you what I think now?

A skilled angler could not more cleverly have baited his hook to catch an unsuspecting fish.

From the Uncollected Correspondence of Lord Lytton

My Own Dear Kind Good Poodle,

It is impossible to express the state of mind I am in. I write only to say *this*; in spite of everything I am so fully convinced of your faith that I implore you to MARRY ME AT ONCE. I do not ask this, my own dear love, as a vague unmeaning compliment in order to have it rejected but I cannot bear the thought of leaving you ill and unhappy without one who ought to be your real support and friend and soother. Come then to my arms for ever, my own dear, dear angel. Let me watch over you and not desert you, no not for a day. My own dearest love, I ask you this as a most earnest favour. Name the earliest day and after that all shall be as you like.

A thousand kisses from your Puppy.

From the Memoirs of Rosina, Lady Lytton

One thought goes through my mind when I review this pile of sentimental drivelling from Sir Would-be Byron Lytton: Why did I not end it all then? Even though he was as often as he could at my bedside, holding my hand and looking into my eyes with what can only be described as Puppy-ish devotion. He was convinced he could still bring the ancient relic who was his mother to accept our union. He promised all sorts of things in a rhapsody of our future prospects with little attention to any of my questioning. In his view, we had a golden future.

Part of me wanted to believe him. As I have written previously, it cannot be said that my marriage prospects were so glittering that I could afford to turn down an advantageous offer in marriage market terms, for all the inconveniences attached. Instinct told me to continue to reject him because of my all too prophetic vision of our future. But now it was Reason which betrayed me. Reason which urged me to take a reasonable proposal when it was offered by a man who was not physically repulsive or stupid.

My God! My God! There is no escaping one's destiny. He clasped my hand tightly and I have been in manacles ever since.

From the Uncollected Correspondence of Lady Lytton

Dearest Puppy,

Your Poodle loves oo forever and ever. She longs for the day when she is finally Mrs Puppy and in her Puppy's paws.

Oo own Rosebud.

From an Unpublished Autobiography by Lord Lytton

I am a novelist. Which means that I know all there needs to be known about the business of telling a story. In order to create a striking narrative, which does not fatigue the reader with unnecessary and excessive information about things which do not matter in the long run, choices must be made and matters which may seem important at the time but, in retrospect, are not should be omitted. These principles guide what I am writing here. Letter followed letter on an almost daily basis in our courtship and one can only be thankful that these tedious pennings no longer exist. But even so, as the Bard has so memorably put it, the course of true love never did run smooth, and in our course the word 'true' is undoubtedly up for debate.

But my belief is that if we endeavour to catch the essence, we also must acknowledge the confusion, particularly when dealing with a creature as wayward as Rosina. Things were said, things were unsaid. We met here in company, we met there in company. We decided this and then we decided something different. Rosina had a remarkable capacity not to stick to the point in question even though I was straining every nerve to behave honourably. Who knows what accommodations I made with myself? She had her physical charms and, if I look around me, few of my fellow authors have had access to a woman as lovely as she was. In her early days that is. So my feelings went this way and that way, propelled by her giddy programme of what she did and did not want to happen. But who wants to read about all that when they know the outcome?

And then there was my mother as unmoving in her opinions as Rosina was fickle. I summarise here a hundred reproachful interviews. Namely, not only was I too young to marry but Rosina's age, parentage and upbringing were insuperable objects to our union. She was the daughter of Mrs. Wheeler, whose mode of living, whose friends and whose principles were all detestable. Rosina was a penniless girl whose education had been flagrantly neglected, which made her vain and flighty. Worse still, she was the spoiled pet of Lady Caroline Lamb, a woman of questionable morals. My mother accepted that I might visit Lady Caroline in the interests of good neighbourliness (I fancy I had invented some dispute over shared woodlands to justify my attendance) but no decent woman, according to my mother, could be seen in her company. She begged me to bring the dangerous intimacy to an end with little acknowledgement of her part in starting it off in the first place. When she wanted to appear judicious, she said she understood why Miss Wheeler's beauty could excite my admiration and how her forlorn and unprotected position could arouse my pity. But – and I can still see her pursed lips and determinedly upright posture as she said this – she warned me against allowing such sentiments to lead me into a marriage which would incur her bitterest displeasure and lead to life-long unhappiness for myself. In effect, she accused me of feelings and motives so unworthy that from anyone else the accusation would have roused my bitterest resentment. From her, it wounded me to the quick.

I regret to say this, but it was as if she wanted to drive me into Rosina's arms. Without her interventions and lectures, I do believe I could have forgotten Rosina. Be that as it may, months of my life were passed as shuttlecock between these two women while I struggled to be as honest and gentlemanly as I could. In the end, of course, my mother proved right but I do believe no full-blooded Englishman of honourable intentions would not at the end of the to-ing and fro-ing between the two of them have vowed to make Rosina his bride.

Perceiving that her threats not only of displeasure and disinheritance were not working, my mother played one last card. Three weeks before the marriage, she accused Rosina of being a congenital liar. She announced that she believed that Rosina was not a few months older than me but two or three years older. What was I to do as the Juggernaut approached and I was crushed underneath its wheels? I agreed to abandon my marriage plans if my mother proved to be right. Irish lawyers were consulted, family solicitors were consulted and they universally agreed that Rosina was the age she said she was. My mother made no comment upon this but, in another part of what now seems her inexorable plan to drive me into Rosina's arms, she started to raise further objections. Enough, I had finally to say, was enough. I wrote to my mother that all her reproaches had made me wretched without moving me one iota from the only path (thorny though it be) which I could tread with self-respect.

From the Uncollected Correspondence of Lord Lytton

You are an angel, my Rose! The delays and doubts are over. I will call upon you at one and tell you what you are about to become. I feel your consideration as it deserves. There can be but one answer to it – and that I whispered to you on the 29th. No, Rose, darling, there is no longer any necessity for a delay, God bless you, my good and kind and generous love.

Your own ownest Pups.

From Memoirs of Rosina, Lady Lytton

His mother did as she had threatened. Never let it be said that the evil old Harpy was not a woman of her word. He was disinherited overnight. Eddard maintained a bold face but I knew that he was devastated. For once I genuinely felt sorry for him. For all his undeniable faults, the Witch Bulwer Lytton played a huge part in their creation.

For my own part, I consulted my uncle, the antithesis in every way of Mrs Harridan Lytton. He was one of the few people genuinely delighted by our proposed union. He was all support and indeed gave me away in full military uniform. He was in full military uniform, I mean, of course, I was in a modest and economical (as circumstances demanded) bridal gown. I made no attempt to inform my mother of my impending wedding because it would only have involved finger-wagging lectures on the rights of women and a drunken flirtation with whatever gentleman was put next to her at the bridal breakfast. Who knows what advice a sensible rational mother might have given me, but alas! no such figure was available.

In an attempt to be just to her, at that time my sister Henrietta's health was very poor and she would have had little time to give to my marital tragedy. My sister, for whom I have nothing but sadness and pity, died very soon after. My mother, alas, lived on and returned to haunt my marital home. Fate or God has a very strange way of organising his priorities.

From the Morning Post, Thursday, August 30th, 1827

On Wednesday last, the 29 inst., was married at St. James' Church by the Hon. and Rev. W. Bentinck, Edward Lytton Bulwer, Esq, third son of the late General Bulwer, of Heydon Hall, Norfolk, and of Mrs. Bulwer Lytton, of Knebworth Park, Herts, to Rosina Doyle Wheeler, of Lizzard Connel and Ballywise.

The bride, who is remarkably beautiful, was given away by her uncle, General Sir John Doyle, Bart., and the happy pair, partaking of a cold collation at the house of Colonel Doyle, Montagu Square, set off for their seat, Woodcot House, in Oxfordshire.

From the Memoirs of Rosina, Lady Lytton

'Remarkably beautiful'. Was that put there by Sir Liar's friends in the press (he already had them as others have plagues of locusts)

to explain why the great up-and-coming had suddenly married beneath him? Who knows? But it certainly wasn't there simply to praise my looks.

And our seat in Oxfordshire? A similar rule applies. Edward had lost his access to his family seat. Mine was crumbling away in Ballywise, if it had not crumbled away altogether. Eddard had, after endless consultations, rented Woodcot as somewhere we could afford and (possibly) be happy.

So much for the press, as partisan and unreliable as ever. I suppose I should say something about my wedding night. I had never seen a man naked before and, despite the rumours spread by Sir Liar, he remains the only man I have seen naked. He was in a continuously Priapic state for most of our honeymoon. I am sure there are worse lovers but undoubtedly there have to be better ones too, more considerate of a virgin's feelings and less proud of the length and thickness of their own member. But enough! The memory of it all sickens me.

Chapter Three: 1827–1833

From an Unpublished Autobiography by Lord Lytton

The morning after our wedding night, I left my wife in contented slumber and made my way downstairs, before dawn was breaking, towards my new study where I wished to contemplate a far more taxing aspect of my recently acquired marital duties. Our servants were not yet stirring so I found myself a candle, lit it and entered. I nearly stumbled over the unpacked boxes of books which covered the floor but finally sat down at my desk, one of the few remaining souvenirs of my former life, and gathered my thoughts. Rarely has a gentleman faced a more daunting prospect the day after his marriage and the all-enveloping darkness outside only added to my gloom.

I own that I had been hoping that my mother might relent in her opposition to my marriage once she had realised my mind was set upon it. In the past few days I had sent loving and dutiful messages, I had sought her forgiveness for opposing her will and I had persuaded Rosina to add messages of admiration and humility. My brothers, however halfheartedly, had attempted to urge reconciliation upon her. We had even despatched a slice of our wedding cake but there had been no response to any of this and the cake, I suspect, remained uneaten.

The loss I felt at this apparently irrevocable falling out with my mother pained me deeply. If only she had been less intransigent, perhaps it would not have been inevitable that Rosina and I married, who can tell? That morning I sat there in the knowledge that I must live not only without maternal approval but also without maternal financial support. I had no choice but to take a long and hard look at our expectations.

My own fortune consisted of a small capital of £6,000 secured to me by my father's will, while Rosina's did not amount to more than £80 a year. She had little or no conception of the value of money and my patient attempts to explain our situation had done little to dampen her unreal vision of our future. She was simply incapable of taking in what I had to say. But then, after all, I was the husband and it was my duty to provide as best as I could in the circumstances. I must be honest and confess that my pride had forbidden me from contemplating the only scale of living which was compatible with our slender resources. The die had already been cast in my choice of Woodcot for our first home, made with a courageous, possibly fool-hardy, disregard of our actual poverty. The house, some six miles from Reading, was a handsome eighteenth-century pile, still unreconstructed in any way, unlike Knebworth. It stood in a well maintained park of some fifty acres. For our current needs, both house and grounds were unnecessarily, even absurdly, large. In addition to that, I had already promised Rosina that we would maintain a carriage and two or three saddle horses. I had further assured her that we should be ready and willing to entertain guests in a becoming and un-penny-pinching way. Whatever might be the cost to myself, and however trying her ignorance was, I was resolved that Rosina must not suffer any degradation in her way of life from her marriage to me; nor should any children which might result from our union ever suffer deprivation.

As the dawn finally broke over the verdant lawns and ancient oaks of Woodcot and light illuminated my lonely desk, I reached what had probably always been the inevitable conclusion, a conclusion some might say was my preordained destiny. I had no choice but to become a professional writer. I was all too aware that it was a difficult decision to make the attempt to live solely by my pen. I knew even then that it would be very different from the protected life of the talented amateur I had been, a spoiled puppy who could write when he chose to please himself or his vanity.

The difficulties were daunting but there seemed that morning a blessed rightness about the decision. The psychic powers who have often served me well gave me no warning of a troubled future and that morning was a rare morning in my life when I felt genuinely optimistic about my future. As the birds started singing and dawn finally broke, the doubts I had experienced disappeared like the dew from the lawns of Woodcot. It seemed as if the growing chorus of birds (blackbirds primarily, as I recall) would fill my ears with the beauty of their sound and its message of hope for ever. I was in control of my destiny.

As well as inspired and relieved, I was, of course, also light-headed from lack of sleep, which is probably why I managed, as the birds sang on, to convince myself that my beautiful wife, still asleep above, and I might be compatible after all. She had enjoyed our night of physical passion, more extended and uninhibited than the time at Brocket, never spoken of before this memoir. She was very lovely at the time of our marriage, though it would not be gentlemanly even now to describe her charms in any detail. Suffice to say, she was responsive and affectionate without any affected modesty or prudish denial of pleasure. I must be honest and record that a flood of affection for her burst over me that morning, because, as throughout this memoir, I am endeavouring to be as honest as I can about what I felt, or, in this case, perhaps wanted to feel.

The consequences for my health and my sanity from the decision made that morning can never be under-estimated. Consider, if you would, the direct consequences of my decision to earn my living by my pen, blessed though my literary career has been with a certain amount of success. Over the next ten years, I undertook a workload which even my harshest critics could only describe as crushing, even while they mocked me for my hypochondria, my touchiness and my fecundity, as if nothing came at a cost. In this decade, I completed eleven three-volume novels, always under the pressure of deadlines and always knowing that, however much success they might achieve, my enemies would mock them. In addition, I wrote poems, plays, a history of Athens and a sociological examination of English life. I also reviewed countless books for the periodicals and contributed essays to many journals, including a much admired series upon domestic economy. And I have not begun to talk (and will not at this moment) about my decision to become a Member of Parliament with all the obligations that entailed.

I do not wish to make myself into a martyr. I chose my destiny that morning. But I would like some acknowledgement of the hours spent at my desk during these years in order to maintain my wife, myself and our children. As it turned out, I was extraordinarily successful – beyond anything I could have conceived as that watery sun made its presence felt. In later years, I put on a brave face and insisted to anybody who enquired (and audiences of schoolboys were particularly keen to learn about my success) that I devoted no more than three hours a day to writing and to reading, less when Parliament was in sitting. At the time I speak of, the pressure was unending and sometimes, with Rosina's dogs (more of them later) barking in the middle distance, I could feel myself close to madness. Even my own wife acknowledged how much I have achieved and there is no more grudging testimony I could cite in my favour.

But let me try to recapture for the very last time that golden morning. Happiness is brief and therefore to be cherished. I have no idea how long I sat there but the sun was already streaming through the window and the candle guttering when there was a gentle knock on the door of my study. I opened it. There was Rosina, still attractively dishevelled from the night before, dressed in a becoming cream silk peignoir. She looked beautiful and, it has to be said, desirable.

'Oh my darling,' I recollect saying as I kissed her delicate neck as a preliminary to further exploration. 'Oh my darling, do not worry. I will provide.' Then I led her back upstairs.

The operations of the authorial mind are strange, even to the authors themselves. Certainly that is true in my case. Where does inspiration come from? Well, in this case, as I entered once again my bride of one night, an exciting notion entered my head. As I proceeded to pleasure her (we Victorians are prudish about these matters but then I grew up in a world where sex was crudely jested about and so I always struggle to find a *via media*) but, anyway, as I pleasured her, I felt the inspiration for my first and possibly best three-volume novel. By the time I had erupted within her, the essentials were all in place.

From Pelham, or the Adventures of a Gentleman, 1828

I have observed that the distinguishing trait of people accustomed to good society, is a calm, imperturbable quiet, which pervades all their actions and habits, from the greatest to the least: they eat in quiet, move in quiet, live in quiet and lose their wife, or even their money, in quiet; while low persons cannot take up either a spoon or an affront without making such an amazing noise about it.

From the Memoirs of Rosina, Lady Lytton

It always amused me greatly that Eddard was so proud of his articles upon domestic economy. They had titles like *Domesticity, or a Dissertation upon Servants; The Kitchen and the Parlour, or Household Politics* and (my own personal favourite) *Long Journeys with Short Purses*. Later ages have marvelled at his ability to conjure up the last days of Pompeii, but I consider these articles took a greater leap of imagination since he knew far less about kitchens and servants than that fatal eruption of Vesuvius. But I must not carp too much about those early days, those very early days, which, compared with what came after, were positively idyllic. His Priapic demands were apparently satisfied by my humble self and no other. The house was certainly a fine one, if isolated, and he was not yet Sir Liar, or at least not obviously so. His mother was in a sulk, which, with any luck, might prove permanent, while my own mother, still the High Priestess of the Rights of Women, had, as yet, shown no interest in visiting us. The neighbours we had were few and exceedingly dull but at least not hostile. I enjoyed our gardens and had excellent relationships with the domestic staff. Above all, it has to be owned, there was a real satisfaction in presiding over a household of my own.

How could I ever think it would last? If I'd realised that I was enjoying the few days of joy in a relationship that otherwise was to consist of nothing but utter misery and humiliation then I would have savoured it much more carefully than I did. But Time moves forward and the clock cannot turn back, which again, I fancy, is said by one of Shakespeare's Kings, but I really cannot remember which.

Eddard had to earn the money to provide for us both and, he never failed to add, for our children, if children ensued. I fancy that was the reason offered for the incessant Priapic demands but I could scarcely argue with his logic. How else could we survive, given his grandiose ideas of how to live and his complete ignorance of the very basics of domestic economy? I fancy I should offer the World an apology for the number of inflated, turgid volumes which Sir Talentless has inflicted upon the reading public but since, I own, I was an accessory to the crime, I can only plead extenuating circumstances. Where else could the necessary money be found? It was only later, too much later, that I realised that a woman might also earn her living by her pen, although the rewards were inevitably smaller, particularly in a world populated by Sir Liar's friends and sycophants.

But let me savour those few moments of happiness. Ah, if only I had known!

Take a deep breath. There, I have savoured. On with my tale.

Eddard had to work hard. This I accepted. He had to spend many hours locked away in his study. This I also accepted, and even did my best to keep the household quiet and wear a smile upon my face when he finally emerged. When we were alone together, he would be preoccupied and often short-tempered, particularly if his every whim was not fulfilled. I never demurred. Even then I had no high opinion of his literary talents, but he was earning us money so he must be supported.

What did become increasingly difficult to comprehend was the amount of time he spent away from home. There was always an excuse offered. A publisher had to be wooed, an article for a magazine had to be discussed, a fellow author had to be consulted. There were so many reasons for going up to London and not returning for days at a time. At first I understood or thought I understood. Later on, I became a sceptic on the matter of this time away from what he claimed was his notion of domestic bliss. But it was some time later before I realised the full nature of his perfidy. Today it is very difficult to recall that I was once a very trusting person.

There were two immediate consequences of my increasing isolation in what turned so quickly from a magic palace into a swamp of despair, a transformation the wicked fairy effects every year in the pantomime to great applause but which in real life is rather more painful. The better consequence was that I began to draw my dogs around me.

First there was a lapdog called Fairy and then there was a Newfoundland called Terror. You have to understand that my objection to Miss Lamb was not that she was a dog (more accurately, a bitch) but that she was a type of dog in which I had no pleasure, particularly when imposed upon me. I have always loved dogs; they are the sweetest memory of my grim and dank Irish childhood and they became the happiest part of my days alone in Woodcot. Dogs are loving and honest creatures. Their needs are simple and their devotion unquestioning. Look into canine eyes and you see no hypocrisy, no deception. If you catch them doing something wrong, like an offering upon a carpet, then they stare at you guiltily and accept their punishment, not that I believe in physically punishing innocent animals. Terror was my delight. He was fearless as he chased the birds across the lawns of Woodcot and brought me dead rats as gifts.

But I also sought human companionship and there I made a fatal mistake. I invited Mary Greene to stay with me. She was older than I was, but we had been friends in Ireland and we had corresponded frequently since I left. She was, I suppose, my chief confidante during all the travails of my engagement and the early days of my marriage, and, because I trusted her, I assumed she was trustworthy. She certainly looked trustworthy. The word 'homely' might have been created specifically to describe her looks. She had judged *Falkland* 'horrid' and full of 'bad sentiments and infamous morals', so she had approached a visit to the home of its infamous author with some trepidation. I think she was surprised that he was not a devil with horns (not yet anyway) and was altogether charmed by the gentlemanly respect Eddard paid to me and the ladylike way in which I presided over the household. After all, she hadn't seen me since my Irish youth and, let it be said, I was rather more a woman of the world now. Anyway, Miss Greene declared herself delighted by her reception since she was spared Eddard's acid asides to me on her implacable dullness. She certainly vowed devoted friendship to me. Even then, I knew she was fishing for invitations in the future, as a welcome respite from her dull Irish bogland, but I still had not the least inkling that she had the intelligence or poor morals to be duplicitous. But then all that glisters is not gold, as Mr. Goldsmith (or was it Mr. Gray?) observed in that poem about a cat drowning in a goldfish bowl. Talking of companionship, I should add that Lady Caroline's heart finally gave out in January of the next year. I had had no contact with her since our marriage, about which I had so determinedly (and foolishly) put her urgings aside. But Edward, ever the nosy neighbour, in search of material, visited her on her sick bed and found her 'dreadfully altered', which is hardly surprising in the circumstances. The 'tapping' procedure she had undergone to reduce water accumulation from the dropsy further weakened her. She was fifty-three. Her husband, to his credit, managed to seem greatly grief-stricken, not simply greatly relieved. A few months later, his father died and William became Lord Melbourne. The rest, as they say, is history.

Did I feel sorrow? Of course, it was sad. But she had lived her life to the full (and how full it had been!) with a complaisant husband who had left her free to live her own life. How many women in our age have been granted that privilege? Certainly, as you observe, not myself.

Anyway, I invited Miss Greene to stay, fool that I was, but then I needed support and companionship in my increasing loneliness because there could be no doubt that I was expecting our first child.

From Pelham, or the Adventures of a Gentleman, 1828

I was a luxurious personage in those days. I had had a bath made from my own design; across it were constructed two small frames – one for the journal of the day and another to hold my breakfast apparatus; in this manner I was accustomed to lie for about an hour, engaging in the triple happiness of reading, thinking and bathing.

(Removed from the edition of 1837)

From an Unpublished Autobiography by Lord Lytton

How to describe my first-born? *Falkland*, after all, is a mere by-blow, of no account in my enduring history as a writer. On the other hand, *Pelham or Adventures of a Gentleman*, which was published in May, a month before my daughter was born, was, for sometime after its publication, the most discussed, most fashionable, most scandalous novel in London. Its author's name was at first a secret, a publisher's ploy which has since lost its savour, but at the time, the secrecy over the authorship almost certainly intrigued readers and stimulated sales. By the time my name was known, the book was such an undoubted success that even my detractors could do little to harm its triumphant progress. I was young (at least as an author) and I still savoured the pleasure of writing. Despite our parlous financial circumstances, I did not feel fettered to my desk as I do now. I revelled in my power to shock, to tease and to provoke, as well as to entertain and instruct.

But how to describe to a later age the sensation it caused? Some explanation certainly seems necessary. Pelham is a dandy but not a dandy in the finical mode of Brummell. Of course, dressing well is part of it and a part I shared wholeheartedly with my creation. Never to be dull or dowdy in appearance was as much a part of my creed as it was of my hero's. I love dressing elegantly. I dared, in a much admired (and vilified) chapter in the second volume, to set down the rules for correct male attire. Everything, from the guiding principles of colour and cut, right down to the importance of coat-tails, collars, canes, cravat, rings and shoe-strings, was comprehensively discussed. I own it was a provocation, designed to irritate the serious minded as well as to amuse the *cognoscenti* and in that it undoubtedly served its purpose. But clothes were only part of Pelham; he is in every way a man who cherishes sensual pleasure and is not to be rushed or short-changed in enjoying it. When he dines out with an epicure, he carries a specially designed set of cutlery – a shallow spoon, a tiny fork and a blunt knife – to guard against his tendency to eat too quickly. He cherishes fine perfumes, fine wines and glorious baths. Yet a man who concerns himself with nothing but his toilette, his menus and the contents of his wardrobe is merely a coxcomb. A dandy is something else. Clothes make the man but the attention to the clothes is about creating an armour, which defends against the absurdities of the old world and can choose what is genuinely worthwhile in the new. Pelham is a philosopher who regards the world and its incessant doings with a jaundiced and detached eye but he is also a man of principle. When offered a place in a new and super-selfish ministry, he refuses to have anything to do with these bogus politicians. He announces (in words which still delight me) that he would sooner feed his poodle on paunch and liver, instead of cream and fricassée, than work with a group of politicians 'who talk much, who perform nothing; who join ignorance of every principle of legislation to indifference for every benefit to the people – who level upwards and trample downwards.' He is an exquisite, cherishing luxuries that many of my contemporaries then regarded as distinctly unmanly, but he is still capable of defending himself successfully with boxing-gloves when needed. He is emotionally detached but he has numerous flirtations and affairs. Indeed, at the end of the novel, I had him settle down to married bliss, like a proper hero. I did not yet see the bitter irony of recommending this fate.

Of course, the literal-minded gentry, who calls themselves critics and say 'We' when expressing their singular (in both senses) opinions, declared that Pelham was a simulacrum of its author. They had said the same of Falkland, a hero of a very different temperament, gloomy and Byronic – the moral and temperamental antipodes of Pelham. Did they condescend to reconcile this contradiction? Of course not. These gentlemen have not the slightest grasp of the creative imagination, nor would they ever acknowledge I have never ever drawn two heroes alike but made each – Falkland, Pelham, Mordaunt, Devereux, the list continues – essentially different. I am more various a man than my critics will ever allow and among them, in these later times, of course I must include Rosina.

I freely admit that, though I was never Pelham, there was a part of me that, as a callow and flamboyant young man, gloried in creating him. The truth, however, is more complex than that, if the critics had deigned to look for it. In the novel, there is a place also for that more enduring part of me, the melancholic and self-doubting. Pelham is essentially a bystander at a tragedy, distinctly of the Gothic School, which engulfs his school friend, Sir Reginald Glanville. It involves rape, murder and the suspicion of that murder falling upon Sir Reginald. For much of the time, Pelham simply watches and observes, before intervening to uncover the murderer and save his friend from the gallows. Here – dare I say it? – lies the originality of what I had created and the conflict within it. In one corner stands the old Gothic world of guilt, revenge, and darkness. In the other corner stands the new world of the dandy, much vilified since, but at the time a shining light of sanity in a mad world. I struggle to explain today the popularity of my novel, not because it is bad (it isn't, even in its rewritten form) but because, forgive me for a cliché, I caught the spirit of the age.

As always, I ploughed a furrow which others followed in order to profit themselves and then denigrate my own achievement. (I expect, of course, my dear friend Benjamin Disraeli from this general censure because his *Vivian Gray* would have succeeded in any time and any place.) Of course, it was galling to see my pioneering achievement mocked or simply unacknowledged, yet, at the same time, the tremendous, nay scandalous, success enabled me to gain the level of remuneration for my work that it deserved. It may be deemed vulgar to talk too much about money, but I am describing a time in my life when I was struggling to make ends meet. My dear friend, Charles Dickens, of a later generation, had no compunction about demanding what his writing was worth, so why should I be reticent? The figures speak for themselves. Publishers who had paid me nothing for *Falkland*, which they regarded as a gentlemanly indulgence, now competed to publish my next novel. I was paid £500 for *Pelham*, then £800 for *The Disowned*, and the substantial sum of £1,500 for *Devereux*; I have never met with a publisher who parted with money out of charity. These are significant sums of money and a significant part of how I became able to support my wife, our child, her dogs and her extravagances.

Rosina had already started to acquire the dogs, which became her unhealthy obsession later in life. The dogs had barked while I was working and left their offerings where I could put my foot into them, but what could I do? The three handsome volumes of *Pelham* were prominently displayed upon the table near her armchair. She was assiduous in drawing my attention to reviews (something I have always tried to ignore) and even assembled a collection of clippings in an embroidered folder sewn by her own fair hand. All this delighted me because

I had not then realised how fickle and partial all her judgements were. She would look up adoringly as I emerged weary-eyed from my study, but, even then, I was not naive enough to believe that Rosina could fully appreciate what I was enduring in these heroic struggles with my pen. She was, after all, an essentially female creature with all the lack of horizons that implies, but at least she professed pride in my achievement and even encouraged me teasingly to follow my own published sartorial precepts in my manner of dress. I could never have predicted the ingratitude and mockery which lay ahead.

Sadly, these days, even my first-born novel is no longer what it was. It barely lasted seven years before it underwent substantial revision. Its dandiacal message was savaged by Mr. Carlyle, who deemed its obsession with clothing unhealthy and unmanly. At least Mr. Carlyle was, and is, a man of some intellectual stature. The book was then subjected to gratuitous abuse by the disreputable crew who ran *Fraser's Magazine*, led by that infamous traitor to his public school upbringing, William Makepeace Thackeray. Criticism can hurt, even when you are able to rise above its pettiness, but I do own that, in later editions, I agreed to tone down my youthful excesses. The age was changing and so, if I am honest, was I. If you wish to find that original three-volume *Pelham*, so redolent of the last days of His Dandyish Majesty George the Fourth, you would have to search through the dusty shelves of some long neglected bookseller. I'm afraid to say that I no longer own one myself.

Rosina and I, despite the terrible burden I had undertaken on that momentous first morning in Woodcot, did manage to have a few happy months together. Or so they seemed at the time. They were certainly the only candidates for happiness together that I could ever nominate, however much those infernal dogs barked.

But then the inevitable happened. As it became apparent that Rosina was pregnant, it also became clear just how mentally and physically fragile she was. Our idyll was quickly over.

From Pelham, or the Adventures of a Gentleman, 1828

'Watch!' said I: '*do* you think *I* could ever wear a watch? I know nothing so plebeian; what can any one, but a man of business, who has nine hours for his counting-house and one for his dinner, ever possibly want to know the time for? an assignation, you will say, true; but (here I played with my best ringlet) if a man is worth having he is surely worth waiting for!'

(Removed from the edition of 1837)

From the Memoirs of Rosina, Lady Lytton

I will never forget the moment when my dream finally ended. When the house of cards collapsed. When I realised I had been living in a fool's paradise... Oh, I beg you, choose your own metaphor, I cannot find it for you.

It has, I hope, become clear that I did not regard Sir Liar with rose-tinted spectacles when we married. I had a fair inkling of his egotism and his vanity, but I also believed that he was sincere in his wish to provide for me and to cherish me. Why else had he flouted the will of his monstrous mother? But he was soon locking himself away in the library, where he breakfasted, while I sat alone in my dressing-room. He rarely dined at home, except when we had guests. And he was forever going off to London pleading the pressure of business. Literary men must apparently interview their publishers, must be ever present in the world of letters, and keep themselves well in view of the public, if they do not wish to incur the risk of falling into oblivion. Eddard lectured me repeatedly on this topic when I questioned these absences, so frequent and so prolonged, even at this early period of our married life, that I could not believe they were prompted simply by necessity.

When I finally attempted to discuss these matters more fully with Mr. Would-be Pelham on one of the rare occasions when he was at home and I had his undivided attention, he turned on me as if I had struck him in the face. Of course, he'd rather stay in Woodcot. How could I complain when I knew that it was to provide for me and for our child to be? When I continued to gently remonstrate, Eddard lost his temper and kicked my lovely Fairy, who was playing round my feet. The startled dog yelped in pain and ran in terror from the room. This was too much for me to bear, but, when I protested, he angrily cut me short and stormed from the room, leaving me shaken and distressed but still unaware the worst was yet to happen.

This episode occurred in the early evening of the 27th May 1828, just a month before the birth of my daughter, Emily. It had become my habit to assist the Famous Author in his researches. When he deigned to inform me of what he was planning, I created a system of cards and wrote upon them whatever I thought might be of use. He plundered my cards at will, but my labours went unacknowledged, although every book he completed during our marriage was supported by the selfless labour I put in to finding the information he required. A loving dedication would have been gratifying, but I never expected it and, unsurprisingly, it never happened. Sycophants like Dickens and Disraeli were acknowledged for their exquisite suggestions, but not his wife, even at the point at which he claimed to love me before anyone else.

Understand, I knew he was working to create money for us and for our future family, however bad the books he created, so it was my duty (that tired old word) to assist his endeavours. Do you think Sir Liar knew anything about prize-fighting when his hero donned his gloves in *Pelham*? Of course not. I had furnished him with descriptions from the sporting journals, which gave him all the information he needed to make these encounters plausible. He would still have made them fight bare-knuckled because that was what the lower-class pugilists still slugged away with. Only the descriptions of Mr Pelham's clothing came from his imagination untouched – or rather from his obsession with matter sartorial. Indeed, given the effeminacy of his first and most convincing hero, one might enquire why Sir Potency was so keen to prove his swordsmanship, as he sometimes referred to the activities of his much loved (by himself) member. The lady doth protest too much. Oh dear, I fancy I have quoted Shakespeare again without knowing the source.

I fear I am simply postponing describing something that was both shocking and frightening to me. We had been in the library all evening. Sir Self-Importance was preparing his next novel entitled *The Disowned*. Would it surprise you that he sent a pre-publication copy to his mother? Self-pity was never far with Eddard. The book was set in the late eighteenth-century and so My Lord and Master required chapter and verse for certain forms of address, and then certain details of costume, and then certain details of what might be in the library of a gentleman so thirty or forty years ago et cetera et cetera.

I had been up and down the step-ladder for several hours and I was worn out and exhausted. Recollect I was heavily with child at the time. While His Majesty sat at his desk, making notes from one of the heavy volumes I had reached down, I took the occasion to lie down upon the sofa. My back was aching and I wished for nothing but my bed.

Then he looked up from his labours and requested me to fetch him another volume – *The Pleasures of Memory* by Samuel Rogers, as I recall, the pompous nothings of the Banker Poet being much to Eddard's taste. It was on one of the highest shelves in the library and would require me mounting to the highest step of the ladder, not that the Great Author had even deigned to look round to see what he had required of me.

I rose, nevertheless, from the sofa and attempted to climb the ladder but the effort was too much for me. I was weary and thought I might faint.

'I am sorry, Edward,' I protested mildly, 'I cannot do any more.'

He turned in angry surprise and demanded what the matter might be.

'I am just very tired, really that is all.' In my weakness I clung to the step-ladder for support, hoping he might come to my aid. He stared at me blankly for a moment and then suddenly sprang to his feet. A look of hideous fury filled his face. He made a vile curse and pushed me to the ground.

I was too shocked to struggle or cry out, but then the next thing he did was kick me in the side with such savage violence that I fainted from the pain.

He must have summoned servants, told them some cock-and-bull story about a fall or a faint, because of my delicate condition. The next moment I recall is awaking in bed, aching all down my left side. My dear faithful dogs lay at my feet and there was Mary Greene by my side. She took hold of my hand, her eyes full of apparent concern, but, when I tried to tell her what had happened, she simply shushed me and begged me not to be agitated. I tried to indicate that I had every reason to be agitated but the response was more shushing and a kiss on my brow as if I was a little child to be pacified. In that way, I was deprived of the one confidante close at hand who might have solaced me and perhaps even advised me. At the time, I thought it was because she was of too naive and religious a turn of mind to believe ill of an apparently loving husband. I know better now.

It was several days before I could leave my bed, with only my dogs as constant companions. When Sir Bully finally came to my bedside on the second day, he made no reference at all to what had happened, although he expressed apparent concern for my health. I felt too frightened and confused to look him in the eye, let alone speak, so perhaps he believed that I could not recall what had really happened. Perhaps he hoped at a later date to convince me that his version of the truth was what had truly occurred, and I was, as ever, a weak-minded woman and a fantasist.

Indeed, I suspect that was his intention on his second visit the next day. He seemed calm though he must have spent an uneasy night. He deserved to. He sat by my bedside and took hold of my hand, although he must have plainly seen that I flinched away and wanted him to let go.

'There, there, my dearest Poodle,' he said in the gentlest of voices, and continued to stroke my hand though my flesh crept at his touch.

I stared into his eyes.

'You do know you hurt me very badly, don't you?'

His eyes met mine and he shook his head pityingly. 'Get some rest, dearest Rosina, you are still feverish and imagining things.'

'I worry for our child. You kicked me so hard.'

'Oh, my poor darling Rosebud. Your Puppy loves you so much.' There was not a flicker of recognition of the words I had spoken. He leant down and kissed my hand before finally letting go of it. My eyes sought his again. He was forced to return my gaze. His eyes were apparently filled with love and concern. I could see not the least trace of guilt.

It was at that moment when I first realised that I had not only married a man of violent and sometimes uncontrollable temper, but a man who could, when it suited him, lie and lie and lie, with the confidence that he would be believed. Miss Greene and the servants gave credence to what he told them and only the dumb loyal creatures who remained at the foot of my bed knew the violence he had done to me.

I could, even now, find some space in a small corner of my heart to forgive the physical attack, cowardly and unprovoked though it was, because I knew what pressure he was under, but the lies were beyond defence – and they had only just begun. He had not even been knighted Sir Liar then.

A month later, on June 27th, 1828, my dear daughter, Emily Elizabeth, was born. In my confinement I suffered very severely and there is little reason to doubt that my agonies were in great measure, if not entirely, caused by the above-mentioned exploit of my amiable spouse.

It is hardly surprising that, after all this, I was in a weakened state though I clung to my new-born babe with all the love a woman can feel for her first-born. But Eddard did not care for this. I do believe he thought he deserved my undivided attention. As he confided to Miss Greene, in an aside which he doubtless thought was outside my hearing, he didn't want his wife's time 'to be taken up by any damned child.'

On the pretext of my weakness, I was not allowed to feed my little infant myself. I protested, I even (something I rarely do) wept and pleaded, but it was useless. Emily was handed over to the care of a neighbouring farmer's wife. After that, I was never able to feel with her the proper affection a mother should. Some bond of nature had been broken and I regret it to this very day. Who knows what would have happened without that kick? Well, at least, she was born.

There. I have set down probably the saddest part of my tale and I see no reason not to blame Sir Liar for denying me my motherly feelings. Then, just when life was at its saddest, my sickly sister also died and my own mother, released from responsibility, arrived on the scene, eager, she claimed, to embrace her darling first grandchild.

From Pelham, or the Adventures of a Gentleman, 1828

'Pelham, I have something of importance on my mind which I must discuss with you; let me entreat you to lay aside your natural levity.'

'My lord,' I replied, 'here is in your words a depth and solemnity which pierce me through one of N.'s best stuffed coats, even to the very heart. Let me ring for my poodle and some *eau de Cologne* and I will hear you as you desire.'

(Removed from the edition of 1837)

From an Unpublished Autobiography by Lord Lytton

In the midst of gathering storms which were shortly to break over our marriage and would never lift, Mrs. Wheeler, Rosina's mother, arrived from the Continent, full of delight, she claimed, on becoming a grandmother. It was difficult to find plausible grounds to deny her entrance to our house, although, fortunately, she based herself with her unfortunate and long-suffering brother in London. It is very rare for me to have agreed wholeheartedly with any opinion of Rosina's, but she had told me her mother was impossible, and impossible she was. It made me thankful for my own mother, even at a time when we were not on speaking terms, and perhaps that allowed me longer tolerance of Rosina's eccentricities than might otherwise have been the case.

Where to commence? The novelist always looks for material but Mrs. Wheeler was never a person whose idiosyncrasies I ever wished to capitalise upon in that way. Indeed, I have never believed that personal attacks, however dressed up, were part of the art of creating fiction, where it should be the imagination which holds sway. Mrs. Wheeler, let it be recorded, drank more heavily than any other woman I have ever encountered. Even in her later most decadent times, Rosina never consumed the same amount. It is never an attractive feature in a woman, and, at table, it made Mrs. Wheeler loud, argumentative and cantankerous. Occasionally, when she talked of the recent death of her younger daughter, she was also lachrymose, but that was perhaps the most pardonable of her moods in the circumstances. She professed enormous enthusiasm over her first grandchild, in her loud Irish way, but with all the specious enthusiasm of that race, and her only encounter with little Emily in person saw her handing the child back to its nurse the moment it opened its lungs in protest.

But, most intolerable of all, were her lectures upon the Rights of Women, based on a book she had coauthored, with the unappetising and cumbersome title of *The Appeal of One Half the Human Race, Women, Against the Pretensions of the Other Half, Men*. Rosina had made clear that she dissociated herself emphatically from her mother's strident opinions, but if Mrs. Wheeler had had her way, women would set about acquiring strength, both of body and mind, and would reject as weakness the soft phrases, susceptibility of heart, delicacy of sentiment, and refinement of taste which makes them women. According to

Rosina, illness had made her but a shadow of her former self but the shadow was more than enough for me. Never have gentlemen been more willing to retire from the company of ladies than when Mrs. Wheeler was at the table. Even I, who have always enjoyed and encouraged intelligent mature women, found her intolerable. Her views were apparently much appreciated in France, but then they had deservedly endured the catastrophe of revolution, and we have not.

And yet in defiance of her principles, she draped false ringlets about her dyed hair and painted her face thick enough to be a modern Jezebel. Though if she did this, as I suspect, to make herself more attractive to the male sex, then she had disastrously miscalculated. Yet it was somehow sad to see pathetic traces beneath the mask of the undoubted beauty she had bequeathed to her daughter. My own mother had so much more dignity in facing age.

I did my best as a host and a son-in-law to accommodate myself to her visits and her often over-emphatic praise of my own talents. To realise that Rosina had done everything in her power to distance herself from her mother and her views was immediately to feel some sympathy for my wife, though I was shocked at how little distress Rosina seemed to feel at the loss of her sibling. There is no doubt that the scars of her upbringing were seared into her very being. It was a matter of great sadness to me that Rosina proved to have no real vocation for the role of motherhood. At first, I excused it by the fragility of her health, which eventually become of such concern that she had to be sent away to Weymouth, barely two months after the birth of our daughter, to undergo a rest cure for her eyes, which were displaying considerable symptoms of strain. Her mental state had also been increasingly depressed, and she entertained many strange fantasies of what was happening around her, which I hoped repose by the sea would lay to rest. It was sad to see my initial misgivings confirmed and her liveliness turning into hysteria.

I must be eternally grateful to Miss Greene, who remained at Woodcot for the first few months after Emily's birth. Mary Greene was a woman of narrow ideas, with strong Evangelical prejudices and a somewhat puritanical view of life, whom my dear wife took pleasure in shocking upon every occasion, either by her extravagance, her recklessness or her mocking humour. Poor Miss Greene took it all in good part, though it was not generous of Rosina to treat her so. She was not a deeply imaginative soul but she had a solidity of sentiment and a willingness to devout herself to others which I found then admirable – and still do. It's a pity that no sensible married lady with a knowledge of the world was available, someone who could have helped Rosina to make the best of her situation and find mental occupation and recreation within her own sphere. But Miss Greene was better than nothing, a great deal better. Fortunately, the wet nurse we found was also a capable soul who ensured that our child was (for the moment at least) healthy.

Rosina did indeed eventually rally, at least superficially, but she was never a mother to our child. There were times when she would suddenly lavish affection on Little Boots, as she nicknamed our daughter Emily, and our daughter responded in loving kind as her mother kissed and caressed her. These outbursts, however, had no consistency and no regularity; they came and went like clouds across the sky. The remainder of the time, Rosina happily left her to the care of others. The truth is that Rosina's affection for her dogs was becoming ever more of an obsession and, if there was a competition for her attention, the dogs would win out over the child on almost every occasion, unless there were guests present.

By contrast with the undesired introduction into my existence of my wife's mother, my own family began to seem more attractive, even reasonable. My older brother, William, had inherited the Heydon estate from my father, but it was so badly mismanaged by the trustees appointed by the Court of Chancery that, when he came of age in 1820, the estate was heavily saddled with debts which he struggled ever after to clear. Perhaps this reduced the amount of condescension he had shown towards me when I was a boy and allowed him to appreciate my struggle to make my financial way in the world. Our middle brother, Henry, meanwhile, had gambled away the modest fortune left him by his maternal grandmother and had yet to make his mark in any other way. So much for the worldly wisdom I had been invited to admire in my siblings.

Whether by coincidence or design, my brother William had rented a house not far from Woodcot with his wife of less than a year, Emily. Our choice of the same name for our own daughter, incidentally, was one of Rosina's whims, however much we might have liked to have represented it as a compliment to my new sister-in-law. It was some consolation to me that my mother had strongly disapproved of my brother's choice, as she had of mine, though Emily was far less of an exotic bloom than my own Rosina. In her case, it seemed to have been her lack of social graces which offended my mother, since her family was not without means. God knows, it cannot have been her beauty. What was of no consolation at all, indeed a cruel blow to me at this time of intense literary labour, was that my mother relented enough with Emily to actually receive her, while my own wife, now the bearer of our first child, remained cast out into the outer darkness.

With little Emily ushered into the world, it seemed a time to try again for a reconciliation. I wrote to my mother, telling her both of her grandchild's birth and of Rosina's resultant ailments, which I hoped might soften her towards her recalcitrant daughter-in-law. I knew Rosina would never be prepared to bend the knee in penitence, as my brother's soft-natured wife was willing to do, but I hoped my mother would respond to the intimation that Rosina was a human being and a mother, and a fragile one at that. Eventually, my letters brought forth a response, friendly enough in my mother's guarded way, but there was no hint that she was willing to see me. Nevertheless, I felt enough encouragement from her response to continue to communicate with her. Perhaps there was one short tight-lipped note for every three or four open-hearted epistles from myself, setting out my anxieties for my child and my ailing wife and the strain of the workload I had necessarily imposed upon myself, accompanied always by affectionate concern for her own health and mental well-being. There was no insincerity about what I wrote. My encounters with Mrs. Wheeler had made me all too aware of how fortunate, whatever her faults, I had been with my maternal parent.

And, of course, I sent her a copy of *The Disowned*. Rosina always twitted me upon the obvious hint in the title, but I thought only of my fiction and what was right for it. Would any serious author name a book as an open reproach to his own mother? She duly acknowledged the book, but offered no comment. Still this was an improvement upon her treatment of the proffered slice of wedding cake and I sensed my mother's steely demeanour was beginning to melt a little.

The critics were harsh upon *The Disowned*, though it sold exceptionally well. Good sales are always balm to the soul of an author, still more to his publisher (who may well not have a soul), even though the publisher knows he will have to pay more for his writer's next effusion. Over the years I have learned to accept damning and often unjustified criticism because, to be honest, I have had no choice in the matter and the answer to my denigrators must be the quality of my work and its continuing success with the reading public.

If you had asked Rosina then what struggles and compromises I was going through, she would have understood nothing and simply complained that my study door was closed to her for too many hours.

My mother didn't understand either. But she had more excuse and, though unwilling as yet to receive me at Knebworth, she finally consented to see me in London for the first time since the marriage had taken place. The estrangement had been too complete for an entire reconciliation to be achieved at once, yet, though the old cordiality between mother and son was not re-established, the dropped allowance was provisionally restored.

From the Memoirs of Rosina, Lady Lytton

Pelham had, I own, a certain wit and bravado, which did for a time make me reconsider my opinion of my husband's talent. But it was a flash in the pan, an attractive moment of cynicism in his endless self-pitying self-importance, inspired, dare I say it, by his encounter with my own down to earth opinions and, yes, let it be said, his Priapic desires being satisfied, completely satisfied, by one intelligent woman. There were moments, I will own, when I found myself beginning to develop a certain sympathy with that opinionated Goddess of Reason, who was my mother.

Soon, however, lingering creative death set in for Eddard in what was probably one of the most protracted death scenes in literary history. The death of Little Nell in the maudlin book by his literary chum, Charles Dickens, seems positively speedy by comparison. For the rest of his literary life, he would never use one word when seven could be usefully employed. It made his books longer, which may have been the original highly practical impulse, but it ended by making them unreadable by anyone of any discernible literary taste. Even the flashy Mr Dickens and the oleaginous Mr Disraeli (chums both) never sunk quite to his verbose depths.

I am describing what is self-evident to any discerning reader of his works, so I should continue with the sad history of the rest of our life together, told as simply as words can tell it. There was no recurrence of my husband's violence to me but the threat was always in the air. I knew it was hopeless to turn to anyone to confide in, so I held my tongue. Despite this, I was peremptorily sent away (I am tempted to say banished) from my newly-born child and my home to a house close to the sea in Weymouth. The house was pleasant enough (as I was regularly reminded) and it was indeed true that I was not well, my eyes hurt, my spirits low, but a degree of interest in my health and some believable expression of affection would have done much to relieve my symptoms. However, it suited Mr Hypocrite of the Homely Hearth to present his removal of me as concern, and the annexation of my daughter by Miss Greene as a caring solution. Then, when she had served her purpose, with Eddard's usual ruthlessness, she was suddenly *de trop*, and poor wailing Little Boots was delivered into the care of his aunt Emma, that wizened carrot of a woman. I have been reproached for my lack of maternal feeling by those not necessarily in the pay of Sir All Proud, but even those few well-disposed towards me simply do not understand the ruthlessness with which my child, my Little Boots, was taken away from me. For appearances' sake, she would sometimes be brought to see me, but her tears had barely dried after the upheavals of her journey and the unfamiliarity of her own mother, before she was packed up and dragged away again to the ministrations of the Carrot. And then Sir Liar had the audacity to spread the rumour that I loved my dogs more than my child, the dogs being the only faithful companions left to me in my solitude. A dear little Blenheim dog called Dash had been added to my menagerie at this time and I own she was my pet among my pets.

There were a few other miserable compensations to my solitude, I admit. My mother was in poor health and showed no interest in leaving London to come and visit me. Her unwilling host, my poor uncle, must have been cursing his lot and embroidering every object in sight, but at least she wasn't bothering me. There was even a certain pleasure in realising she was in a position to embarrass and badger Eddard far more than she could do the same to me.

Eddard, meanwhile, had been fawning upon his own Gorgon of a mother. There's no doubt that she had money aplenty and even I felt compassion for the hours he spent locked away creating his turgid masterpieces. I could even rejoice at their success with the public, although my respect for the public was permanently destroyed. When Eddard claimed with some justification that he needed release from his endless literary struggles (although, interestingly enough, when he did achieve financial release, he had become such a literary threshing machine, that he could not stop emptying his withered bales on to the market), I couldn't totally condemn him for wooing his mother with a passion he never put into wooing me. But even in private correspondence, he could not stop himself over-egging the pudding, in his increasingly verbose style. How else to explain the letter which Eddard's brother, William, copied on to us in a rare gesture of opacity? Her Starched Highness had obviously received the impression that I did not only have eye troubles but I was going blind in one eye. *How much she is to be pitied*, runs the letter in increasingly unconvincing terms. *How did Rosina lose her sight? Is the eye lid closed over or is it open? Is she likely to lose the other? Do let me know. Et cetera. Et cetera.*

Well, you can read this communication in a variety of ways. In my eyes (officially at this point apparently rapidly losing all sight), this represents gloating over the spoils of victory. Against her advice, Eddard had married a blind woman. But there is, I will admit, an alternative interpretation. Not that she cares for me, that would be absurd, but that this ridiculous old iceberg of a woman was trying to find a way to reconcile herself to the son she had cast away. Without him, where else could her withered affections find outlet? If the price to be paid was my relegation to blinded victim, a Lavinia or whatever that daughter is called who gets her tongue and hands chopped off somewhere in Shakespeare (how fortunate I am to have obtained a copy of the Bard before Dr. Bowlder got his hands on it), then I accepted the capitulation gracefully, not least on behalf of my Little Boots. In those days, my husband, otherwise Mr. Pelham or Maltravers or Devereux, or whatever the latest pretentious name of his leading fictional character happened to be, was still susceptible to guilt. He had not quite become the hardened Sir Liar of later years. So it came about that, after my earnest entreaties and significant improvement in my health, I was allowed to move to Tunbridge Wells, which had a certain fashionability and was not quite so estranged from the metropolis.

Here my dear Little Boots was allowed to be with me more regularly. Perhaps even Eddard realised how bad it looked in the eyes of the World that he kept a mother apart from her child. As a little girl, Emily was certainly the best little thing that ever was, and could sit by my side for hours on the sofa amusing herself. She was barely a year old but she could talk, and she could walk, and she had little golden curls all over her head, but not a single tooth yet. And if she wanted something ever so much, she would grab hold of a candle or a paper knife or whatever it might be, I just had to look at her seriously and say, 'No, Little Boots mustn't have that', and she would put it down directly and look up from under her eyelids to see if I was angry. And if I looked very grave, she would put her little paws round my neck and say, 'Tiss Boots'. And Dash, my little Blenheim dog, she simply adored. So much so that anything she liked was called Dash, even her father when he deigned to visit. Oh, the futile affection poor Emily wasted upon that cold-hearted man!

But I must not torment myself with remembering moments of happiness, because my Emily's fate was so unbearably sad and I must recount that in its place. For, in retrospect, there were still moments of happiness to hold on to and Eddard, in part from feelings of guilt I like to imagine, had begun again to woo me. After what had happened in the library, I could never again trust him, but at least his temper was under control, and his love-making had at least the semblance of a respect and affection for my being. If there were mistresses at that time (and almost certainly there were), I had yet to learn of them. And, above all, I wanted what was best for Little Boots and whatever other offspring we had, although I had no desire to turn into a breeding machine like the Withered Carrot, who died some seven years later, for all her pains, after having produced six uniformly ugly-looking red-haired children.

Yet there were always ulterior motives with Sir Liar. A dog does not lie when it looks into your eyes with affection and devotion, but a husband usually does. Mr. Pelham had begun to earn money, substantial sums of money, from his pen (mightier than the sword we must never be allowed to forget) and there was other good financial news. The old iceberg, his mother, though still declining to acknowledge me, had nevertheless begun to thaw somewhat and she had promised to restore his allowance. He must have grovelled and pleaded and said God knows what about me to shift the unshiftable, but finally there was money, money enough for a very different sort of life.

So Sir Specious had undoubtedly another motive in attempting reconciliation. He needed to look well in the world because he had acquired a splendid new town house in Hertford

Street. If I had been absent or disaffected, the picture he wished to paint for Society of his admirable domestic life (important now he was aiming for respectability rather than scandal) and the hospitality he needed to offer to further his career would have been compromised. He knew I would make an engaging and decorative hostess who could shine in company (though I say it myself), so I had to be placated. And, why did I agree? Does that question need an answer? I had been starved of wit and conversation and access to my child so, naturally, I agreed to our move together into this fashionable new world.

Foolishly, I had convinced myself that there would be a new beginning. Woodcot was let to another, Weymouth and Tunbridge Wells were left behind, I was returning to London as a hostess for literary evenings which would cause Miss Benger to eat her shrivelled old heart out in envy, not least because she would never be invited. We had money. We had prestige. We had an adorable child. Even our mothers were no longer our enemies. We were, in many people's eyes, a handsome and successful couple deeply in love.

Hope springs eternal in the human breast, as some idiot once said.

From Godolphin, an Abandoned Novel, Circa 1829

It has been said that marriages are made in heaven. Very possibly, but heaven imports the raw material from earth. The workmanship may be admirable, but the stuff might be better.

From an Unpublished Autobiography by Lord Lytton

The special pleading I made on Rosina's behalf with my mother is something she could not, and would not, ever acknowledge. I bombarded my mother with news, messages, pleas, with a frequency even I thought excessive. When we moved to Hertford Street, I returned again to the topic with increasing fierceness, even though it might endanger the *rapprochement* I had achieved with her. I was very firm. I live in the same town as you, I wrote, but you refuse to visit my wife or enter my house. My brother also displeased you by his marriage, but you enter his house and visit his wife. You say that you can distinguish between the two cases. But the world cannot take the trouble to understand such a distinction. It merely sees that, the two brothers being both of age, and having both married gentlewomen, you are sufficiently reconciled to both our marriages to see both

William and myself, but also observes that your visiting the wife of one and not the wife of the other is a marked insult to the wife unvisited. You may say, I continued, that the world does not occupy itself about the matter, but, unfortunately that is not the case. In the first place, the world always gossips about dissensions in families, however humble, but I pointed out that, in my case, I was very much a marked man. Every man who writes is talked of, more or less. The affront to me is therefore more known, and so more wounding, than it would be if I myself were less known. Besides, what can it be but galling in the last degree for our carriages to pass and no salutation? For me to come to your house, and attend your receptions alone, and you never to be seen at mine? For my wife to be asked about you by persons who do not know the matter, whilst your name is sedulously avoided by those who do? It is, I concluded, an affront, not offered once and then over, but of daily, hourly occurrence, which perpetually occasions me the greatest unhappiness and the deepest mortification.

I laboured long and hard to effect a reconciliation between Rosina and my mother. And my mother, let God above give praise to her severe soul now lodged in Heaven, finally agreed to come to Hertford Street and pay a visit to my wife. Rosina's response? Well, I was not present, so I have only their deeply divergent accounts to base my opinion upon. Rosina claimed to be so offended by my mother's high and mighty tone that she felt humiliated in her own home, and therefore felt no obligation to provide my mother with access to her grand-daughter. All of this recounted to me with satirical imitations of my mother's manner of speech and adverse comments upon her antediluvian dress sense. My mother was more Stoic. She simply stated that she had been made to feel unwelcome and she would never willingly repeat the experience. My conclusion was clear. With her usual sense of contrariness, Rosina had thrown away an opportunity for reconciliation for which I had laboured long and hard. I could do no more.

I could have done no more even if I had wished. I was wrestling with the spirit of Demons in my writing and my prostration of mind was such that I sometimes believed myself mad. My skin was erupting with nervous rashes. Indeed, I sometimes wonder if Rosina wished me to be tipped over the abyss into insanity to justify her own deeply partial view of our life together. Who knows? But, if I am honest, it seems only justice that in the end she was the one who has toppled into the abyss. I had striven for so long to reconcile her distorted and naive views of the world with the brutal truth of how it is and, after my struggles, I am relieved to be vindicated.

The mind slips between the past and the present. Let us, for the moment, stay with the past, which, because it is irrevocably fixed in time, is easier to describe. In the eyes of the world, Rosina and I held court at Hertford Street. I was now a highly successful author, even though a part of me had had to be banished to achieve that success. The envy of the world, and in particular the envy of *Fraser's Magazine,* always plagued me.

On the other hand, I had acquired friendships which would sustain the rest of my life. Benjamin Disraeli, to name but one, was an aspiring author to whom my work gave inspiration in its satirical insights into a fashionable society he had yet to experience for himself. His dress sense had a wildness that even I could not aspire to, but there was always a wit and shrewdness there that served him so well in the future.

And there was the delightful Count d'Orsay, the handsome exquisite, who both fulfilled the vision of my Pelham and proved it was possible to be a figure of elegance but also a human being of rare kindness and perception. The attempts to blacken his name recently, I totally despise. Then there was his close friend, Lady Blessington, an authoress of rare talent who, like me, had to learn how to write in order to provide. When I first met the two of them, her husband had just died of an apoplectic stroke, leaving his depleted estate in disarray and so Lady Blessington laboured not only to support herself but the Count and his wife, Lord Blessington's daughter by his previous marriage. I am proud that I was able to assist the launching of her literary career.

Oh how I delighted in Lady Blessington's company! I have remarked before that I have always relished the company of older, more tolerant and understanding women. Recollect at this point, I was still in my twenties, and longed for a sympathetic and intelligent ear. Mrs. Cunningham, Lady Blessington, Mrs. Stanhope (of whom more later) form my *beau ideal* of the feminine sex. Rosina was too frivolous, my mother too judgemental. These were the women the gypsy had instinctively directed me to. If Mrs. Wheeler had not been my wife's mother, and filled with absurd notions about femininity, she would have been of the ideal age and maturity to understand me, but, to reverse a paradox, ailing or not, she was her daughter's mother. At least I have given you some notion of my intimates in this expanding social circle. I do not want to proceed with a self-congratulatory list which would simply tire both my reader and me. Suffice to say, for the first time in my life, I could feel myself at home in my world, not simply an intruder. If Rosina had been a different person, maybe the idyll (and idylls I acknowledge must inevitably end) might have endured longer. I went to my clubs, I attended evenings at the homes of the fashionable and the talented (not, I will acknowledge, categories that necessarily duplicate) and was able to entertain in my own home, presided over by a household God, a Lares (I mean Rosina) who could in the best of circumstances and moods seem totally benign.

Rosina, of course, never developed the least talent for domestic economy. We are talking of a woman who had the names of her dogs printed upon tiny visiting cards, which she used to leave with her own upon her friends and neighbours. Still, for the moment, she was a hostess more attractive to the eye than most and her superficial wit impressed all but the most discerning. Let it be recorded that Mr Disraeli came away from his first encounter with her enchanted. Of course, by the third encounter, the magic had vanished but his was a more discerning eye than most.

With the increased expense of Hertford Street and Rosina's total impracticality as a housekeeper, there could be no respite from my literary labours, despite the renewed financial support from my mother. How many nights, after lively social encounters both abroad and at home, I have struggled to my desk to pen another chapter or (if the grape had hit me too hard) dragged myself early the next morning to perform feats of disciplined imagination only the mighty Disraelis and Dickenses of this world could understand though they did not have to struggle as I did, given their lower social origins, with the notion that these literary labours were beneath them.

My fate is to be an innovator, whose innovations have been annexed by others and my own pioneering contribution forgotten. This is always the fate of the labourer who cuts the first swathe through the cornfield. While my wife bickered, my mother carped and my mother-in-law lectured, I had to continue to write and to continue to surprise a reading public, both ardent and fickle.

My new novel, *Paul Clifford*, was set in the criminal world of the late eighteenth-century. I had once made the mistake of inviting Rosina to help me with my researches. She was heavily pregnant but had complained so often of being excluded from that part of my life, that I thought it might occupy a mind, which found it difficult to settle to anything in a sustained fashion. On one evening, I recall particularly, she became so listless that I begged her to go and rest. But she insisted that she wished to continue helping me. Half an hour later, barely able to concentrate, because of her ostentatious sighing and yawning (her dogs had, thank God, been banned from the library) I begged her again to go and rest and leave me with my literary struggles. Her reply was mock surprise and coy satirical remarks about how my poor over-heated brainbox needed to cool down. She clearly had no notion of how disruptive she was being when, in her view, she was doing exactly what I had asked her to do. If I had descended into argument at this point, then a hundred details, a dozen of insights, the interlocking fragments of story, would have been lost to me, only to be recovered with immense effort. So, I confess, I spoke to her harshly and she left in tears.

Heaven alone knows how she represented the cause of her tears to the world but, disturbed though I was, I had nevertheless to force myself to sit down and continue my story.

In *Paul Clifford*, I resolved to treat my hero, a criminal and highwayman, with understanding and respect. The old style moralists believed criminals should be unequivocally condemned both in words and in practice. The gallows was the answer to all social problems. I dared to disagree. To understand how criminals become criminals is not to approve of what they do, but to give them a humanity which speaks to our own humanity. For the slightest of crimes, pick-pocketing, born out of hunger, and parental neglect, my hero is placed at a tender age in a prison, where the boy is corrupted by the very punishment that ought to redeem him. And then, when finally he is arrested again for his crimes as a grown man, despite the transparent good in his character, he is condemned to be hanged right away, as our society's easiest way of getting rid of our own blunders. In my novel, I allowed my hero to escape with his lady love to America, but I (and, I hope, my readers) was under no illusion that this was the common good luck of convicted criminals, who might have done no more than steal a horse or set fire to a barn.

I was vilified by the envious and the hypocritical for writing an immoral book. And then, when I had blazed the way and taken the blame, others leapt in and reaped the benefits of my creation of the so-called Newgate novel without any of my seriousness of intent. Other writers made money and reputation out of tawdry tales of Dick Turpin and Jack Shepherd, where social justice and moral teaching were lost in simple sensation. (Are you hearing me, William Harrison Ainsworth?)

But I should be philosophical. *Paul Clifford* sold exceedingly well, beyond even my expectation, and the reading public responded warmly to its stirring tale and the gusto of its telling. What I still struggle to understand – not because I want to apologise, far from it – is where my radicalism, my care for an underclass ignored by most of my own social peers, came from? Certainly not from my mother, who feared the mob as if the French Revolution was at her door. Certainly not from Rosina, who dismissed any discussion of politics with a satirical shrug. There is nothing in my background or in my domestic circumstances to explain my growing sense of indignation at the injustice and inequality of the England I contemplated.

Whatever the explanation, whatever the initial motivation, in the battleground which was England in the early eighteen thirties, I found myself, instinctively and without question, allied to the forces committed to radical change.

Which is why, despite all my commitments, I decided to take on the burden of seeking to be a Member of Parliament.

The Opening of Paul Clifford, Published 1830

It was a dark and stormy night; the rain fell in torrents—except at occasional intervals, when it was checked by a violent gust of wind which swept up the streets (for it is in London that our scene lies), rattling along the housetops, and fiercely agitating the scanty flame of the lamps that struggled against the darkness.

From the Memoirs of Rosina, Lady Lytton

Many people, I am sure, imagine being the hostess of widely reported and much envied parties for the rich and famous, while married to a man, for good or ill, regarded as a leading author of the day, was a role profoundly to be wished for. The truth is, as the truth often is, very different. Days of isolation, ignored by my eternally busy husband, followed by hours of intense social activity. The Irish part of me, the only part of my Irishness I fully appreciate, enjoys spending time with like-minded people, enjoying relaxed conversation full of laughter. Real relaxation and real laughter, however, were always distinctly lacking at the parties my Lord and Master demanded in Hertford Street. There were always alliances to be made, people to be impressed, people to be wooed, in Master Eddard's evenings. I found myself longing for the simple charms of Miss Benger's soirées, a longing I could never have believed a couple of years before. There were guests at Miss Benger's who were self-promoting (Sir Liar among them) and dull beyond redemption (Sir Liar border-line), but there was nothing poisonous about the atmosphere, nobody who could lie and lie and be a villain. Alas, another quotation from the Immortal Bard for which I have no reference.

So there was little pleasure to be had in the poisonous creatures who haunted our drawing-room. Some are mercifully sunk into the obscurity they richly deserved. But a certain Benjamin Disraeli has done rather well, I understand. He and my husband were as thick as thieves, at this time, when they both dressed like masculine whores and thought themselves the epitome of the *beau monde*. Somebody had clearly told the Semitic (for all his protests) Benjamin that the best way to be remembered is to dress in a fashion that can never be forgotten. Eddard was tasteful by comparison. I remember him once with long, black glossy ringlets that were taken for a wig. The women (obsequious nonentities, not me) were allowed, with his encouragement, to pull his curls to satisfy their curiosity as to their authenticity. The excitement was visible in his face and I do not like to speculate what other parts of his anatomy. He was dressed at the time in green velvet trousers, a canary coloured waistcoat, low shoes with silver buckles and lace at his wrist. Other ladies (including his later wife) found him attractive. I simply shivered.

Were these men she-men? My Eddard and his Semitic friend cared more about their appearance than any woman I have ever met. And I have not yet begun to consider Alfred Guillaume Gabriel Count D'Orsay (I hope you are impressed that I have researched his full title). He was the dandy they all aspired to be. Handsome, broad-shouldered, narrow-waisted, he was Mr. Pelham personified, in a way poor spindly anxious Eddard could never be. The men, Eddard, Semitic Benjamin, Mr. Sparkler Dickens, were all besotted with him. The ladies, and for once I am not alone here, were less attracted. Apart from poor Lady Blessington, most women recoiled from his over-scented, over-exquisite presence. That was certainly my own experience. He was clearly trying hard, too hard, to ingratiate himself with me, but there was something cloying and distinctly unmasculine in the way he went about it. I reeked from both his charm and his perfume. There were times when I felt like fumigating the whole house after the departure of Eddard's male companions, the cigar smoke and the brandy fumes blending with some of the heaviest scents the human nostrils could endure.

Here you reach the endless hypocrisy of Eddard's circle of liberated Romantic souls. Count D'Orsay was welcomed and adored by his male friends. There were many eulogies upon the cherubic quality of his countenance and the rugged muscle of his body. Poor hard-working Lady B. was meanwhile *persona non grata*. I suppose that I should have felt some sympathy for her for my life with Sir Sodomite seemed positively dull by comparison. She was a Tipperary girl who'd married a penniless Lord and she'd laboured away at her novels (not good, but better than Eddard's) to support her husband and the exquisite Count, who was then married off to Lord Blessington's daughter by a previous marriage. By the time I met Count Exquisite, Lord B. was dead and Countess D'Orsay was suing for divorce. Shall I tell you the only solution to the D'Orsay / Blessington *ménage* which makes any sense? Lord Blessington allowed it all to happen because he was in love with D'Orsay. Lady B. had had (it's well known) dalliances with men who were violent and Priapic and her womb was destroyed. So the exquisite Count was a relief because he made no sexual demands at all, just stood around looking decorative. The injured Harriet, Lady B's step-daughter, eventually put in for divorce, from a marriage which had produced no children. So the Count was impotent, Lady B. was frigid and Lord B. loved his own sex, so who could blame Lady Harriet for escaping? Well, only the Count's male friends, who continued to worship at his shrine. I do not call Eddard Sir Sodomite for nothing.

Meanwhile, the ladies who were allowed to attend our parties were uniformly dull, polite approving adjuncts to their self-satisfied husbands. Most of them were also dowdy. Only Mrs. Stanhope (of whom more later) had any style or looks and the appeal of that was negated by her cow-like stupidity, only matched by the bullish complacency of her banker husband, who, rumour had it, accepted money for access to her charms. In company of women like these, I began to feel nostalgic for poor departed Lady Caroline. On some of the dullest evenings, I even liked to imagine her leaping out naked from under one of the dishcovers.

I continued meanwhile to be the recipient of Master Eddard's Priapic demands, only because he wished me to conceive a son to impress his mother, and elicit her further financial support. Do I sound cynical? As he came within me, he uttered words of passion and of devotion, but sometimes he uttered a name and that name was not mine and it wasn't even the same name every time.

It was a matter of private amusement to me that, even with his mother's restored allowance, he claimed we were still comparatively poor. Compared with whom? He simply could not contain his extravagance. His furnishing mania filled our London house with pictures, furniture and statues until it burst. He insisted upon holding lavish parties, with out-of-season foods and rare wines which he bought to impress with little more knowledge of the grape than myself. And yet, in the midst of all this extravagance, he had the audacity to upbraid me for the weekly bills and even withheld the house-keeping money in protest at *my* extravagance.

So why did the most driven and exhausted writer in the world (his own estimation) decide to become a Member of Parliament?

I think I can remember the very night when Eddard first developed a social conscience. He would like the World to believe it came from God and his magnanimous nature but, like most things in his life, it came from his mother. I remember Eddard was lying exhausted from his Priapic exertions and he started crying. We were still at the point at which I could ask him why. He talked about injustice, by which he meant how differently he and his brothers had been treated. There you have it.

Do you think Sir Liar could ever care about anyone except himself? Never believe a word he has said about caring for others. He is just talking about the fact that his relatives all preferred his brothers and his father (clearly a man of taste) hated his guts. Is this superficial? Only if you believe that those magnificent abstractions, Duty and Honour, really rule people's lives. With Sir Liar, I know better. Until this time, Master Eddard had displayed little or no interest in politics. He was entirely consumed by his literary efforts and his social self-importance. Yet he decided to aim at a seat in the House of Commons even before the thought had entered the noddle of the dandiacal and ambitious Semite, Mr. Disraeli. Oh, and how Eddard must envy him his success.

But to continue. Not long after he had vented his tears (and other fluids) upon me, a misfortunate befell his brother, Henry, hitherto the black sheep of the family (though later a successful diplomat, which makes what I am to tell you deeply ironic). There was a by-election in 1830 in Hertford (Mary Tudor had Calais engraved upon her heart, my suffering heart should have Hertford) and Brother Henry became one of the candidates. But his candidature did not last until polling day. He withdrew, and remained in Brussels, where he already held a minor diplomatic post (God alone knows why he was given it). There was much speculation about why he had fled. And then the truth began to emerge, as it will, even when the evil-doers are rich and powerful. Brother Henry, obsessed with money like his siblings, had accepted a bung (a word I learned from my – unacknowledged – study of *The Newgate Calendar* for one of Sir Liar's novels) from the Second Marquess of Salisbury, a former M.P. for the seat but also, alas, a member of the opposite party. In a word, he had been bought. It's unfortunately very common for a candidate to buy, give or perhaps sell votes at an election but it was something really new to buy or sell a candidate.

You can imagine how vaustly distressed the aged mama was by the juicy scandal that subsequently developed. There were people who declared that Henry Bulwer would not be able to step foot in the country for a long time to come (not knowing he would become a famous diplomat). Even Mrs. Lytton's poker back and pursed lips began to wobble under the strain of the gossip and the ill-feeling in the neighbourhood. Not surprisingly, she sought the advice and comfort of her youngest son, and, even less surprisingly, in view of the continuation of his allowance, he rushed to her side. Apologies were demanded, denials were made, Henry was advised to say nothing and stay away. William was a pompous oaf, but basically decent, but Henry was a much nastier, less trustworthy creature (perhaps he was born to be a diplomat). So I rest my case. Eddard became a politician to spite his brother – and, as always, to appease that formidable antique Volumnia, his mother. I fancy that she is in *Coriolanus* (Volumnia I mean) but I cannot be sure.

Politics for Sir Liar have always been about vanity and revenge. If he really cared for the poor and needy, he could have spared some of the money he lavished upon Louis Quatorze clocks. But, most important of all, by seeking election, he salvaged the honour of the House of Lytton, which means that his mother loosened the purse strings still further, just so long as she did not have to encounter me. He became M.P. for St. Ives. Hertford, for all its closeness to

Knebworth, was in the circumstances not really an appropriate seat in which to stand.

You will doubtless tell me that the Reform Bill was a great achievement and Eddard helped it to happen. Certainly our large industrial cities gained a voice and the rotten boroughs lost theirs. But, consider, at the end of all this: one in five male adults had gained the right to vote, some five per cent of the total population. How do I know this? Because after being lectured night and day by Sir Sanctimonious on his great achievement, I enquired from others the truth of the matter. Meanwhile, all over the country the infatuation of the Common People was astonishing. They seemed to look upon this new Bill as a sort of patent steam engine Miracle Worker. I recall, one night a ragged drunken fellow in the street crying out details of the King's Speech with the following surprising appendages. He informed anybody who would hear that, once the Reform Bill was passed, they'd all have their beef and mutton for a penny a pound. Every one would be as fine as peacocks then for a mere trifle, to say nothing of ale at a penny a quart in which, he continued, drunker by the moment, you may drink His Majesty's health and His Majesty's ministers' health and the health of the glorious Reform Bill's health – all without a ruining of yourselves. At this point the dogs started barking loudly and I had to close the window on the inebriated orator and his hopeless dreams. Probably the Peelers, then newly invented, took him away. Poor deluded souls, they gained nothing from the heroism of Sir Liar and his cronies. Fortunately, his new activities as an M.P. left him with little time or energy to harass me over my failings. I still dreaded his rages, but there was to be no repeat of the violent assault in the library. This was because I was pregnant again, and my Lord and Master had convinced himself that I was bearing his son and heir.

From Eugene Aram, a Tale, 1832

I lived but to feed my mind; wisdom was my thirst, my dream, my aliment, my sole fount and sustenance of life. And have I not sown the whirlwind and reaped the wind? The glory of my youth is gone, my veins are chilled, my frame is bowed, my heart is gnawed with care, my nerves are unstrung as a loosened bow: and what, after all, is my gain?

From an Unpublished Autobiography by Lord Lytton

By the start of 1833, some five years after I had sat in the study in Woodcot, faced the rising sun and accepted my destiny, I was exhausted. Once before, the endless hours of literary labour had taken their toll upon me and my constitution and I had been forced to rest for a couple of months, but this time the collapse was total. Painful disfiguring rashes erupted all over my body. Sleep constantly eluded me, as I spent the night in endless mental and physical agitation and rose to another day of travail. Several have described me as looking like a man who had recently been flayed alive. My interior being was probably in even worse shape. The record of what I achieved in those years shows, without question, that there was no malingering or hypochondria in my state. I have always had a sensitive, melancholy, introverted nature, for all my public success, but I had been pushing myself towards the physical and mental abyss and there was serious danger that I might tumble down into its dark and desperate blackness.

Even Rosina roused herself from her habitual self-absorption and devotion to her dogs to express concern. I was, of course, her sole provider and if I foundered then little would be left for her to survive upon, but there was, at least to my eyes, a genuine affection in how she started to attend to my health and well-being and hush the dogs when I went by. What further indication of how much she cared than that she took the radical step of writing to my mother, begging her to invite me to Knebworth and force me to rest? My mother later showed me the letter, in a rare attempt, for her grandchildren's sake, to shore up a marriage she had nearly destroyed. In her epistle, Rosina urges my mother to lock up the library, hide all my papers and never to leave a pen or pencil within my reach. She recommends that my mother should not let me have any dinner till I had ridden seven or eight miles. If only she had found a way to express her touching anxiety more directly, perhaps things might have turned out differently. But, no, why delude myself? Rosina's affection for me, once so genuine and all-consuming, had dwindled to the passing concern she would show for a sick puppy.

As a young man, I had adopted a Byronic pose aimed at showing a cynicism about the world and all that it contains. The dramatic change brought up by the intervening years was that I did believe in purpose and progress, even though my battered spirits sometimes led me to doubt. I remain proud of being part of the group which engineered a remarkable change in our corrupt electoral system and created the Golden Age of politics which ensued under Queen Victoria. There were no visible wounds, but the fight was brutal and I was only sustained by my principles and my colleagues. I lived the dangerous life of a Radical member of a Tory society, when the country was aflame with riotous disorder and sympathy with Reform was seen by many as a sign of a perverse, even dangerous, state of mind. And then, because I trained myself rigorously to become an accomplished public speaker, few will credit the agonies the exposure to the common eye causes me or the endless internal dialogues of doubt and self-criticism which dog my every speech to this day.

But let me count the political work of those years an achievement and one which delighted my mother, after the unhappy experiences of my brother, Henry, in the field of electioneering. And let me also, for a moment, relish my literary accomplishments. For I now completed what was perhaps my finest achievement to date, *Eugene Aram*, the tale of a high-minded scholar, who, years before, had been driven by dire poverty to assent to a deed of violence wholly alien to his nature. The story was already well known but I honestly believed that I had transformed it by the intensity of my identification with the suffering hero / villain. Eugene settles in a remote village and falls in love but, before his marriage can take place, his accomplice returns and betrays Aram, who is imprisoned, tried and sentenced to death. Some of my finest historical novels were still to come but Eugene Aram's story consumed me with a fire that both excited and enervated me. It took Europe by storm and became one of the most enduringly popular of my fictions. Few, except my most talented peers – Benjamin Disraeli, Charles Dickens – can begin to understand the mental labour involved in such a book or the agony of identification with a flawed but sympathetic hero. Again, my imitators simply vulgarised what I had done by parading vicious criminals as objects of sympathy without either understanding their interior life or offering any illumination of their motives.

I do not believe any author in modern times has suffered so much sustained ridicule from a collection of hacks and would-be wits as I have. They envied my success and the money I have made, but it went beyond that. It is as if they had a personal vendetta against me. I always maintained a brave face, but the crudity of the attacks of *Fraser's Magazine* and its unholy crew hurt me deeply. It was undoubtedly a contributory factor to my physical collapse, although, proud man that I am, I would never ever admit it.

Let me, however, record the one achievement in this sad time of which I am undoubtedly proud and no one can take from me. I acquired a son, Robert, a delightful child, whatever his later shortcomings. Emily, of course, I also adored, but her reticent nature and continuing ill-health made her an object more of affectionate concern than pride. Which brings me, of course, back to their mother. Sadly, Robert's birth rekindled no obvious spark of maternal feeling in Rosina. At my suggestion, therefore, her admirable Irish spinster friend, Miss Greene, graciously agreed to return to attend to both son and daughter. If only Rosina could have been made to care, how much might have been different.

At the time of my breakdown, however, for breakdown it must ultimately be called, she was my wife and the mother of my children. When I conceived the ideas of a continental tour to restore my ailing constitution, there was not a doubt in my mind that she should accompany me. I still believed that there might be some chance of reconciliation because I knew that was best for my children. I did not want them to grow up in an atmosphere of acrimony and distrust.

With these thoughts in my head, I proposed to Rosina a tour to the Continent. Pleasure lover that she was, and is, of course she accepted. In my debilitated state, I needed to hope that we could settle our differences and somehow make a life together, and that task might be easier in a foreign country with no crew of yapping dogs in tow.

We left Miss Greene to supervise the care of the children. The dogs were entrusted to servants who claimed to love them (and I wish I had instructed to poison them all). I had made my peace with my mother and, for all my anxieties, I felt, after my labours, our financial future was secure.

Believe me, for Robert and for Emily, I honestly wanted to save our marriage.

From Godolphin, an Abandoned Novel

When once in a gay and occupied life a husband and wife have admitted a seeming indifference to creep in between them, the chances are a thousand to one against its removal.

From the Memoirs of Rosina, Lady Lytton

Once I had looked into the eyes of a husband who denied he has violently assaulted me, I knew in my heart that I could never wholly trust him again, but I still struggled to believe him on all occasions that I could. He was, after all, the father of my two children and, by his own lights, a tireless labourer in the literary field. It was sad to see him, a man barely thirty, emerge from his study, red-eyed, blotchy faced, spreading and pasty-faced with copious grey already in his hair (the corsets and the hair dye were to come later). In order to avert what looked like an inevitable collapse, God forgive me, I even secretly contacted his mother, who had heaped upon him the heavy burdens that seemed to be killing him.

I myself had never been in robust health since the vile attack preceding Emily's painful birth and dear Robert's birth proved not much easier. As I have indicated, I was not created to be a breeding machine like the Withered Carrot (who died early for her pains). I had struggled to recuperate and was too weak ever to suckle my son, a great sadness. He was an adorable, dark curly-haired child and I counted myself lucky to have produced two such angels.

Dear me, Shakespeare's book of fate has somehow found its way back into my head but I push the Immortal Bard out again with a determined effort. The truth was that, although I lacked the obvious stigmata so apparent in the Great Author's countenance, I was in a poor state myself. Do I need to name the causes? I had had a difficult recovery from the birth of my second child. My mother's ill-health was causing me anxiety, principally, it must be owned, anxiety that she might attempt to come and recuperate with us. Then there was the constant dread of Eddard's sudden and ferocious rages, now aggravated by his physical and mental debility. And, perhaps worst of all, the strain of a thousand noisy dinner parties I did not wish for, attended, for the most part, by people I did not want to see.

I can still recollect the morning when Eddard appeared at my breakfast table with a lightness in his step and something approaching a smile on his face. He took my hand, called me his Angel Poodle for the first time for many a year, and asked me whether I thought I would like to go on a Continental tour with him. I believed, against all experience, that I saw affection and hope in his eyes and a genuine concern to make things better between us. My own frail nerves longed for new experiences, for new cities, new museums, new galleries, and also for a respite from all the cares of family (the two mothers rather than the two children) and the endless round of London social life. I could see no reason to refuse and we spent some of the happiest evenings of our married life discussing our itinerary. We both agreed that it would be ideal to ask Mary Greene to come over to take care of the children. For a miraculous time, it seemed as if our desires and our hopes, at least for the next few months, were at one.

Alas for my trusting soul. We had barely been aboard the vessel an hour out of Dover, when I came up on deck to see Mrs. Robert Stanhope sitting there, all wrapped up, with my Lord and Master at her feet and her contemptible wretch of a husband, that Westminster Pandarus, looking on.

Chapter Four: 1833–1836

Letter from Rosina Bulwer Lytton to Mary Greene, 1833

Remember, too, that the only way to work upon Emily is through her pride. In order to have any chance of rooting out faults in so young a child, the best way is first to try and turn those very faults to account; and then time and common sense may do more towards banishing them than all the precepts in the world. All I ask is that if she is going out in a hurry, and *orders* a servant to tie her shoes, put on her bonnet, or anything else, you will not allow it to be done till she asks in an humble and proper manner; and that when she makes an unfeeling speech about anyone, or anything, you will not let her see you laugh at it because it may be worded in a clever or worldly manner. Poor, dear child, it is *much, much* kinder to check these things in her now, than to let the world break her spirit for her hereafter, as it most assuredly will.

From the Unpublished Travel Diary of Lady Lytton

Paris. – September 1833.

Mrs. Robert Stanhope (I refuse to acknowledge she has a name of her own) grows no more tolerable upon closer acquaintance. Yesterday we visited the Cathedral of Notre Dame. We made our way through busy, dirty, narrow streets and there it was, rising above them, a Gothic pile like no other (Mrs. Lytton excepted). During the Revolution, our guide explained, many of the treasures of the cathedral were either destroyed or plundered, the 13th century spire torn down and a set of biblical kings beheaded unceremoniously by the mob who believed them to be former Kings of France and presumably thought, as they'd beheaded one King, they may as well behead them all. Even Pups was silenced as we gazed up in admiration at the delicate filigree work of the Rose Window. And then Mrs. R. Stanhope spoke. She pronounced the Cathedral 'charming'. I could not believe my ears but from the little smile on her plump face, she thought she'd said something rather splendid. This is truly a woman with a tiny mind.

Not long after, we lunched in an over-heated restaurant in a rather more salubrious part of the City. Our guide assured us the food was the finest Paris can offer. In which case, the food in Paris leaves much to be desired and I have served better in Hertford Street. Towards the end of the meal, Mrs R.S. began to yawn ostentatiously. She pronounced herself tired and wished to return to the Hotel. Pups nobly stepped in to offer to accompany her back before Mr. S. could put himself forward, not that I believe he had any intention of doing so. With simpering excuses, the Cow-Like rose and, taking Pups's arm, left the restaurant. If they for a moment entertain the notion that I cannot imagine what will occur when they reach that hotel, then they must think me blind and even stupider than Mrs. R.S. herself. I was forced to remain in the company of Mr. Stanhope, that buck-toothed runt of a man. We made small talk of such banality it could be entitled infinitesimal talk. I do hope Pups is not hoping that I will fall for Mr. S. and solve his problems. To be fair to Mr. S., he displays as little interest in me as I in him. Is Pups paying this man for his wife's services? That was the rumour and I wonder now if it's true. Mr. Stanhope has, he informed me (several times and at great length) substantial investments, both domestic and foreign. And yet Pups always seems to be picking up the bills.

We lingered long enough over our luncheon to ensure that when we reached the hotel, Pups was in our suite, affecting surprise that I had been delayed so long. Much ill-judged teasing on the subject. A humourless man like Pups should not attempt to tease, particularly when he is in the wrong. As I intimated to him in no uncertain terms.

I do wonder if Pups has finally taken leave of his senses. A child of five (dear Emily's age) would have no difficulty in understanding our *ménage à quatre* and there are acquaintances here in Paris who will doubtless relay their impressions back to London.

Pups certainly looks no fitter or less haggard than he did when we commenced our trip. As you sow so shall you reap, say I.

Venice. – October 1833.

Neither of us is in love with Italy, and therefore I devoutly hope we may be back in dear England by the end of December. If Mrs.

R.S. pronounces one more magnificent building 'charming', I shall probably push her into one of Venice's odiferous canals. Even her husband is talking of the need to return to England, which shows the guiding atmosphere of our party.

The travelling here may be divided into three classes – plague, pestilence and famine. Plague – the mosquitoes. Pestilence – the smells, and Famine – the dinners. Indeed, I should like Venice very much more, but for the unprincipled mosquitoes. My face is in such a state that I look as if I have had the small-pox. My only consolation is that the fair-skinned Mrs. R.S. suffers even more than I do, and her face resembles a badly executed sewing sampler.

The *gondolieri* here speak with the greatest affection of poor Lord Byron and tell you with such pride that he made a tragedy out of the Doge Marino Falieri. Difficult to imagine a hackney cab driver in London displaying such enthusiasm for a literary figure. Pups was duly impressed and no doubt hopes to find his name on the lips of the *gondolieri* in years to come.

The Doge's Palace exceeds anything one could dream of in the splendour of its architecture and its paintings. From the Palace you pass over the Bridge of Sighs to the dungeons of the Inquisition. These were not half as horrible as I had expected except one, where the criminals used to be beheaded, to which there is a stone door, in which are round holes for the blood to drain out of. This door opens under a black shiny arch, with innumerable slimy reptiles up and down. To this black arch is moored a black boat which, with the black hollow sounding water splashing against it, was, by the torchlight with which we saw it, more horrid than I could have imagined. This boat was to take the dead bodies out to sea.

In my mind's eye, Mr. and Mrs. Robert Stanhope's headless bodies were on the top of the pile.

I do wonder if Pups may not be beginning to tire of them too. He has been affectionate, even amorous, since we arrived here. But I want nothing to do with him.

Florence. – October 1833.

The entrance to Florence is certainly beautiful, being completely crowned with vineyards, plantations of silver olives and orange, lemon and pomegranate trees, and nobody could be disappointed with the Grand Duke's Gallery. Apart from that, Cheltenham or any other little watering place in England is twenty times a prettier town.

Our window looks upon the Arno. How fine that sounds, and yet it is a dirty, little, narrow, ugly, muddy river, covered with little ugly Feluccas in which are coarse, ugly men in little more than a state of semi-nudity, shovelling up the mud all day long. In short, the Westminster Bridge part of the Thames is a hundred times handsomer. Even Mrs R.S. omits to say how charming it is.

One thing I do like in the travelling here is a little sort of Pomeranian dog, which belongs to the postillion and often rides a whole post on the off horse and keeps its seat perfectly. The jockeymanship of this little dog impressed me deeply, as I told the postillion in whatever mixture of languages we could manage.

But, of course, out of loyalty to my own darlings, I never kiss or pat any of the dogs, only order them to be fed.

Mrs. R.S. is visibly fading in the heat and talks again of returning home. I say nothing to dissuade her.

Rome. – November 1833.

I am knocked up with sight-seeing, and so thoroughly disappointed and disgusted with the whole place that I want only to take to my bed. This is without exception the most dirty, barbarous and dismal place I ever saw, and its magnificent buildings, and still more magnificent ruins, look as incongruously out of place as if you were to see rubies and diamonds the size of a pigeon's egg upon a very coarse, very dirty, and very ragged kitchen floor. The Vatican, St. Peter's, the Colosseum, the Capitol and the Church of San Giovanni Maggiore are splendid beyond conception, and so are the innumerable fountains about Rome; but all the water in them would not suffice to purify the disgusting filth of its streets. The streets are given over to the cult of Cloacina.

I try to maintain due reverence with difficulty, particularly as I feel the four of us are hardly in a state of grace. At San Giovanni Maggiore we were shown the staircase (*soi-disant*) that our Saviour descended to be crucified, which they pretend the Emperor Constantine brought from Pontius Pilate's house at Jerusalem. We were also shown half of the table off which our Saviour ate the Last Supper, and as many pieces of the true Cross as would suffice to build a man-of-war.

I cannot wait to leave this place. My only consolation is that the rest of the party seem even more dispirited than I am. Pups complains about the food, but is eating like a horse. Or indeed, given the culinary habits here, may even be eating a horse.

Mr. Robert Stanhope on the other hand has acute stomach pains. Hopefully, he will either die or elect to return to England.

Naples. – November 1833.

Well, we are in Naples; it is beautiful and the only place in Italy that we have not both been disappointed in. Our hotel is beyond comfortable – it is luxurious. The man who keeps it has been all over the world and spared no expense in fitting it up. The furniture is quite magnificent, with loads of Persian carpets, ottomans, sofas, tabourets, easy chairs – in short, he has put the cooks and furniture of France, the comforts and cleanliness of England, and the fine arts of Italy, into his house, which, after the dirt, misery and starvation of all the other Italian inns, is not a little delightful.

Mrs. R.S. has been tearful at breakfast. I think Pups has had enough of her.

Mr. R.S. talks of their return. He's done that many times before but I do think this time he means it. His runtish little face is showing the strain and his buck teeth are gnawing at his lower lip.

Finally, I feel I have arrived at a place I believe I will enjoy. We have not yet been to Vesuvius or Pompeii, for I want to rest after the endless sights of Rome, where every evening I was so knocked up that I felt more and more the truth of the observation of Mrs. Ready, the friend of the Irish Minstrel Tom Moore, who exclaimed that she 'had seen too much'.

Naples. – November 1833.

They have gone. Whisper it not in Babylon but they have gone. I was gracious but felt no need to express any deep regret. I felt almost sorry for clumsy Pups as he made his farewells and kissed Mrs. R.S. delicately upon the cheek as if it was the only part of her body he had ever directly encountered. Mr. R.S. meanwhile was giving indications that he had had enough. A return to London followed by the dissolution of the marriage and her social exclusion is a result profoundly to be wished for.

Naples. – November 1833.

We have had an adventure at the library here. The old woman there is exceedingly crabbed, and Pups wanted her to lend him one book more than his subscription entitled him to. She refused. 'Much indeed I should think such a chap as you should know about libraries.' Pups laughed at this, which put her into an additional fury, and snatching the book out of his hand, in which he had written his name for the subscription, she put on her spectacles to read it. She had no sooner done so than she exclaimed, 'Now I shall be happy' and throwing her arms round his neck (a proceeding he would willingly have dispensed with), said: 'Take all the books in my shop, Miraculoso Giovanestro,' and still holding him tight by the coat called in her daughters, three pretty black-eyed girls, and vociferated to each, 'Ninetta, questo Pelham; Beatrice, questo Eugene Aram; Elizabetta, questo Devereux.' And then wiping the pen he had written his name with, she told the daughters to lock it up carefully. We made our escape as soon as we could. Pups affected much embarrassment but, to tell the truth, I think he was secretly delighted to know his fame as a writer was reaching down towards the toe of Italy. Later that day, we paid a call upon Sir William Gell, the distinguished archaeologist. He is old now and crippled by gout, but still hard at work upon his *Pompeiana; the Topography, Edifices and Ornaments of Pompeii*, or so Pups informed me in impressive tones. Sir William is famous for taking Sir Walter Scott round Pompeii and publishing an account of it, so Pups hopes he will do the same favour for him. I do fear Pups is starting to collect material for another novel, he is so terribly bad at doing nothing, particularly without Mrs. R.S. as diversion. His temper is already visibly fraying again.

To be honest, I was dreading meeting some dry as dust old scholar, but luckily Sir William has a seraglio of dogs, which I was happy to pet while Pups established his credentials as a serious author. Sir William has taught one of his dogs to speak, but no sooner was he taught to speak than he taught himself to swear – not the first clever dog who has perverted his talents. Still, a man who loves dogs as much as I do has a great deal in his favour.

Sir William ended by agreeing to show us round the ruins, though the poor old soul will have to do it in a wheelchair.

Naples. – November 1833.

We have just returned from our visit to Pompeii and Vesuvius and I am exceedingly glad we did it in the winter months, for in summer I think I would have expired in the heat. Sir William was most instructive, perhaps too instructive, but no one could fail to be impressed by the poor dog, twisted in agony as the lava engulfed him. Pups had that air I know all too well of the important author in search of a subject, so I got little from him as we walked through the site.

Fortunately, Sir William had got up a party, so we were not alone. I am sure he gets many requests to be a cicerone, so you can hardly blame him for saving his energy by combining us. There was a group of Italian nobility, or what passes for nobility here, with the ladies saying, 'Bello' at everything they were shown, with a vapidity which unfortunately recalled for me Mrs. R.S. And a couple of English gentlemen, so wary of damaging their boots in clambering over dust, that I suspect they were sodomites here to enjoy the lax ways of Southern Italy. But there was also a rather distinguished-looking dark-haired gentleman, travelling alone, somewhere around our own age, who approached me while Pups was pumping Sir William with questions about the drainage.

He introduced himself as Prince Alexander Lieven. He is from a German Baltic aristocratic family, clearly of some significance as they have served as advisers and diplomats to the Tsars of Russia. The most modest of men, this information had to be elicited by polite enquiry. He has exquisite manners and his thoughts upon the transience of humanity inspired by what we had witnessed had a simplicity and power I'm afraid Pups can rarely aspire to.

Naples. – November 1833.

Pups is obsessed with the ruins of Pompeii. Poor Sir William is probably regretting ever taking us there. He is being bombarded with questions about street lighting, furniture, gladiatorial fights and the surviving frescoes (some of which must be salacious as I was not allowed to view them). Poor Pups! He is making himself ill again with worry.

I am fortunate in having found a congenial friend in Prince Lieven. He has hired a very elegant carriage and we have been on trips all over the Neapolitan coast. The November sun and sky beat our June one, with flowers and fruits growing in the open air that would shame the produce of our July hot-houses. Today we did the exquisitely beautiful drive to Terracina and back. The most bold and beautiful sea possible, girt with rocks crowned with arbutus and heath and broom in full bloom, a smooth, silver-sanded beach with dwarf trees of myrtle and rose geraniums in full bloom. And then there's Mola Gaeta with its myriads of terraces, one above the other, of orange, lemon, magnolia and pomegranate trees with their golden fruit, silver blossoms and emerald leaves. In short, all their fairy-tale paraphernalia on at once, making the air one long breath of flowers.

I was heady with pleasure when we returned.

Naples. – December 1833.

Edward has just left the room. I cannot bring myself to write Pups in the present circumstances.

I had returned barely an hour from a trip round the Bay when he burst into the room and began upbraiding me for my infidelity. My infidelity? As if his own had not been displayed across Europe in the most blatant fashion to the citizens of Paris, Venice, Florence and Rome. As if I had not had to swallow my pride and appear to smile in public to acquaintances from London we have encountered in our travels, who are undoubtedly capable of making two and two make four and informing the fashionable world of their conclusions.

I protested that I have not even been unfaithful, unlike his self-righteous self. I confessed that I could not help contrasting the tender attentive attitude of the Prince with that of a cross, ungrateful husband, who gave more time to the drainage systems of Pompeii than he did to me.

This at least is what I tried to say but My Lord and Master was in such a violent rage that he did not take in a single word that I said. Was I in love with the Prince? he kept demanding over and over again. Since he would not listen, how could I explain how attractive it was to be treated with respect as a woman of beauty and intelligence? It's many years since my Lord and Master played that game. Once he'd won me, he all but abandoned it. Whatever words he did hear of what I had to say, simply increased his rage. There was no understanding, no allowance. He could bring his mistress on holiday but I could not spend time alone (with servants in attendance) with a handsome and charming man without driving him into apoplexies of fury.

My Italian maid was in earshot. On one count, this was embarrassing, because one wishes one's servants to have a sense that their masters and mistresses maintain their calm and dignity on all occasions. On another count, it was a blessing. However much he raged, Pups turned Wolf was not going to physically attack me as he had done in the past. Not tonight anyway.

Trembling with rage, he finally left the room, slamming the door behind him.

I am shaking too.

Am I in love with the Prince? Now the shouting has stopped, I still don't know the honest answer. Maybe it is a flirtation, maybe it could in time have gone further. Of course, there was no understanding in my husband's diatribes that he might have contributed to my attraction to the Prince by his own shortcomings.

All I am certain of now is that Edward, with his violent rages, lack of sympathy with my situation and his endless hypocrisy, has killed all affection I have ever felt for him.

Naples. – January 1834.

Alone, I went for a drive along the old and cherished paths. When I spoke to the Prince, he was regretful and understanding, but he has an important diplomatic role to play and cannot be party to the scandal which Edward would undoubtedly create if his wishes are not respected. He has kissed my hand and said goodbye.

Edward (never ever Pups again) has insisted that we return post-haste to England. He demanded that I reaffirm my love for him. This was his condition for forgiveness. How could I possibly oblige him by telling an untruth?

The result is that he has vowed that he will never live with me again. To me, the return to England feels like going back to prison.

I cannot stop thinking about that poor little dog, twisting and turning in agony as the molten lava of Vesuvius enfolds him in its clutches for eternity.

From the Preface to The Last Days of Pompeii, 1834

On visiting those disinterred remains of an ancient City, which, more perhaps than either the delicious breeze or the cloudless sun, the violet valleys and orange groves of the South, attract the traveller to the neighbourhood of Naples; on viewing, still fresh and vivid, the houses, the streets, the temples, the theatre of a place existing in the haughtiest age of the Roman empire – it was not unnatural, perhaps, that a writer who had before laboured, however unworthily, in the art to revive and to create, should feel a keen desire to people once more those deserted streets, to repair those graceful ruins, to reanimate the bones which were yet spared to his survey; to traverse the gulf of eighteen centuries, and to wake to a second existence – the City of the Dead!

From an Unpublished Autobiography by Lord Lytton

There are many things in my life I deeply regret. I would never claim to be a perfect human being. I suffer and I have made others suffer. My faults are as numerous as my virtues. All this I freely acknowledge. I have really no defence for choosing to invite the Stanhopes with us on our Continental trip, but at least I can attempt to explain.

I have always suffered from strong sexual needs. This is more a curse than a blessing in my view. I envy men who can live ascetic bachelor lives or those whose desires can find satisfaction with one woman. I genuinely believed I had found that singular satisfaction with Rosina, but, alas, it was not to be. After the birth of our first child, her acceptance of my advances was severely circumscribed, and, after the birth of our son, she denied me altogether. What was I to do? I had had my taste of the world of prostitution as a young man and I had no wish to re-enter that sordid world where money is the only real point of contact between two sexual partners. Besides, I have no interest in the more perverse and degraded services women of the street can offer. I do not wish to be whipped or humiliated nor do I wish to whip and humiliate members of the female sex. I like women, I enjoy the company of older, intelligent women, as I have mentioned before; they are among the most valued companions of my life. It is a matter of record that I have spoken on numerous occasions in the

House in favour of bettering the inequitable lot of married women. But the sexual drive, alas, was always there, as it was particularly at that troubled period in my life, and, though I do not expect to be exonerated from blame, I do wish it to be noted that I have always sought out willing partners, never forced myself upon any woman, and I have always considered their pleasure as well as my own, which, as I know from the boisterous chat of some of my male friends in the club or in the House, is not how all men regard women. I detest their talk of whores and cock-teasers as much as I deplore the sanctification of women as angels of the house, with never a sexual bone in their body.

Ah, how unfortunate it is that Rosina withdrew her favours from me! It precipitated a tragedy for us and for our children, which might otherwise have been avoided. If there had been continuing physical union, it might have mitigated the emotional tensions between us. I will admit inviting Mrs. Stanhope and her husband to join us was never going to please her and I must admit the charge of insensitivity. However, the alternative would have been a frustration within me that would have led either to sordid dalliance or to an explosion of savagery out of frustration. Please let it be noted in this context that, again unlike many of my eminent contemporaries (I will not mention their names for they would never forgive me), I have never fathered illegitimate children. I have fathered but two children in my life, my dead daughter and my still living son.

If only Rosina could have understood or even softened enough to let me share her bed in the welcoming warmth of those glorious mornings in Naples! Instead, she chose to throw herself at Prince L., a man of considerable standing and diplomatic status but perhaps lacking the more essential quality of how to behave as a gentleman. He was constantly outside our hotel with a carriage and horses, offering to take my wife on various excursions. I had become preoccupied with the immensity of the history of Pompeii and my discussions with the totally admirable historian of the sites, Sir William Gell. My imagination was at bursting point, filled with the vistas which were opening before me of an ancient city, filled with life and intrigue and love, suddenly engulfed by the remorseless flow of volcanic lava. I mention this to explain why I took so long to understand. I have little or no doubt now that Prince L. had a sexual liaison with my wife, something simple enough to arrange in the lax morals of Southern Italy, where for all its beauty, vice lurks not far below the surface.

She denied it, of course. What else could she do? Her wonderful Irish grey-green eyes breathed a sincerity and an indignation that somebody, who had never looked into them before, would be tempted to believe. So here we come to an essential difference. I am an imperfect being and I acknowledge it. I brought my mistress on our trip because my wife denied me access to her bed and her complaisant husband suffered, I believe, from some aberrant form of sexual inadequacy, poor fellow. But I do not deny these things. I even suggested discreetly to Mrs. Stanhope that it might help my cause with my wife if she and her husband left us – in the hope that Rosina might finally see the way to reconcile the two of us – between the sheets.

Rosina, on the other hand, was adamant that nothing had ever taken place between them, even though the driver of the Prince's carriage had told my attentive and trustworthy courier otherwise. I did not wish to view the soiled sheets but I knew they were there, in some sordid dwelling just outside the periphery of Naples.

She denied outright, but then, when she understood my questioning came from knowledge, she became defiant. She declared that she was in love with Prince L. and she wished to spend the rest of her life with him. To fall for a hardened seducer is understandable, to believe that an unprincipled rake, who has whored his way through Europe, actually cared for her was a sign of the onset of the deep delusions which finally engulfed her with a power beyond the lava of Vesuvius. I tried to persuade her of the true nature of Prince L. I endeavoured to explain to her the dire consequences for her children of her behaviour. Her ears were deaf. There was not a moment of self-criticism, an inkling of self-blame. I was, apparently, questioning her very being. She claimed to be madly in love with him but never to have entered his bed (obviously not his personal bed but a sordid mattress somewhere in a complaisant peasant dwelling in the Neapolitan hinterlands). My own view was exactly the opposite. He had entered her repeatedly but love was simply a pleasant cover for a set of ugly acts.

I had no choice. With Rosina in the state of defiance she was, we would have to return to England, before a full-blown scandal destroyed her reputation. I am fairly certain that the love of her life, Prince L, never communicated with her after she returned to England. He had too many other mistresses to bother about her. Our return was full of bitter squabbles and recriminations but Rosina, never once, expressed any regret for the course she had pursued or the damage it could do to both her reputation and mine. She took the children to stay with Miss Greene in Gloucester, while I myself settled into bachelor chambers in Albany, Piccadilly. The separation was not yet complete but I doubted even then that we could ever fully live together again as man and wife.

Yet the imagination works in strange, often mysterious ways. On one hand, our Italian trip had ended in disaster; on the other, my creativity had been sparked in a way I could never have anticipated. The ruins of Pompeii filled my mind with vivid images of life as it must once have been there, before disaster struck. I was immeasurably fortunate in making the acquaintance of Sir William Gell, whose *Pompeiana,* then still in draft form, was the inspiration for my book, and a constant source of reference whilst I was bringing my characters and their daily life on to the page. Sir William was, alas, already in failing health, but he spent some of the very last drops of his fading life in showing me the site and patiently instructing me in the finer points of his discoveries. The novel is dedicated to him and I hope his spirit will believe that I have not betrayed his trust nor itch to correct my copious footnotes which provide the support for my imaginations.

The Last Days of Pompeii is, of course, the one title which will always kindle reminiscence of my work. It is not my best novel, several other titles come to mind, but it is the title forever associated with my name. I have learned to accept that. Much of the work was written in Naples, but, on my return to England, I was, indeed, too much occupied with political matters to have a great deal of superfluous leisure to complete it. (I had become, by the way, since the Reform Act which took away my previous seat, the Member of Parliament for Lincoln, a picturesque part of the world, where, if I am honest, I did not spend nearly enough time.) I had to wait for those not unwelcome intervals when Parliament goes to sleep, and allows the other objects of life to awake: dismissing the weary legislators, some to hunt, some to shoot, some to fatten oxen, and others – to cultivate literature.

How strange it is that a book written in the midst of the turmoil of my marriage and at a time of great mental depression should, when finally completed, have a marked liveliness, and even lightness, in much of its tone, as so many of my friends and contemporaries commented. Indeed, Glaucus, my hero, is a very different figure from my previous haunted guilt-ridden protagonists, a dignified young man of Greek heritage, both principled and stoic, resistant to the more sordid temptations of the city and true throughout to his love, Iole. At the end, I allow the lovers to escape from the doomed city, led by the blind slave girl, Nydia, who is used to navigating her way around Pompeii in darkness. The two lovers find peace in Athens, where they become Christian converts and find true happiness. Blind Nydia, alas, who secretly loves Glaucus, must unselfishly sacrifice herself by drowning in the sea to leave them to their idyll, but this is a novel which supposes it is possible to walk away from a huge natural disaster and survive. There is no Eugene Aram lingering here, wishing his own self-destruction.

My readers, of course, responded to the evocation of Pompeii as a thriving city and a dying ember. The story has been told since but I was the first to tell it. Dear Isaac Disraeli, my good friend Benjamin's father, wrote to me that it was the finest and most interesting fiction that we have had for many years. No mean historian himself, he told me I have achieved more than all the erudite delvers had done: I had made the place alive. The reader can enter the city whenever he chooses. He can be a trembling spectator at a tremendous tragedy of nature. In his words, 'I was overcome by the phantasma, and was glad to find myself once more in the solitude of my armchair.' I could, of course, accumulate examples of the praise my book received – and the envious criticisms of my many embittered rivals. Lady Blessington told me, 'There is more true poetry in your *Pompeii* than in fifty epics, and it alone would stamp its author as the genius *par excellence* of our day.' And so on. For a man who felt frail and battered within his heart, I own these tributes were manna to my unhappy soul. How strange to be, on one hand, the most appreciated and admired of men and, on the other, a man who felt circumscribed by a failing marriage and black clouds of self-doubt and depression.

There has been a pattern to my literary career, as I have already noted. The very pigmies who mocked my achievements then went on to steal my ideas to pen their own inferior imitations. The silver coin I had fresh minted would swiftly become grubby copper farthings in the hands of the opportunistic and small-talented. But, surprisingly, the vivid inspiration of Italy and its landscape had not yet exhausted its impact upon me. Hot on the heels of *Pompeii* came a book, which I do consider among my finest, *Rienzi, The Last of the Tribunes*, a tale of fourteenth-century Rome, drawn again from impeccable historical sources. I mention it here because Rienzi is a dreamer, drawn by circumstances into political action, where, for all his good intentions and desire for reform, he finds himself compromised and ultimately destroyed. The fault is partly in the failure of the greedy, apathetic and capricious Roman populace to grasp the opportunities offered by Rienzi's challenge to the established order. But then Rienzi himself is flawed, too caught up in his dreams to understand the forces he seeks to confront. He ends up awash in the very corruption he seeks to reform. Why dwell on this? Because *Rienzi* is my most mature meditation upon the way forward for reform in turbulent political times, a reflection of the turmoil I experienced as a politician in this troubled decade, attempting to guide the ship of state into more equable waters. As I write at one point, 'Better one slow step in enlightenment, – which made by the reason of a whole people, can not recede, – than these sudden flashes in the depth of the general night, which the darkness, by contrast doubly dark, swallows up everlastingly again.' This was to be the hard-earned lesson etched into my soul by the political struggles that lay ahead and it is remarkable I had already anticipated them in the fate of the idealist, Rienzi.

In the case of *Rienzi*, the appropriation of the fruits of my imagination by others took an even more insidious turn. In Germany, a certain Herr Wagner seized upon my hapless hero and turned him into a bawling fat Teutonic tenor at the centre of an interminable Romantic opera. I confess I have never heard this work but this much has been reported to me. I should not worry, I suppose, because this Herr Wagner will doubtless soon sink back into the musical obscurity he so richly deserves.

Alas, I have no choice now but to return to the chronicle of the greatest misfortune of my life. Hertford Street, inevitably, had to be let, and I rented for Rosina and the children Berrymead Priory in Acton. It was a pleasant enough retreat on the high road to London, from which it was separated by open fields until Notting Hill and Bayswater.

I struggled to spend as much time in Acton as I could for the sake of our children, although the black clouds stemming from overwork were already beginning to descend once more. However, I became even more painfully aware of the gulf between us. In me, the family instinct has always been strong. I had been brought up in close personal intimacy to my mother, to whom, for all our differences in the past, I continued to be devoted. I take pride in my lineage and have always endeavoured to add to it in my own person. Rosina, on the other hand, was insensible to any family ties. She was the child of separated parents, for whom she entertained neither love nor respect. She hardly ever saw her father and, when she did, they quarrelled. He was dead long before I met her. Her mother, meanwhile, remained alive, though in poor health, but had never shown her true affection or, for all her fine principles, ever given a thought to her proper education. Her brother had died when she was still young and there had never been any bond of intimacy or affection with her sister, Henrietta, who, her mother had made clear, was her favourite. I remember that she once remarked of one of her uncles that the news is 'he is dirtier than ever. That can scarcely be possible, as he always looked like a chimney-sweep in a vapour bath.' It was said with her usual quick wit but it gave me an insight into why she was so ill equipped for family life. The truth is that she was not even drawn to her own children by any strong maternal instinct. Of course, she desired them to be happy and well-behaved, but she never showed them the same affection which she bestowed upon her dogs. They were beautiful, proud children, and they did not want to cling to their mother or beg for loving attention, but each time I visited, I saw the distress in their eyes. Miss Greene had already begun to be a greater object of stability and affection for them.

Despite all this, I went back whenever I could (whenever I could endure it, to be honest) but the experience each time was more gruelling than the last.

Whenever I arrived, and whatever the circumstances, we had not sat down to dinner five minutes before Rosina would start saying the most insulting things to me. I prefer not to specify their nature, but accusations of debauched parties and sodomitical practices were the least of this. On one occasion, I returned to find one of my best loved shirts, trimmed with lace and adorned with the most exquisite needlework, had been incinerated by my wife on a whim. These provocations came every time I visited and on one occasion, overworked and preoccupied as I was, I behaved in a way which I deeply regret to this day.

From the Memoirs of Rosina, Lady Lytton

Berrymead Priory, the villa which Lord Mount Vesuvius took for me and my children, had not been inhabited for years, and therefore looked like the very abomination of desolation, the grass growing right up to the front door. When we first arrived at this damp, dreary, desolate place, there was not even a bed for me to lie upon. Sir Niggardly will tell the world that I do not know how to run a household, but, with the miserably inadequate funds he allowed me, I somehow managed to make it habitable for the sake of Robert and Emily.

When the author of *The Last Days of Pompeii* came to visit, he was a volcano waiting to explode and we dreaded the moment when the lava of his rage and impatience would engulf us. The book is actually one of his more amusing efforts because, if one tires of his mawkish story of suicidal self-sacrificing blind girls and evil Egyptian priests conveniently flattened by falling pillars, one can at least engross oneself in the footnotes, which are full of fascinating information, courtesy of dear Sir William Gell, fortunately dead before he realised how ruthlessly Eddard had exploited his generosity. The Great Author, though, remained very much an active volcano and the children cringed in terror when they saw his rages building up. When he saw me teaching Robert, now five, his letters one evening on arrival, he bit his lip sharply and asked why that damned child wasn't in bed yet? Poor frightened innocents, they felt they were responsible in some way for their papa's angry purpled face, and stentorian breathing. How could I tell them the explanations lay principally in the baleful influence of his (now fortunately fading) succubus of a mother?

Even so, I was not prepared for the molten eruption which occurred one day when, comparatively, Vesuvius had been at his most amiable. He had even deigned to spend several days in a row with us and we were seated at dinner before his return to London, the ever-present Miss Greene having decided for once to dine with neighbours. The servants had been instructed to leave the room and not return till he rang, whether in anticipation of what happened or not, I have no notion.

He then enquired, mildly enough, whether I was going to the christening of Mr. Fonblaque's child that evening, the Fonblanques being a family close by and Mr. Fonblanque being an author of considerable talent but little success. I replied that I was going with Lady Stepney. His response was extraordinary. He exclaimed angrily that, 'My mother calls her that ugly old woman!' He then repeated the same statement a dozen times in succession as fast as he could. Without warning, he had become a mad man.

I realised the volcano was on the point of eruption and decided it was best to flee while I could. But as I rose from the table, he called out, 'Do you hear me, Madam?'

I turned towards him as calmly as I could and replied, 'Of course I hear you!'

He then demanded in language I do not wish to transcribe why I didn't answer him. I replied that I did not consider his observation required an answer. At this juncture, he seized a carving-knife and rushed towards me. His eyes were filled with fury as he neared me and hissed, 'I'll have you to know that whenever I do you the honour of addressing you, it requires an answer.'

I was genuinely alarmed for my life now but managed to get out the words, 'For God's sake, Edward, take care what you are about!'

My urgent plea seemed to bring him to something like his senses. He stared fixedly at the knife, trying to make sense of why it was in his hand. Finally, he let it drop to the floor.

I breathed a sigh of relief, but my relief was premature. Suddenly, he sprang towards me and grabbed hold of me fiercely. He brought his purpled face close to mine. Again there was frenzy in his eyes. I struggled in his grasp, but, before I could get free, he pulled my face still closer to his.

Nothing had prepared me for what happened next. He opened his mouth and then, with one ferocious bite, made his great teeth meet in my left cheek.

The blood spurted out of me. The agony was so great that my screams brought the servants back. My husband, rooted to the spot, stared in surprise at the blood, as if he was not the cause of its flowing. Presently Cresson, our excellent cook, to prevent further outrages against my person, seized him by the collar. Edward broke from his grasp, and seizing one of the footman's hats, rushed out of the house into the carriage, which was fortunately waiting to take him back to London. I was left wounded and shocked and I will be eternally grateful to the servants who comforted me, treated my wound and saw me to my bed, where I sobbed my heart out.

When, the next day, Edward wrote a grovelling letter of apology, saying that he was a vile wretch, who was fit only to live on his own, and he seriously contemplated abandoning his work and his country, I could only reply that these seemed excellent ideas.

From the Unpublished Reminiscences of Mary Greene

I shall never forget the first scene of violence I witnessed between them. I saw her turn upon him with fury and throw back whatever he said. And at the end, after a fearful scene of mutual recrimination, he rushed out of the room saying, 'We never then meet again except upon our mutual death-beds.'

From an Unpublished Autobiography by Lord Lytton

There is no excuse for what I did. I accept that I am guilty. Except that in Rosina's version, as I have heard it from Miss Greene and others, our argument was over something trivial. It was not. In the most persistently sneering and sarcastic tones, Rosina had taunted me for engaging in forbidden acts with both Benjamin Disraeli and Count d'Orsay. Others too, probably, though I cannot recall all the details of that distressing moment.

She indicated that I should not be let within half a mile of my children because my sexual tastes were so vile. Out of nowhere, her mocking voice struck at all I held dear. She used the children I loved, and she cared for less than her foul-smelling old terrier, as an instrument against me.

When I started to get angry, she proclaimed as a matter of fact that half of London knew that I had used violence against my mother, who had had often to declare herself indisposed until the bruises receded.

Of course, the charge was vile and untrue and the provocation extreme. But there is still no excuse and I can still only offer a poor explanation for something of which I am deeply ashamed. My wife will always deny the vileness of what she said that night, probably the last night in our lives we could look into each other's eyes without seeing deep loathing reflected. She will always maintain the trigger was trivial but it was not. Nevertheless, she had been cruelly degraded and I stand eternally degraded in my own eyes. I repeat that there are no excuses to be made for my behaviour.

If matters could have been left with my abject apologies, then, perhaps, and this 'perhaps' was even fainter and less vital than the one I clung to when we went on our Italian tour, we might still have held on to our marriage. That was not Rosina's way. She had won a round in our battle because I had lost all control, but, instead of being understanding for our children's sake, if for no other reason, she chose to give as much publicity as she could to an affront nothing but frenzy could extenuate. She told the servants everything, which was to be expected, but then she took the occasion to vindicate herself to my mother, already in failing health. Fortunately, my mother could not credit her outpourings, but, of course, I was made the theme for all the malignity of London. My friends trusted me, my enemies believed worst than the worst. Was there any gain to anyone in these revelations once I had knelt at her feet and begged forgiveness? Nobody was helped and our children, in the eyes of the world, were harmed.

Do not think that I did not interrogate myself about what had happened. I had frightened myself as well as Rosina. I found myself reverting to my adolescent frame of mind. I possessed a temper so constitutionally violent that it amounted to a terrible infirmity. She should, after our years together, have understood that it was inhumane to tamper with so terrible an infirmity as mine. The years have brought some peace but even material success, both literary and political, cannot completely eradicate my sense of my own worthlessness. If only Rosina had comforted me, instead of provoking me.

I cannot bear to linger long over the next eighteen months of my life. I kept, as always, busy as an editor, M.P. and writer. I even began work upon a first play – *The Duchess de la Vallière* – which had some modest success on the London stage. But these triumphs remained more ashen than the ruins of the House of the Tragic Poet in Pompeii, my model for Glaucus's house. My heart and stomach were in a state of constant tension, tightening still more when it came time for me to make another visit to the Priory. My mother saw my debilitated state whenever I visited her at Knebworth, and she gave me all the love and support her reserved and stoic nature was capable of giving to me. She urged me to show patience with Rosina, for the sake of the children and for the honour of the family name, to which any divorce would be deeply damaging. She even began a friendly correspondence with Rosina, sending her thoughtful gift of game and fruit from Knebworth, and found it in her heart to show some understanding of my wife's plight, knowing as she did of my volatile temperament. I could not suffer to remind her of her role in making our marriage inevitable for me as a matter of honour, nor could I bear to tell her that this was all too little, too late.

There was some consolation in knowing that Mary Greene was also there often to keep an eye on the children and to bring some order into a household which, on occasion, seemed to serve primarily as a hotel for an ever-increasing pack of barking, yapping competitive dogs, who left their excrement wherever they chose.

Who knows how long we might have gone on in this unendurable state? Miss Greene was beginning to show concern for the welfare of the children, a concern which had started to make her reconsider her loyalties. She reported to me that Rosina, who came from a family of heavy drinkers, was keeping company with a Miss Fraser, a neighbour all too obviously addicted to strong alcohol. It was all she could do, Miss Greene reported, to stop Robert and Emily from seeing their mother after she had been imbibing brandy with her neighbour. Apparently, a bottle of spirits or wine would be consumed overnight.

Even at this distance, I do not know whether to be sorry or relieved that Rosina's intemperance precipitated the final breakdown of our marriage.

From *The Duchess de la Vallière, 1837. Act Five*

The Duchess de la Vallière in the habit of the Carmelite nuns, passes down the steps of the altar. She sees one of King Louis' courtiers.

> Duchess: Lauzun! thou serv'st a king, whate'er his faults, Who merits all thy homage: honour – love him. His glory needs no friendship; but in sickness Or sorrow, kings need love.

From the *Memoirs of Rosina, Lady Lytton*

My Acton home being more a prison than a home, I began to reflect somewhat upon the principles my mother had so often and so determinedly enunciated, often to my annoyance or boredom. There might, after all, be something in them. I came to resent the fact that I had to assume the name of Lytton or Bulwer as a blot or blister, because it denoted the smothering of one personality by another. My literary efforts were returned to me without comment, as if no married woman could possibly pen anything worthy of serious consideration. Put brutally, a wife is no better than that humble garden shrub, the cotoneaster, to be treated as ill as possible without the slightest attention, save by throwing a little cold water on it whenever it attempts to put forth anything new. Would I were as hardy as the neglected examples in the Priory garden.

However, as time went on, it became clear that I was not even to be allowed to handle those areas of responsibility which a wife and mother was supposed to handle without interference. Sir Niggard always lectured me upon my extravagance at the least opportunity, even though everyone I knew, even those who were not my friends, acknowledged that I learned to manage affairs pretty well on a very limited budget, a very limited budget having been a constant in my married life. Sir Miser even grudged small luxuries for Robert and Emily, although his dandified appearance always attested to how much money he saw fit to spend upon himself.

But I had not previously experienced so much interference in my handling of the children, partly from Eddard himself but partly from Mary Greene, who, I learned all too late, was in league with him to alienate me from my darlings. For example, Robert came to me praising himself for having saved some of his grapes (a gift from a neighbour) and given them to his nurse. I told him that he had much better not have been guilty of this piece of generosity if he thought so much of it as to boast about it. He had been told off before for being a selfish child, who did not share with anyone, even his gentle-spirited sister, so he stared at me and did not seem to know what I meant. He started to cry, whereupon Miss Greene appeared on the scene.

I explained to her that the secret of forming really estimable, lovable characters was surely not to praise them for doing right, but to make them very much ashamed of doing wrong. We all know persons who are extremely tenacious of their character but not at all particular as to their conduct. I don't know what a narrow-minded Irish virgin is supposed to know about rearing children, but she looked at me as if I was mad, before leading my weeping son away. I had made my point to him so I did not stop her. Perhaps I should have done so because I began to realise everything was being reported back to my Lord and Master.

What upset me even more was an edict handed down from on high, and enforced by Miss Greene, whenever she had the chance. Children, I was told, should not play with dogs. Dogs are flea-ridden and of uncertain temper; they might bite the children suddenly (a pretty amusing injunction coming from a man who sank his teeth in my cheek) or knock them over with their boisterousness. Both Emily and Robert had always adored my dogs, so I saw no reason to obey this order. If a child is scared of a tiny nip from a lively dog then the child will be scared of most things for the rest of its life (and certainly should never acquire a partner like Sir Liar). Well, that is my opinion, and surely it should have been sufficient, but, whenever Miss Greene was around, there was a great deal of fussing, and a great deal of tutting, and little anxious exclamations of, 'Now, do be careful with Feste, Emily, you know what your father has said,' or, 'Robert, don't tease the dog like that. You know, it may lash out at you.' In the end, the children became so self-conscious that their playful times with my canine friends were all but ruined.

There was little doubt in my mind that I was being punished for a flirtation started in justifiable revenge for the humiliation and neglect my husband had heaped upon me. And so I was left isolated, in an uncomfortable house, while My Lord and Master was free to do whatever he wished in his bachelor apartments.

Every now and then, I was grudgingly allowed to go to London to make necessary purchases, primarily for the children, and, when I met up with Miss Benger and others well-disposed to me, they hinted as delicately as they could that Sir Priapic was up to his old tricks. Various names were mentioned more than once, notably a Miss Laura Deacon, the former mistress of a Colonel King, so obviously all too familiar with the duties of a kept woman. I even began to feel a certain limited respect for the bovine Mrs. Stanhope, who had at least dared to meet my eyes when we dined together, and was now cast into the stygian outer darkness unless the Pander of Westminster had found another purchaser for her charms.

I do my best to laugh now at the humiliation and the hypocrisy, but the truth is that I became very ill. As Sir Liar's visits became less and less frequent, and it became clear that my visits to London, however few, were not to be countenanced, my health in my dank surroundings deteriorated so badly that, with crying and coughing and violent agitation, I burst a small blood vessel. Oh my God! I remember mentally addressing the Deity, my God! When will you take me? May it be soon!

The Deity, if he ever heard my prayers (forgive me God if I sometimes doubt it) obviously had other plans. The end of my earthly existence was fortunately, or perhaps unfortunately, still far distant, but God certainly allowed matters to come to a final head on February 23rd 1836. My Lord and Master was expected to dine with me at Berrymead Priory, a rare honour granted me, and I had endeavoured to arrange a meal which would be to his satisfaction. He did not arrive. The disappointed children were sent to bed but I waited supper until nine o'clock in the hope he might still appear.

Finally, a groom arrived in haste with a note saying that he was very ill, and quite unable to leave his chambers. Alarmed, I fully believed this statement and at once started for London, taking with me medicines and other comforts for my ailing spouse. He was, after all, still the father of my children and the provider for their future.

I arrived at his chambers in the Albany around eleven o'clock at night. I rang and rang but received no answer. This puzzled me because, given Sir Liar's *soi-disant* illness, surely his man would be on hand to answer the door. Concluding, after ringing and ringing, that maybe, after all, my husband was out and the servants in bed, I was just about to go away, when Eddard suddenly opened the door *en chemise*, with his dressing-gown hastily thrown over his shoulders, though it has to be said he seemed in robust health.

Upon opening the door, he was so taken aback at seeing me standing there that I actually saw him stagger with rage and indignation. I remained firm as a rock because, after all, I had come there in good faith to succour him. But then, behind him, I saw something which his attempts to block my view failed to cover. Through the drawing-room door, I saw our cosy silver salver with tea for two on it, and Miss Laura Deacon making a precipitate retreat into the bedroom, unfortunately dropping, after a Parthian fashion, in her flight, all her arrows, namely her bonnet, shawl and the rest, on the sofa.

Sir Liar affected not to notice what I had seen. Instead, he demanded, with a considerable use of expletives, what I thought I was doing by turning up at that time of night. I replied with, I think, considerable calm and dignity in the circumstances, that I had come because of his note, with its circumstantial details of his illness, which, I added, now appears, like himself, to be an incarnate lie. I could see windows being opened and heads appearing out of them to hear us. I had nothing to hide so I continued, despite poor Sir Liar's frenzied attempts to hush me. He finally began to look ill enough to justify the lying note he had sent me. As more windows, and even doors, opened, I took the rare opportunity to make the facts about Sir Liar and his mistresses known to the world. Maybe I should have restrained myself for our children, but the endless humiliations had been too much for me.

Sir Liar could neither close the door upon me nor invite me in to discover the undoubted presence of Miss Deacon (from a brief glimpse, a rather more overweight and less attractive woman than I had imagined). When I had said what I had to say, and windows were being discreetly closed so that the neighbours could not be caught in the act of over-intrusive and unhealthy interest in the affairs of others, I turned and rushed back to my carriage.

I describe it cynically now, as I must everything which concerns Sir Liar, but when I returned home, I reached first for a penknife, and then for a dinner knife, in an attempt to end my agony. Fortunately, the servants heard my anguished exclamations and rushed to disarm me. I am grateful for what they did, because I knew there was a battle to fight and I was not going to surrender abjectly. That would have been to say that men are always right and women must always knuckle under. That cannot be how the Universe was designed by God. When press reports appeared next day of what had happened, I remembered Eddard had enemies as well as friends, and that, lonely though I felt to myself, there were those who would support my struggle in the battle which was to come.

From an Unpublished Autobiography by Lord Lytton

It was probably inevitable but would it had happened in another way. Rosina's deliberately loud and incessant babblings outside my Albany Apartment made any corrections of her false impressions impossible. She had come there late at night, clearly inebriated, and rung the bell violently. My sole servant (I do not have a fleet of them as Rosina always implies) was out, and I am not generally in the habit of answering my own front door.

The ringing continued and, eventually, ill and worn out though I was – I went at last to answer the door and there was my wife, the smell of brandy wafting about her. She immediately started a storm of suspicion because she could see *two* tea cups upon my tray. There are any number of explanations for that, but she chose the worst and made a scene before her own footman and the porters of the Lodge as well as any one of my neighbours in earshot, and exposed both herself and me to the ridicule of the town. A young lady, who could provide witnesses who can attest she was elsewhere on this particular night, was engulfed (ah, how Pompeii echoes within me!) in scandal, more accurately, tittle-tattle.

But this was the end. The nettle had to be grasped, even though there was no dock plant or jewelweed plant to hand. Why could there not have been a proper divorce? God knows, I would have longed for that. The honest answer is that my behaviour would not bear scrutiny in a court. I have explained, as candidly as I can, why I have had sexual congress with other women than my wife, but there are two important considerations in making this information public. The first is that I would have to surrender all hope of high office if my adultery became public and that would have dismayed others in my party as well as me. The second is that the names of a number of eminently respectable women (I refuse to name names) would have had their names dragged through the dust, because, given Rosina's late night address to the world in the Albany, she would have had no compunction about naming the names I refuse to name.

And Rosina? She had committed adultery with Prince L. and possibly others, so, if we went to court, she risked losing everything, unless her extravagant denials were believed, which, even she knew, would be to ask the impossible. Honesty, in this particular affair, was undoubtedly the worst policy. Neither of us opened the floodgates. We went for a deed of separation.

From the Memoirs of Rosina, Lady Lytton

My uncle, having recently recovered from a severe paralytic stroke, and being, in addition, a thoroughly honourable man of the old school, there was no one to properly represent my interests. The Deed of Separation was, in all aspects, in favour of Sir Liar, but at least I was finally free. If the money had been regularly forthcoming, I could have maintained myself and my children on what had been provided, even though Sir Liar had thousands more from his trashy books to spend upon his mistresses, discarded as quickly as they had been acquired.

When I signed that Deed of Separation in the presence of witnesses, without, fortunately, my Husband (the last time, I swear to God, I will ever employ that word) being in attendance, fool that I was, I really do think I believed this might be the end of the matter.

From the Deed of Separation:

This Indenture is made the nineteenth day of April, One thousand eight hundred and thirty-six, Between Edward George Earle Lytton Bulwer, of Acton in the County of Middlesex, Esquire, of the first part, Rosina Anne Bulwer his Wife, of the same place, of the second part.

Whereas the said Edward George Earle Lytton Bulwer hath proposed to allow unto or into trust for the said Rosina Anne Bulwer during the said Separation the yearly sum of £400 as a provision for her maintenance and support, and a further yearly sum of £50 for each of the two children of the Marriage so long as he, the said E.G.E.L Bulwer, shall consent that each said child shall remain with the said R.A. Bulwer to clothe and maintain them.

Interlude: June 1858

The Prison Diary of Rosina, Lady Lytton

On my first night, I was informed that the rule of the house at Hill's is that we are allowed about two inches of candle to go to bed with, for fear of some mad incendiary choosing to set the house on fire, and then the door is double-locked on the outside. As I am not either mad or incendiary, and am in the habit of making my ablutions, and reading, and saying my prayers before I go to bed, I protested that I could not do so within the light afforded by just two inches and so effectually resisted the candle rule, but could do nothing against the locked door.

It is perhaps needless to record that I hardly slept a wink, even though my mind and body were hideously fatigued. My anger at Sir Liar's treachery was more powerful, thankfully, than my fears. The tears on my face came from rage, not self-pity. By this outrage, he has undone himself for all eternity. I persist in believing (I have to persist in believing) that he cannot lock me up here forever, however much his sycophants in the press try to cover the matter up.

Miss Ryves, for one, will, I know, do her best after she had made her departure from Dr. Thomson's house in Clarges Street to let the world (but not in this case, his wife) know what has happened.

All the same, to be locked up in an institution which houses any number of lunatics, dangerous and possibly incendiary (in the manner of the first Mrs. Rochester in that vulgar trash by the eldest Miss Brontë) has disturbed me deeply. I fancied a thousand time I hear a mad cry or a despairing scream come from somewhere in the building. A bark, alas, I did not hear, and I miss my dear dogs so much.

If madness is the yardstick for incarceration, then surely Sir Lunatic should be here, not me.

One thought only has caused me amusement this grim night. Somebody will have to pay to keep me here, and, since it cannot be me as I am all but penniless, then it must be Sir Liar, a man who hates to spend money upon any cause except himself. If I could devise a way of running up a high bill here, then I must endeavour to do it, although the opportunities may be small, apart from an increase in candle consumption. Perhaps it was this thought which enabled me to drop finally off into sleep.

The next morning, I was greatly frightened, because the first time one awakens in a strange place, one cannot for a few seconds remember where one is. So I was alarmed at seeing the great six-feet-high keeper standing over me. She said words to the effect that, 'I came to call you, but your Ladyship seemed in such a happy sleep, I did not like to wake you.' A happy sleep! I examined the giantess's rubicund countenance (she drinks and who can blame her in the circumstances?) for any trace of irony in her statement. But irony saw I none. Later, I told Hill (all obsequiousness and sweaty anxiety, I suspect aristocratic wives are not often within his walls) that this must not happen again, but the keeper must wait till I rang. He then said he meant to get me a personal maid the next day. I agreed that this was necessary, if only for the pleasure of adding to the items on Sir Niggardly's bill for madhouse hospitality.

The next night, as I tried to sleep, I heard a dog barking. A young terrier from the sound. I confess that it made me finally cry bitterly at the cruelty of my lot. Mrs. Clarke is an excellent woman but she has not the least idea in the world of how to comfort my puppies.

The maid has arrived and she is even more strapping than the giantess, a proposition that I could not have envisaged until I viewed her. Wider rather than taller and dark rather than fair, but in every other way the equal of my female Hercules. I fancy a breed is specially developed in this neighbourhood to answer the needs of the asylum. After all, who knows when these Amazons might be required to wrestle to the ground a possessed Mrs. Rochester with a candle in her hand and a notion to set the whole place on fire?

Her name is Sparrow, which suggests God (or the Domesday Book or whoever gives us our surnames in the first place) has a wicked sense of humour. She is dull beyond dull and has no more idea of her proper duties as a maid than a bricklayer would. Indeed, a bricklayer is a methodical man and Sparrow has no visible means of arranging her thoughts that I have been able to discover.

Everything is so atrociously bad at this fine house that I really cannot eat. I do believe Hill is beginning to fear I will die upon his hand. He came to me this morning, more sweatily obsequious than ever, and said: 'What can I get you? What do you have for breakfast at Taunton?' To which I replied, looking him directly in the face, 'What I am not likely to have here, Mr. Hill – an appetite.' Collapse of Stout Party, as the execrable Punch has started saying.

Sparrow feels more like a jailer than a maid, not surprisingly, because that is what she is. She is never there when I want her and always there when I don't. What I suffer from most in this intensely hot summer is the drinking water. Sir

Liar would wish the world to know (he has tried this before) that I am addicted to alcohol, brandy in particular, and the spirits have affected my spirits. But I am a water-drinker and the water at Taunton was among the best I ever tasted in any part of the world. Here at Hill's, the water is horribly tepid and bad. When I tried the soda-water, that was equally bad. I dread being asked to join the ladies, who pick strawberries, in this dreadful heat, but I think that is one martyrdom I may be spared. They are simple, lost souls, given a little physical recreation. I am not lost, nor indeed, simple.

I am thoroughly wretched, without my clothes or books or a single thing I am accustomed to. Hill, it's true, is very anxious to send for *all* my goods and chattels to Taunton, which I will most certainly not let him do. As I told him, it is not worthwhile for the very short time, I am sure, public indignation will allow me to remain incarcerated here in his stronghold.

I have just had a visit from the Commissioners in Lunacy. They were Dr. Hood, Dr. Conolly, and Mr. Proctor (Barry Cornwall, the writer). He was by far the best and most gentleman-like of them, as you would expect from the man who is the dedicatee of *Vanity Fair* (a finer novel than any by Sir Talentless or Cockney Gent. Dickens). They listened to my statement about what had happened with marked attention. Then Mr. Proctor said, with a shrug of his shoulders, 'Those letters, I confess, startled me.' The letters he alluded to were two I had written to Sir Edward (as I was obliged to call him) touching some of his infamies, for there is *no* vice that he has left unexhausted, and no virtue unassumed. But, as I told Mr. Proctor, the charges in those letters were no inventions of mine; and I gave him my authority, which was, that when I was at Geneva, my old friend, the Comtesse Marie de Warenzow, came to me one morning, and said that she must read me a paragraph in a letter from her niece, Lady Pembroke, which read, 'That wretch, Sir Edward Bulwer Lytton, has just been drummed out of Nice for his infamous conduct.'

Then, before these Commissioners, I turned to Mr. Hill, who stood, like a footman, at a respectful distance in their presence, and I said, 'Now, Mr. Hill, I have been here nearly a fortnight in your house, can you say from your conscience – if you have one that I have said, done, or looked, any one thing that could in any way make you think I was not in the full and clear, aye and very analytic possession of my intellect?'

The Commissioners' eyes were upon him. Hill wagged his head, twirled his thumbs, and rolled his poached egg orbs fearfully, as he mumbled in a low voice, 'I'd rather not give an opinion.' Then he began sonorously clearing some imaginary obstruction in his throat, and reminded the Commissioners that they would be late for their trains.

From the Somerset County Gazette and West of England Advertiser, July 13th 1858

The circumstances under which Taunton has lost one of its inhabitants are so extraordinary and so shocking, that, as may be supposed, they have greatly excited the minds of people generally. Upon those persons who were on terms of intimacy with Lady Lytton (they were only few, for she evinced little inclination to mix in society, and it was pretty well know that her pecuniary means were too limited to allow her doing so), upon those personal friends the first mention of her incarceration fell like a clap of thunder when the skies gave no sign of an approaching storm. They could not credit such strange information with truth; but when convinced of its veracity, their exclamation has been, 'Good heavens! Lady Lytton in a *madhouse*! For what? Who can have sent here there? She is no more mad than I am, or any one else.'

From the Times, July 14th 1858

LADY BULWER LUTTON.

We are requested to state upon the best authority that all matters in reference to this lady, about whom certain statements have appeared in some of the public journals, are in process of being amicably settled by family arrangements to the satisfaction of all parties concerned.

From the Daily Telegraph, July 15th 1858

Sir Edward Bulwer Lytton has succeeded in hushing up the scandal of his wife's arrest and conveyance to a madhouse at Brentford. The matters in dispute, so say the persons interested, will be arranged to the satisfaction of all concerned. For the sake of the lady herself, the public will rejoice that such a compromise has been extorted from the Secretary of State; if the victim be content, no one has a right to complain, but it must be remembered that Sir Bulwer Lytton alone has gained by the suppression of enquiry.

From the Private Diary of Edward Bulwer Lytton

I dined this evening with Dickens at our club and he played the part of an honest and concerned friend to the hilt. I know he meant it well but it grated. He pointed out that now that the papers had carried reports of Rosina's incarceration, and there could be no doubt that this was at my instigation, my enemies would be prepared to make hay with my reputation and, if possible, destroy my career as a politician, perhaps as any sort of public figure, for the rest of my life.

I reminded him of the provocations I had endured from Rosina over the years and he nodded understandingly, before assuring me that he had no doubt I had been provoked beyond endurance, but, and here the Inimitable Boz gave me his famous look of understanding and complicity, that is not how the public will see it. We two may know that Rosina is unhinged but, unfortunately, she is not so transparently unhinged as to convince others that is the case. She's not like Thackeray's wife, another crazy Irishwoman, who tried to drown herself, and was retired into decent suburban obscurity (with an understanding keeper) without the least protest from anyone, Mrs. Thackeray included. Rosina, alas, Boz continued with a worldly sigh, will never be the Silent Woman and will never be obviously mad enough to the superficial eye to justify her presence in a lunatic asylum.

He then gave me a most amusing account of madwomen he had known, with imitations, but, I confess, I was not in the mood for Boz's ebullience. Eventually, he subsided and I asked him what he thought I should do. 'You have to let her out,' he pronounced, 'and pay her enough money to persuade her to hold her peace and leave the country.'

I protested that these tactics had never worked in the past. She had always been like the pantomime Clown who says, 'Here we are again!' during the transformation scene in order to bring about the Harlequinade, where characters are hit, tripped and generally humiliated in a way I have never found amusing. Boz, it goes without saying, adores pantomime.

He shrugged in his Inimitable way. If you don't deal with her, you will be the laughing stock of London. Believe me, he said with a Boz-like knowing look, I am severely tempted by your suggestion that my darling wife should be shut up for ever in an asylum, like Thackeray's sad wreck of a spouse, particularly an asylum which is civilised and well appointed and does not make one look like a miser in choosing it, but (the Inimitable's eyes up to the ceiling) it will never happen. All the same (the Inimitable's eyes finally meet mine), I am very grateful for your suggestion, as I have been able to mention it to Catherine and it has made her contemplate her situation.

We both of us drank a great deal. It was painful to know that he is almost certainly correct. Now it is known abroad, and my enemies have wind of it, I will probably have to compromise and allow her out of the asylum. My hope is that the severe shock will persuade her to make some sort of understanding, financial and otherwise, with me, which will put an end to the humiliations she has heaped upon me over the years. Having scared her, that, I fancy, is my bargaining card.

It was only later, when I was back at the Albany and struggling fruitlessly to find some mental repose, which would allow me to sleep, that I realised how angry I was with Dickens. His wife is an amiable soul, transparently sane, though indubitably dull. Mine is a deranged Harpy, who pursues me relentlessly to destroy me. He has found a mistress, again an amiable and accommodating soul, despite her career as an actress, who is excellent at hiding herself away and thinks only of how to accommodate (in every sense) the Immortal Boz. Some of his friends have protested, even ceased to be his friends, because they think he is treating Catherine abominably. But nothing is public, nothing is printed, and the reading public still fawn at his feet.

Whereas I, for all my achievements, find my private life made public and my enemies poised to destroy me. I could not sleep, did not sleep. And Rosina haunted my dreams as she has so often in the past. Dickens will succeed because his wife is acquiescent, loyal to her children, and sane.

Rosina is not any of those things. We are in a struggle to the death.

Chapter Five: 1836–1857

1836–1838

From the Unpublished Reminiscences of Mary Greene

The first sight of Rosina Wheeler (as she then was) I shall never forget; her figure, face and air were so superior to anything I had ever seen before, that I was quite charmed with them, as well as with her sweet voice and manners. She was just eighteen and came to pay a call upon my family, who were near neighbours of her father's in Ireland. From the character we had heard of Mrs. Wheeler, and the way in which the young lady had been brought up, we were all far from anxious for her acquaintance. Though I was taken immediately by her appearance, I was also much disappointed to find that she was merely making a pretence of filial duty in saying it was a wish to be introduced to her father, which was the cause of her coming back to Ireland. She confided to me later that her real reason was to follow a young officer who had been an admirer of hers in England, and whose regiment had been ordered to Ireland; and I, who was nearly old enough to be her mother, was perfectly shocked when she told me she corresponded with him, and when I saw the impassioned manner with which she kissed his letter, which she always carried in her bosom.

All her faults, however, I regarded then as the natural consequences of her bad education, and believed she could overcome them – encouraged by the admiration she expressed for everything right which she either heard or saw amongst us. Secure in the bosom of a loving and stable family, of fine religious principles, I had no inkling of how my fate would become tied to hers.

From the Memoirs of Rosina, Lady Lytton

I did not think that I could ever again be shocked at the hypocrisies of the world after so many years spent in the baleful company of the Great Liar himself but even I could scarcely credit what happened once the Deed of Separation was complete. That old wretch, my saintly mother-in-law, who occasionally gave five hundred pounds to Bible and Missionary Societies though she quarrelled with every rector on the Knebworth estate, took it upon herself to invite not one but two of her son's mistresses to stay at Knebworth, an honour rarely granted to the mother of her two legitimate grandchildren (God knows how many bastard grandchildren there may have been and even God has probably lost count). Mrs. Stanhope seemed a model of propriety and decency compared with those who followed. Miss Deacon (also known as Mrs. Beaumont and Mrs. Sellars with ne'er a sign of a Mr. Beaumont or a Mr. Sellars) was the star of that drama which Sir Liar's many enemies entitled 'The Mysteries at the Albany', the sharer of the fatal teacups. As I have said, she was the former mistress of a Colonel King, and, as damaged goods, Sir Shameless acquired her at presumably bargain prices, which must have pleased his niggardly soul.

Just when the World could not imagine an even more shameless hussy to join his Harem, along came the dreaded L.E.L. as she signed herself – or Laetitia Elizabeth Landon, to give her full name. Miss L.E.L. had a certain reputation as a poet in the 1820s and there were those so infatuated with her poetry (or her) that they compared her achievements to those of Lord Byron. Her star faded quickly but her notoriety did not. She lived openly, apart from her family, in Hans Place with two scurrilous drunken journalists, Maginn and Jerdan, so perhaps adding even Sir Liar to her menagerie of lovers was a step up the social ladder. But then, to cover his steps, in 1838 he gave her away in marriage to a Mr. McLean, who was Governor of the Gold Coast, so off they sailed. Four months later, she was dead under what were described as 'tragic and mysterious circumstances' involving a dose of prussic acid. Pray do not ask me to mourn her loss.

In any case, that was some two years in the future. For the moment these two whores frolicked around Knebworth with the approval of my church-going mother-in-law, while I had to cope in rather less picturesque circumstances. I own that, in the wake of the Deed of Separation, I was in too distraught a state to plan properly for my future and that of my two orphaned children. It was Mary Greene who proposed a solution. She made arrangements for myself, my two children, our two servants (imagine how many Eddard retained at this time) and, needless to say, the Irish virgin herself, to occupy part of a large house five miles from Dublin, inhabited by Mrs. Shaw, Mary's widowed sister. Well, one of them had to manage to get married. I should be grateful to Mary Greene for providing me with a temporary home, albeit back in Ireland, but I felt like a condemned woman. The injured party had been punished and the guilty party left free to do as he wished. The dogs enjoyed the country walks but the rest of us were in very poor spirits. It is customary, I believe, for the first quarter of a stipend legally agreed to be paid in advance, but my beggarly stipend of £400 a year was not paid until four months after, so I was in the greatest possible financial distress. Hearing of this, Mrs. Disraeli, an old acquaintance of mine, now shackled to the egregious Dizzy, sent me a measly £20. But my parish allowance finally arriving on the same day, I sent it back to her by return of post with many thanks. I gather that, on the strength of this, the vulgar wretch boasted to everyone of her kindness in having lent me money.

My dear children Teddy (as we all called him) and Emily were a huge consolation to me in these trying times. Their father's meanness denied them the luxuries they had become used to, but they did not repine. Mary Greene spent a great deal of time taking them for long walks through wind, rain and mud, despite their obvious discomfort, as if punishing them for their fallen state. I realise that I should have objected but I was in too low a frame of mind to make my objections public. To be honest, being back in Ireland depressed me deeply. The world I had always hoped to escape from closed once more around me. I confess that I often envied my fellow Irishwoman, Lady Blessington, lording it (or rather ladying it) over her London salon, even if she did have to endure the attendance of Sir Liar.

If only my spirits had been higher and my perceptions more aware! I own that it hurt me when Miss Greene began to show the cloven hoof and taxed me with having made a perfect lodging-house keeper of her widowed sister, because fine people and fine carriages called only upon me, and then added insult to injury by leaving cards or invitations for me but none for Mrs. Shaw or Miss Greene herself. I could hardly reply that I had done my best to persuade my acquaintance to include the two sisters, but every one of them turned their eyes up to Heaven at having to entertain so dull a pair. But that was the least of it. Mary Greene may have hymned the joys of letting fresh Irish air put colour into my darlings' cheeks but I know now what was behind those long walks. She was pouring poison into their ears about their own mother, who loved and cared for them. No wonder they came back from those walks and looked at me with timid and fearful eyes. The sanctimonious St. Mary must have been telling them that I was a selfish monster surrounded by dogs who only wished to bite and infect them. And if by any chance I went on a rare visit to some country house, I would be greeted on my return by the children, the poor little unconscious accomplices, saying, 'Oh, Mamma, look here! Wasn't it kind of Auntie to give me this doll!' or 'this pony' or whatever the thing might be. 'Auntie' if you please and the gift usually sent by me or bought by Miss Greene with money I'd given her expressly to buy them.

I descended into the gloom my ancestral homeland always infected me with. Is there anyone anywhere who can believe in those carefree, stupid but canny

Irish peasants, forever singing, joking and dancing, who infect our literature now? The Irish are brutish people, and even Dublin, for all the elegance of its buildings, is but a shadow of even the most backward English city. I have cousins still alive who stink and sweat and fart (forgive me) from dawn till dusk without an ounce of soap between them. There was but one bright spot in this mire (literal as well as metaphorical) of despair. This was our nearest neighbours, the Humes. Mrs. Hume, a woman whose obvious beauty and intelligence had been destroyed by illness, was still somebody one would choose to sit with at her bedside and discuss the poetry we both loved. William, her devoted husband, was a man still in his prime, handsome, cultured (for Ireland) and finely mannered. I lacked a kindred spirit, who loved poetry and literature as I did. I lacked intelligent male company. Put simply, I lacked any appreciation of whom I was or might be. In the circumstances, it was completely comprehensible that William and I chose to spend time together.

What the Master of the Knebworth Harem and the Irish Virgin chose to make of it is entirely another matter.

From the Unpublished Reminiscences of Mary Greene

I cannot in all honesty say that either parent was well suited to the task of raising their two children. Mr. Bulwer was always too involved with his labours, political and literary, to see much of his children and, when he did, he was a stern, often difficult, father, expecting much of his children in terms of obedience and affection, without offering any reciprocal warmth or encouragement. Mrs. Bulwer was capable of showing affection to her children, sometimes smothering them with kisses, promises and gifts, but they were like dolls to her, to be played with and then discarded. She would sometimes scold them bitterly for nothing or make it hurtfully clear that she found them tiresome and wished to be left alone with her dogs. I did my best to mitigate the excesses of both parents but I own that I came, in time, to feel for Teddy and Emily's sake that Mr. Bulwer's consistency of approach, however harsh, was to be preferred to the emotional fickleness of his estranged wife.

From an Unpublished Autobiography by Lord Lytton

The woman who had taunted me with my promiscuity was, of course, no sooner separated from me and settled in Ireland than she became involved with a married man of the poorest possible character. Mr. W. Hume had no more proper consideration of his crippled wife, a woman apparently of considerable sensitivity and culture, than the lowest Irish beggar displays for the tattered drab whom he abuses and then kicks into a ditch. He thought nothing of gallivanting around the country, often in my wife's company, while his poor wife languished at home.

Believe me, I tried to make the best interpretation I could of what was happening in Ireland. After all, my children were there and I did not want to believe they were being exposed to their mother's sexual degradation, even though the reports I began to receive from Miss Greene were hardly reassuring. Perhaps not everyone will understand the extent of my forbearance. As the law then stood, I alone was entitled to the custody of my children, but, at the time of my separation from Rosina, I had not insisted upon my legal right and instead had allowed her to keep our two children, for whom I made financial provision as well as for her, though little thanks I got for it. I believe I hoped that Miss Greene, at that point very much her friend not mine, would prove a sufficiently mellowing influence on Rosina's intemperance (both temperamental and alcoholic).

Besides, and I must be honest, these were times of artistic achievement and I simply could not afford to let myself be diverted from following the flow of my creative imagination. Even my political career had to take a back seat. Apart from essays and tales in *The New Monthly Magazine*, *The Amulet*, Heath's *Book of Beauty* and numerous other periodicals, this was the time of the appearance of *Rienzi*, which had greater sales (and indeed acclaim) than any other of my books over the coming years. I also published the first two volumes of my *Athens, its Rise and Fall* in 1837, a work which won the praises of many classicists of my acquaintance, although, of course, it was eventually to be superseded by the more complete and elaborate history of Mr. Grote.

But perhaps the most important development in my literary career came because of my growing friendship with William Macready, an actor of extraordinary intelligence and versatility but also (more unusually still) a man of firm moral purpose, who saw it as his mission to raise the standards and quality of our plays and their presentation in our sadly decadent theatre. I had played my own humble part in Parliament in proposing in 1832 a Committee of Enquiry into the laws affecting dramatic literature and the condition of the drama.

I managed also during this time to make significant steps towards the establishment of a dramatic copyright. The commonest invention in calico, as I said in my speech to Parliament, a new pattern in the most trumpery article of dress, a new bit to our bridles, a new wheel to our carriages, may make the fortune of the inventor; but the intellectual development of the finest drama in the world may not relieve by a groat the poverty of the inventor. The instant an author publishes a play, any manager may seize it, mangle it, act it, without the consent of the author, and without giving him one sixpence of remuneration. Those days, thank the Lord and my endeavours, are now past.

I failed to make any headway, alas, in reining in dramatic censorship, which invested the Lord Chamberlain with a power more absolute over what could and could not be said in a new play than the comparable powers of the monarch himself. Surely, I argued, since the moral tone of the stage will always reflect that of society itself, public taste and the vigilant admonition of the public press might safely be trusted for the preservation of theatrical decorum. These words fell on deaf, nay hostile, ears, as did my suggestion that the Government might remit a portion of the taxes made upon the two main theatres in order to encourage them to take a more high-minded view of their task. The French Government, I pointed out, devotes little short of £80,000 to the support of the theatres in Paris, while we simply see them as a source of taxation. The English have ever been at heart Philistines and so the idea of giving money to encourage the arts was greeted as if I had proposed that naked dancers should parade through the House of Commons. Although, given the predilections of many of my fellow Members of Parliament, that was probably their idea of a cultural experience.

I mention all this to explain why I immediately found common ground with William Macready, undoubtedly the greatest Shakespearean actor of our age. He urged me to write for the theatre. My poor *Duchess*, as I have already recorded, met with but modest success, in part, both Macready and I believed, because of the envy and hostility of the ignorant and vindictive. With my second play, *The Lady of Lyons*, therefore, I insisted that it be produced anonymously, as I was determined to see how it would be received before acknowledging myself as author. Macready disagreed with me but my wishes prevailed. The play was produced in February, 1838, and was a conspicuous success. The sour and twisted faces of those carping critics who had praised it to the skies when the name of the author was finally revealed were, I own, a balm to my suffering soul. Indeed, I do not wish to boast but I am confident that to this very day its title will raise a nod of acknowledgement in every true lover of the theatre. For two generations it has been the ambition of every rising actor and actress to play the parts of Claude Melnotte and Pauline Deschappelles. With *The Lady of Lyons*, my later historical drama, *Richelieu*, and my satirical comedy, *Money*, I do believe, without false modesty, I have created dramas which will survive well beyond my lifetime. If the partial aim of an author is to achieve immortality, then my dramas are as much of my claim to a tiny eternal corner in literary Elysium as my novels.

If Rosina had remained by my side, I honestly doubt whether, even with the encouragement of a divinely gifted theatre practitioner like William Macready, I would ever have dared to enter an arena so public as the theatre. Her carping words and satirical looks would have destroyed any scrap of confidence I might have had, long before the theatre-going public had had their say.

Meanwhile, ensconced in Ireland, Rosina, who, after all, was born there, would tell anyone who would listen (an ever dwindling number of people) that she, along with our children, had been condemned by our separation to a life of squalor and deprivation, while I lived a life of luxury and debauchery in the Great Metropolis. She had no inkling, for example, of the efforts I made in Parliament to improve the lot of the Irish peasantry. After a visit I made there upon diplomatic business, I was left charmed by the grandeur and variety of the scenery but the wretchedness of the people made my heart ache. I confess never to have heard a word from Rosina's mouth about the Irish peasantry that was not mocking or satirical in her usual way. She cared nothing for them and did less, while I ploughed an unpopular furrow in Parliament to bring them succour.

In this, I was encouraged by the support of dear Lady Blessington. My friendship with her was not only a joy in itself, since I relished the company and confidence of so intelligent and experienced a mature woman of the world, but I also appreciated her valiant attempts, as a fellow Irishwomen, to ascribe Rosina's wrongheadedness to her hot-headed and impetuous Irish heritage. But then Lady Blessington had survived this heritage to become an authoress of great distinction, the Platonic companion and patroness of the most elegant man of our age, Count d'Orsay, and the hostess of a salon to which the whole of literary London craved entry. If only Rosina had learned how to turn her Irish blood to so good an account. You may well understand why I was often in the widowed Lady Blessington's salon – and, of course, how the World wished to turn our friendship into something it most emphatically was not.

As politics faded for the moment from my life, I received an honour which both delighted and surprised me. In June 1837, King William died and our Gracious Queen, Victoria, succeeded. Lord Melbourne was gracious enough to signify his appreciation of my services, both political and literary, and recommended to the new Sovereign that she should confer upon me the title of Baronet. This honour I received a year later on the occasion of Her Gracious Majesty's Coronation in 1838 and I became, to the fury and derision of those who envied me, Sir Edward George Earle Lytton Bulwer.

I should have been on a summit of happiness at this time, but Rosina managed, as was her wont, to poison everything. She constantly claimed poverty and yet spent money like water, as she paraded herself around the worst sort of Irish society in the company of Mr. Hume, a man apparently both vulgar and garrulous in the manner of a certain type of Irishman. The children were increasingly abandoned to the care of Mary Greene, a woman, who, for all her limitations, at least had their best interests at heart. The impending weight of my new honours and the public expectation attached brought me to a momentous and painful decision. The children clearly meant nothing to Rosina and I felt I was left with no choice but to reclaim Teddy and Emily for my own. Miss Greene agreed to continue to look after them, with all the care and affection they had become accustomed to.

Rosina protested wildly, as was her wont, though, in my view, she should have been grateful to be disentangled from a burden she showed so little care for. Indeed, I do believe if I had really wanted to punish her, the worst punishment I could have devised was to insist that she spent every day, every hour, for the rest of her life in the company of our children.

From the Unpublished Reminiscences of Mary Greene

Some, I know, accused me of depriving the children of their mother but they know little of how she behaved towards them, in those rare times when she was not absent on her endless social round. Her rages would drive poor Teddy to tears and the affectionate embrace he received after merely confused him. She would buy them expensive presents but want no part of their everyday life.

It is sad for children to be parted from their natural mother and be left in the care of their doting old auntie, but at least she stayed with them and dried their tears and taught them to say their prayers and trust in God. And God is my judge, I think it was best for the children even though eventually I was to give up my family and friends in Ireland to be with them as they grew towards maturity.

God must also be thanked that none of us had any inkling of Emily's sad fate. As my dear beloved Dr. Johnson writes in his immortal *Rasselas*, 'Human life is everywhere a state in which much is to be endured, and little to be enjoyed.'

From the Memoirs of Rosina, Lady Lytton

In May, 1838, a Bill was introduced by Mr. Talfourd in Parliament, to give a wife who had been separated from her husband the right of access to her children. The chief promoter of this Bill was Mrs. Caroline Norton, a woman who for all her preachiness (reminiscent of my own Mama), had been cruelly and unfairly treated by her wastrel of a husband. An eloquent speech in favour of the Bill was delivered by none other than Sir Liar. Can satire deliver anything more preposterous? For at that very time, he was giving instructions that I was to be denied access to my children, who were to be left in the custody of the Irish Virgin Snake in the Grass herself.

I still strongly suspect that Sir Niggardly's prime motive was to deprive me of access to the measly one hundred pounds a year which, out of his thousands, he had magnanimously allotted to the upkeep of his only children (his only legitimate children, I should say).

It is impossible to describe the grief and pain I felt. I cannot dwell long upon the subject. Suddenly my children were no longer mine to hold and to love. Even to write to my dear Teddy and Emily, I was obliged to rely upon my former friend, Miss Mary Letitia Greene, to hand my letters (and gifts) to them if she chose (and I suspect she usually didn't).

Of all the cruelties Sir Edward (as he was now titled, in a fine example of the satirical and cynical tendency of the World) ever inflicted upon me, this was the worst. Night after night I cried myself to sleep and the nights when sleep finally came were still all too few.

To Robert and Emily Bulwer from Their Mother, June 1838

To My Children:

> When round my heart you did entwine
> Those little Fairy arms of thine,
> My cheek grew wan!
> I asked – will thought of me e'er rise
> To sadden their now cloudless eyes
> When I am gone?
> Ah! No, alas! I fear me not,
> For childhood's love is soon forgot.

1839–1840

From Cheveley, or, the Man of Honour, 1839

'Good Heavens!' exclaimed the old lady, wringing her hands as she approached the door, 'where is De Clifford?'

'Where we must all soon be,' said Lee, solemnly, 'before that tribunal which has but one witness – our own soul! and but one judge—the Lord God who made it! Here,' continued he, pointing to the body as the men brought it forward, 'here is what was your son. And now, having returned good for evil, and brought you your child, who hoped to rob me of mine, I'll go to what was my daughter.' So saying, the crowd gave way, and Lee walked rapidly through it and disappeared.

'Stop—secure…' said the old lady, pointing after him; but, before she could finish the sentence, she sunk down in a fit on the corpse of her son.

From the Memoirs of Rosina, Lady Lytton

It might be imagined that the recently elevated Sir Edward Liar might have thought he had achieved enough when he took my children away and threw me upon the mercy of the world with but a pittance to support me. But that requires one to believe that he was capable of compassion or moderation or any sympathy with the needs of any soul except his own. Instead, he was predictably mortified when I proved that I too was able to earn money from my pen with my first novel, which went through three editions and made me enough money to mitigate at least for a time the poverty of my circumstances. Of course, Sir Envious Little Talent did his best to suppress my book and threaten publishers who might wish to publish any future novels with dire consequences. He had the support of that despicable crew of Dickenses and Disraelis, but for the moment at least he did not succeed in suppressing a book he claimed was aimed at ridiculing him.

Well, if the cap fits, say I. Lord De Clifford is devoted to his old witch of a mother but much less to Julia, his beautiful but sorrowing wife; he has a predilection for governesses and has spawned a bastard on a village girl on his estate. Her indignant father is framed for stealing to silence him during De Clifford's election campaign. De Clifford wins the election by making a speech of indescribable patriotic humbug and sanctimonious tributes to the virtues of the contented family, delivered (I own myself pleased with this) 'with all the bashfulness peculiar to hackneyed speakers and girls of fifteen.' He dies by falling off his horse and the Dowager Lady De Clifford collapses over his dead body. This, alas, I own is fantasy, as is my creation of the honourable and caring Marquis of Cheveley, an aristocrat in every way in contrast to De Clifford, who loves Julia from afar and is finally rewarded with her hand. It is painful to report that no man of Cheveley's sensitivity and distinction has ever paid court to me in reality but, after all, this is fiction. Well, that part of it anyway. If the discerning public understood some allusion to my husband in De Clifford and to his mother in the Dowager Lady De Clifford, who am I to say they are wrong? There was something delicious in knowing that Sir Liar, in order to protest publicly at the truth of my portrait, would have had to acknowledge it was based upon his ignominious self.

All this was some balm to my wounded feelings (and my dwindling purse), but I no longer felt at home either in England or Ireland, and so, following in my mother's footsteps (God help me!), in the autumn of 1839 I headed for France – more specifically for Paris. I was accompanied by Mr. Hume, in need of recuperation from endlessly caring for his ailing wife and I own that I felt more secure travelling with a respectable and gentlemanly male companion, for a single woman is very much the object of unwanted attentions and adverse comments. Nor was there any word of censure or rejection from the eminently respectable social circles in which I now moved, a fact that should surely speak for itself about my still (to this day) blameless character.

But, needless to say, this state of things was anything but agreeable to Sir Twoface, who now began to set on foot enquiries as to my character and behaviour, in the hope of eliciting something scandalous, or at least unfavourable to my reputation.

Reports came from Bath, for example, where I had lodged before my journey abroad, of a gentleman (*soi-disant*) who had turned up and quizzed my landlady about whether she had ever seen anything to believe that Mr. Hume was otherwise than on the footing of a friend? She refused to countenance his increasingly impertinent questions. How could I support the extravagance of my manner of life if I did not receive money from Mr. Hume? Had I not been up with him all night in my dressing-gown? Was it true that Mr. Hume had made me a present of his carriage, upon which I had had his coat of arms removed and my own inserted? That he had ruined himself for me and I had broken his wife's heart? Could a person sleeping in the garret above hear the door between the dressing-room and my bedroom if it opened in the night? The friend who reported all this said Mrs. Stockman (the landlady) had indignantly refuted all these questions, though it took her two hours to get the 'gentleman' out of her house. The friend added that this was alarming in two ways (many more than that, by the way). Firstly, because Mrs. Stockman suspected that one of her servants, a dissolute wretch subsequently dismissed, had been paid money to spy upon me and Mr. Hume – hence, she would hazard, the question about what could be heard from the garret. Secondly, there could be no doubt I was being closely watched by someone who knew every circumstance of my life, even the most minute particulars, and would use these particulars to worm his way into the confidence of anybody who might betray me, even though there was nothing to be betrayed, save by a mendacious, venal and drunken servant.

The account from Bath was not the only report I received of an intolerable surveillance of every detail of my life by the paid minions of the man who was, alas, still my husband and the father of my children. But he had money and I had little, even from the earnings of my own pen, so how could I fight back? Though God knows an investigation of Sir Twoface's personal life would have yielded rich pickings.

I own there are those who, when I tell them of this particular time in my life, cannot credit what I tell them. I have seen the disbelief in their eyes, as if I suffered from strange delusions and was not entirely in my right wits. But my time in Paris, residing in the Rue de Rivoli, made clear to me that my persecution by the paid dirt-stirrers of Sir Liar (now a baronet and therefore authentically Sir Liar, rather than Mr. Liar, with his deceptions multiplied I would say by the tainted honour he had been granted by that tight-fisted little miss who had become our Queen) was to be unceasing.

I have said that my acceptance by the social elite during my *séjour* in Paris was both welcoming and attentive. There was only one fly in the ointment. Eddard's middle brother, Henry, the wastrel who had gambled away his fortune, was now, Lord love us, Secretary of the English Embassy in Paris. This was an early stage in what went on to become what is described as a 'distinguished' diplomatic career. Henry, from my limited experience of him, though less odious and unprincipled than Eddard (possible because he had had very little contact with his ghastly Mamma), was still one of the most conceited, dull-witted and socially inept men you could ever hope to encounter. But then in England, if you have the right social background, and have attended the right school and the right university and joined the right Clubs, then a lack of intelligence or ability is no disqualification to advancement. I remain amazed to this day that Henry's diplomatic skills have not managed to set in motion a major war.

But that is by the by. Soon after my arrival in Paris at the end of 1839, I attended a *soirée* given by Lady Aylmer, the wife of one of our most distinguished diplomats there. The entire Corps Diplomatique was there (many of them tedious beyond words but that is diplomats for you) and that inevitably meant the egregious Henry was present. I had no advance warning so when I saw him in the distance I did my best to avoid a direct encounter, not an impossible undertaking in such a thronged and distinguished gathering. Our eyes may have met once across the crowded room but no more. God knows, there was more engaging company to be had there than Eddard's dreary brother. Imagine my dismay therefore when reports appeared in two English journals – the *Morning Post* and the *Court Journal* – of an alleged encounter between myself and Henry Lytton. The latter is undoubtedly the more offensive version:

Her Ladyship (that is myself), who, it is said, had gone to the soirée with the express intent of insulting her husband's brother, made a dead stop as he passed, and placing her arms akimbo, commenced a series of grimaces that have scarcely been equalled since the best days of Grimaldi, and continued her vulgar gestures until Mr. Bulwer had passed beyond her sight. The affair has created a feeling of disgust in the minds of all persons here, and it is probable that her Ladyship will not have another opportunity of displaying her grotesque performance either at Lady Aylmer's or elsewhere.

This was insupportable. I easily obtained an apology from the Paris correspondent of the *Morning Post* for the much milder version of this canard he had penned, but the *Court Journal*

(*Court Jester* more like) declined to apologise, because its editor was in the pay of Mr. Henry, on whose miniscule diplomatic triumphs inordinate praise was inevitably bestowed. As always, I attempted to rise above the attacks of my enemies with the silent contempt they deserved. But my solicitor, Mr. Hyde, insisted that we should instantly bring an action for libel and it would be an opportunity to show in open court what the amiable Brothers Bulwer were capable of in point of truth and honour. Mr. Hyde was, unfortunately, over sanguine. This account had come from an anonymous correspondent, whom the Editor undertook never to employ again (though as he was anonymous who could possibly tell?). It was impossible to prove – and, it was indicated, impertinent to suggest – that either of the Brothers Bulwer could possibly have had an involvement in such low matters as slandering an estranged wife. At the end of the trial, it is true, I obtained as verdict fifty pounds and costs against this seedy scandal sheet passing for a newspaper, but my triumph very possibly only served to heap fuel on the fire of the brothers' black malice, for from that time on the plot began to thicken. Again, bear with me if what I now recount seems implausible.

I should mention here one friendship made in Paris of immeasurable consolation to me in these trying times with Mrs. Frances (Fanny) Trollope, the distinguished authoress of *The Domestic Manners of the Americans* and over thirty novels. She was then in her early sixties, a short, plump woman but with eyes that sparkled intelligence and sympathy. She had married a man whose reckless financial mismanagement had destroyed the family fortunes. He had died but a few years earlier in Bruges, broken and bankrupt, while Mrs. Trollope had continued to labour to support their family by her pen, despite the tragic loss of several of her children to consumption. To say that we understood each other is an understatement. She saw at once the struggle I was enduring to make my living by my pen and was generous in her praise of *Cheveley*, a book whose truth she immediately grasped. Our friendship, alas, was not to endure (mainly I suspect because of the poison spread by the minions of Sir Liar) but at that moment in Paris she was an angel, the mother I wished I had possessed, a champion of women, and married women in particular, without the endless sermonising of my own mother. Her support gave me courage in the ordeals which now threatened to engulf me at a time when I felt I had been punished enough and begged to be left alone.

Further outrages followed swiftly upon my success in the action for libel. One evening, I went to the Tuileries, where there were great illuminations to celebrate the then King's birthday. All the servants turned out to see them too. On my return from Court, while my maid was undressing me, she indicated that Phoebe wished to speak to me. Phoebe was my cook and I could not imagine what she could want at that time of night. Could it not wait till morning? But, no, Phoebe had particularly requested to see me that very night. The good soul was full of apologies for the intrusion but she wanted to tell me that every time she had stirred out over the last fortnight, she had been followed by two Englishmen – one large, fat and red-faced, the other lean and sallow. This night, however, they had finally entered into conversation, offering her a box of bonbons and an invitation to go to the illuminations with them. She refused but then they started with questions about me, my habits, my callers, the impertinent questions I had come to recognise that Sir Liar's minions would always pursue me with. Phoebe, as I now began to appreciate, was cleverer than she looked and had managed to dissemble and answer like a simple fool, in order to find out what they were about. I praised her for her good sense.

They asked her questions about whether there were nights when all the servants were sent away and, when they returned, did they find the drawing-room locked and would they be prepared to swear that was the case for three or four hundred pounds? It is difficult to know whether the devoted Phoebe or I was more indignant at the implications behind these impertinent enquiries. Finally, the fat brute had said he would be very like to come and have tea with her some night when her mistress was out, because, he persisted, Phoebe was a very pretty woman.

'I told them that's a lie for I'm as ugly as the business you seem to be upon,' she had replied. They had laughed heartily but persisted in saying they wished to come and visit the first evening her Ladyship was out. And here the good Phoebe had an idea for which I cannot praise her enough, namely that if we could get the wretches into the house, and I could have a lawyer here to confront them, then we could catch them in a trap of their own making. I praised Phoebe for her behaviour and her suggestion, tipping her handsomely.

I sent next morning for my French lawyer, Monsieur Ledru, for I had realised the excellence of Phoebe's plan. It would convince those I had to contend with in Paris, who mouthed apathetic English twaddle as to what motive dear Sir Edward could possibly have for such conduct or indeed his brother, so beloved of the salons, et cetera, of the true malice of their intentions.

Put simply, the trap was set. Phoebe donned her smartest cap and made a Barmecide preparation of a great display of tea-things and vacant muffi plates. M. Charles Ledru and two *gens d'armes* were in attendance. M. Ledru advised me to have no light but the firelight in to the drawing-room but then to leave the door ajar that led into the little boudoir where I used to write of a morning, and, moreover, to leave the key in my *secrétaire*. It was necessary to prove that the purpose of the fat spy was to tamper with my papers, so he had to be caught *en flagrant délit* in order to arrest him. I accordingly unlocked the iron box in which they were generally kept and took one or two packets of Sir Liar's letters, red-tape-tied and temptingly endorsed, giving the heads of their contents, and laid them carelessly on the slab of the *secrétaire*.

The trap succeeded admirably. Led along by the resourceful Phoebe, the corpulent crook was literally seizing the baited packets when my lawyer rushed in and collared him. He barely had time to turn his angry reproaches on the laughing Phoebe when I appeared, followed by the two *gens d'armes*. Blaspheming in language even Sir Liar might have blenched to use, the spy was duly taken. His lean partner in crime, who was lurking outside, was also seized and charged. M. Ledru informed me that they were two English attorneys living in Paris, by the names of Lawson and Thackeray (no relation to the author of *Vanity Fair*, I believe) and their chief business consisted in doing dirty work of the same kind as that in which they had so signally failed on the current occasion.

Nevertheless, I initiated an action against these two legal ruffians, partly to demonstrate to the world that I was indeed truly being persecuted but also, I confess, for the pleasure of making it necessary for Sir Liar to come to Paris to defend himself. What cared I if the newspapers made hay with his reputation, even questioned mine, when he was to receive the humiliation he so undoubtedly deserved?

The trial was set for two months later and meanwhile Mrs. Trollope was invaluable in her support and practical advice. She had survived for many years in a world of male jealousy and intrigue and had no doubt about the perfidy of men, particularly male authors. (How sad it is that, after her death, her novelist son, the over-prolific Anthony, saw fit to denigrate in his mealy-mouthed fashion his own mother's fine literary achievements.) She also gave me invaluable advice about my second novel, *The Budget of the Bubble Family*, which I was engaged upon at the time, a necessary labour for my sanity but also for my finances, as preparations for the trial were costly. She urged me not to mention the infamous Bulwers in my dedication, because, as she wrote to me, 'Stand before the public clear of them, dear friend. Your literary reputation requires it. That you have been sorely tried is true – but you have that within you that ought to enable you to rise unscathed from it all.'

How inspiring she was – the book is dedicated to her in acknowledgement of the confidence she gave me at this crucial time. How I wish to have had a mother like her, wise and strong, but not a shrewish preacher. I still often ponder why she chose to distance herself from me in the years to come.

Meanwhile, in the interim before the trial, there was much dirty work doing, for Mr. Loaden, my husband's odious man of dirty affairs, was loose in Paris, playing his old game of bringing my name into disrepute. His *modus operandi* was as follows. He went about ringing at every door where I visited, and whenever he could gain admission, commenced operations by saying, 'My dear madam, I understand you are intimate with Lady Bulwer; now, really, as you have daughters, I come to warn you she is not a person with whom you ought to allow them to associate.' He met, however, with much the same indignant reception and summary dismissal at every home he called, and had nothing left but to go to M. Ledru and say that he had come, for Lady Bulwer's sake, to try and get him to persuade her to withdraw her action against Lawson and Thackeray, as it would be her ruin. An equally dusty answer was received there.

The odious Loaden and his associates had, however, another trick up their slime-covered sleeves. My intention, once the trial was over, was to take a much needed vacation and visit Italy with a large party. I was on the lookout for a travelling servant, and one morning a slip of paper which had been left with the porter was sent up to me, upon which was written, 'If Lady Bulwer will call on Madame—, No.—, Rue de—, between two and three this afternoon, she will hear of a most excellent travelling servant, who can be highly recommended.' I put the piece of paper on the table, resolving to go if I had time, but was busy all morning, writing to my English lawyer, Mr. Hyde.

Luckily for me, my next door neighbour, Sir Henry W. dropped by. He was an excellent linguist and used obligingly to copy any letters or papers, which this charming conspiracy had given rise to. I showed him the slip of paper and asked, if he had time, that he would call at the address and inquire after the character of this servant, 'as men can always better find out the character of men-servants.'

He turned nearly white in horror when he glanced at the paper and, without another word, he seized his hat and rushed out of the room. I did not see him again till dinner-time, when he came in, accompanied by M. Ledru. Finally, he could explain to me their morning's adventure. Apparently, I had had a very narrow escape from yet another low plot by Sir Liar's associates. The address I had been directed to was that of none other than one of the most notorious houses of ill fame in all Paris. When Sir Henry arrived with M. Ledru, whom he had brought along as an extra witness, who should be walking up and down, eagerly looking for my arrival but Henry Bulwer! He was accompanied by a Mr. Hansworth from the Embassy. 'Hansworth,' Sir Henry explained, 'is a great ass, but, hang it! I acquit him of knowingly being an accomplice in so diabolical a plot. He, of course, was innocently decoyed into the stroll, no doubt to be an eye-witness of your abandoned infamy in going to such a place.'

My nerves – and finances – were at stretching point by the time the case came to trial. Thanks to the spies around me, and the plots against me, I felt I was living in a house made entirely of glass into which the curious could peer. But, nevertheless, the plotters could not shake me, even with the zealous advice of Lady Blessington, that Irish Messalina. Sir Liar was intent on shifting the whole responsibility onto Lawson and Thackeray, who had, he claimed, acted as they did without any authority from him. There is little doubt that his casuistry would have been smashed to pieces if he had once been obliged to take the witness stand, before a court packed with his social equals and journalists from every major newspaper in London and Paris, and the last shred of disguise would have been ripped from the infamies of his corseted form.

The case came to court in July 1840, but, alas, nothing is ever simple or straightforward with the law, particularly when dealing with the rights of women. M. Barrot, appearing for my husband, in a long legal argument, contended that neither the English nor French laws authorised Lady Bulwer to proceed in this case, without the consent of her husband, which he, from consideration for public decency, thought proper to withhold. My own advocate spoke powerfully against this insufferable attempt to suppress the truth, but he did not prevail. Many were disgusted as their worse opinions of the Black-Hearted Baronet were confirmed but the case was dismissed.

With the help of Mrs. Trollope, I continued to pursue other possibilities through the French courts and to keep the newspapers informed of my husband's hypocrisy and immorality, though I was checked at every turn by the infamous brothel-visiting brother. Eddard, meanwhile, continued to do everything in his power to blacken my name. That, I eventually became inured to and when I moved later in the year to Florence, even he seemed to have tired of spending his precious money on futile persecution (God forbid that he should spend it providing a decent way of life for me).

Alas, he had the power to deliver one last cruelty. He had succeeded in denying me all further access to my children. Now he put a stop to even the feeble pretence of a correspondence which had existed between me and my dear children. To be truthful, it had never been anything on their side beyond the six stereotyped lines of Miss Green's dictation, commencing with the *obbligato*, 'Dear Mamma.' Still the words, meaningless though they were, had been traced by their little hands, and were therefore precious to my poor fractured heart.

Now even this faint reflected ray of happiness was denied me.

1841–1844

From Zanoni, a Rosicrucian Tale, 1842

Did Zanoni belong to this mystical Fraternity, who, in an earlier age, boasted of secrets of which the Philosopher's Stone was but the least; who considered themselves the heirs of all that the Chaldeans, the Magi, the Gymnosophists, and the Platonists had taught; and who differed from all the darker Sons of Magic in the virtue of their lives, the purity of their doctrines, and their insisting, as the foundation of all wisdom, on the subjugation of the senses, and the intensity of Religious Faith?—a glorious sect, if they lied not! And, in truth, if Zanoni had powers beyond the race of worldly sages, they seemed not unworthily exercised.

From an Unpublished Autobiography by Lord Lytton

During Rosina's clumsy attempts in Paris to hold myself and my brother up to ridicule, it had become clear that she cared nothing for the harm all this was doing to her children's reputation or for the distress it might cause the rest of my family. To most people, her claims of persecution seemed like the rantings of the madwoman she subsequently became, but she managed to convince enough respectable members of society (not to mention the monstrous regiment of women authors who rallied to her cause) that she was much wronged. My own inclination, born of concern for Emily and Teddy, was to deal with our disagreements in as private a way as possible, but it was clear this was no longer possible. After the first of her cheap and sensationalist fictional attacks upon me and my family, particularly devastating to my mother, who was viciously caricatured, it became apparent that she considered nothing to be private, everything was fodder to her revenge.

Let us be clear. It was Rosina who moved our conflict into the public sphere, not me. She had decided to spare nobody and therefore, in my view, she could no longer be spared retaliation herself. Firstly, I had given her control of our children and she had abused that trust, abandoning them to cavort around Europe with a married man of little social consequence (and reportedly the possessor of the worst wig known to Mankind). Secondly, I had let her insult my brother in a vindictive attempt to destroy his diplomatic career and, lastly, I had seen libel after libel on my character published or conveyed in other means to anyone she met. The poison would spread unless I acted.

Of course, it was essential that the last connection she had remaining with our children should be severed. It hurt me deeply to deny Emily and Teddy even written contact with their mother, as I have such a high regard for my own, but better they were left undisturbed in the care of Miss Greene rather than be exposed any more to the rantings of their mother.

The gloves were off, as I believe the saying is in the boxing community, when the bare-knuckling begins. Steps had been taken to investigate Rosina's notoriously wayward and immoral way of life in Paris and much evidence was found but, alas, my efforts were frustrated by the ineptitude of the investigators I employed. They far exceeded the brief I had given them, which was to report the simple truth, not to attempt to alter or inflate it. As the trial approached, I had no illusions as to the glee my expected humiliation would cause to my many enemies. In their minds, the trial was decided against me before it even started and my wife's picturesque imaginings (backed by a French lawyer venal even by the standards of French lawyers) took on the appearance of gospel truth. Henry and I hesitated about whether it would be better to burst the blister (I apologise for the vulgar but expressive idiom) and allow the trial to proceed, given the evidence we had accumulated against my wife. But discreeter counsels prevailed. The battle was public but the fewer scraps of juicy gossip thrown to the dogs of the press, the better for my children – and my ailing mother. I had no choice but to close down the trial as quickly as I could and let Rosina depart for Italy soon after, chastened by the realisation that her mad fantasies would be questioned and disputed at every turn.

Since Rosina, apart from her paltry earnings from her despicable attacks on my family disguised as novels, had no other income than that I had agreed to give her, I was able to always maintain a certain amount of control over her wayward soul thereafter. Whether Mr. Hume of the bad wig and worse morality accompanied her on her subsequent travels or returned to his ailing but loving wife, I have no idea and could not in all truth care less.

It was not only on the domestic front that I found myself yearning for peace. As I explained to my daughter, Emily, attending Parliament was a bit like attending school, except that it is even harder work and considerably less instructive. By

1841 my ability to listen to tedious debates and verbose speeches had reached an end – for the present – and I was less and less convinced there was anything more that I could usefully achieve beyond what I had achieved in my early years in Parliament, achievements of which I was duly proud. I longed to get my hours of sleep back, proper sleep, not fitful dozing on the backbenches while Sir Robert droned on, rousing myself now and then to cheer on Lord John. The last achievement of which I am proud, indeed the last speech I made in Parliament as a Liberal member, was in support of a resolution for the immediate abolition of Negro Apprenticeship. After the abolition of slavery, Parliament had kept its faith with the planters, but not with either the Negroes or the supporters of abolition, who believed that the slave should contain no taint of his former servile condition. The fact was that all the old abuses continued, and hideous cruelties were still being perpetrated. I spoke last and the motion was narrowly carried, in part I was led to believe to my own efforts.

Certainly the Anti-Slavery Society chose to publish my speech as a pamphlet.

Oh, yes, these were achievements, but the cost to my basically solitary nature became increasingly hard to endure. I have never been a clubbable man or a good joiner of any club or association, so even the company of my Liberal colleagues, with their braying laughs and endless allusions to hunting, fishing, shooting or whatever other fatuous activity occupied their leisure time, became barely tolerable. After every book I have ever written, there has been a period of fatigue and depression; at times when I pushed myself too far, I had driven myself close to utter mental and physical collapse. I had given politics as much as I could bear. Despite urgent pleas from many members of my party to stay, I retired as member for Lincoln in 1841.

Life is an illusion that passes fleetingly before our eyes while our soul is heading somewhere else. That does not mean that Life, as we may know it, cannot cause us pain meanwhile. Somewhere deep in my soul, I allowed myself to believe that, now that I had abandoned Parliament and Rosina had fled to Italy, there might be a blessed time of calm, recuperation and reflection, in which, for the first time in my life, I might be able to look at what I have and what I had achieved, rather than endlessly punishing myself for the manifold failings and disappointments I had also experienced. I honestly did believe that I might achieve some sort of personal happiness here and now. Vanity of vanities, says the Preacher, vanity of vanities! All is vanity.

There is no happiness here in the material life we are all compelled to lead. I have come increasingly to believe that life is to be endured, because it cannot be relished except by the lunatic, the drunk and the dissolute, and it is brutishly short. All of this became apparent because, at this very moment of expected relief, my mother became seriously ill.

I had always known that I would be distressed by my mother's death but what followed shook my very soul. I am of good aristocratic stock, I am literate, highly educated, and (without undue modesty) of above average intelligence. None of this prepared me for the pain which now ensued, my tormenting doubts or the conclusions I reached after she died.

If I ever feel tempted to forgive Rosina, I will always hold this in my mind. Her so-called novels, which I cannot bring myself to name as works of literature, caused my mother unbelievable distress. For a woman of great personal pride and dignity to realise that she has been held up for public ridicule in the most offensive and vulgar way was something she found hard to bear. She attempted to brush it away but there was always someone, ostensibly caring, who wished to condole with her on the injustice of the portrait, rubbing thereby salt into the wound that it might, for all its vile absurdities, be seen as a portrait.

My mother did not immediately go into physical decline, but we (my brothers and I) were all convinced that Rosina's cruel lampoon was the beginning of the end. She was approaching seventy and had worn herself out fulfilling her responsibilities as a landowner in order to pass on to me in good order the Knebworth estate. When she was dying, my brothers, insensitive male folk of the kind I often encountered in Parliament, displayed no inclination to be with her. I am sure it pained my mother and I cannot quite forgive them to this day, but, compared with the ruin Rosina had visited on her departing soul, it was nothing.

For my own part, I spent the week my mother was dying by her bedside. I did not want the distractions of literature or politics because I knew that this passing was something I needed to understand if I was ever going to make sense of what Life is – or might be. I am well aware that many would think this unmanly, but if this concern for my mother was unmanly, then I would prefer not to be a man. Of course, there were nurses present, so we were rarely truly alone but the years rolled away and, when I held her hand and looked into her eyes, I was the rejected boy whom nobody loved except his mother. Her strong spirit slowly ebbed away as her body yielded inevitably to the call of what lies beyond our life. She was very weak and in great pain, so she rarely spoke. I just held her hand and occasionally stroked it.

One early evening, however, as I sat by her side, her eyes opened wide and when they looked at me, I knew they knew me and only me.

'Edward,' she whispered, taking hold of my hand.

'Dear Mamma,' I responded, stroking her hand, 'I want to thank you for everything you have given me.'

Her eyes already indicated that she was moving into a different world but I knew that she heard me. I poured out the gratitude I felt for her support and her love and clasped her hand with an intensity born of the knowledge that the next time I clasped it, it would be cold as ice.

'I am so sorry.' Her voice was so faint that I barely heard it. Sorry for what, I asked. But there was no reply. Everything she had ever done for me, her love, her concern, flashed before my eyes. Her breathing became Stentorian. I started to break into tears, tears which would not stop. Reproach me, if you wish, members of my Clubs, mock at me, sneer at me, but, I will never deny it, I cried and cried without cessation.

One last time, she tried to speak. My mother was always a Stoic but she held out her feeble hand to try and console me. I squeezed it with all the energy I had in my body. Then it started to grow cold in truth. But, as I looked into her face as the eyes glazed over and the limbs stiffened, I experienced a moment of illumination. I knew what she was trying to tell me. This was not the end. When I had overcome my grief enough to look again, she lay there, cold, her body but a husk, but the something that had gone from her, her vital power, where had that gone? I could not believe it had gone nowhere.

I realise that conventional religion has an answer, which has to be taken seriously by all members of the Christian Church.

Her soul had gone to Heaven to be united with God and his angels, for assuredly it would not have gone to Hell to shriek and scream under the torments of the Devil and his minions. I have respect for the Church of my country but – and I apologise for the affront this will give to those who wholeheartedly accept its beliefs and naturally assume I do too – I do not believe its truths are the full truth. There are more things in heaven and earth, Horatio, than are dreamt of in your philosophy.

I am all too aware that what I wish to write about now will earn me the ridicule and disapproval of those who are very much of this world and will always remain so. But I have become used to the shallow jibes and they have not shaken my deep beliefs, beliefs deepening in the hours, days, months which followed my dear mother's death.

There are powers beyond whose force we have only begun to understand or, more accurately, to recover from a past where they were comprehended and codified in documents since regarded as childish pagan nonsense. The imagery may be archaic, I own, but the truths are eternal. The rationalist who believe all nature obeys the rules of science, which will, in the end, explain everything, continue to mock at the writings of the adepts, the Rosicrucians, the mystics, because they see only our flesh, our spirit confined in this world. I do not want to denigrate Science, simply to have its limitations acknowledged.

Rosina, though, of course, she knew nothing of Science, was always happy to invoke its infallibility on those occasions when I had tentatively (and unwisely) attempted to talk of such matters in the early days. She would enquire at breakfast if I had had any messages from the fairies, with other shrill, bright remarks, or opine that perhaps if I consulted the cards, I could divine what we would be eating for supper that night. I endured all this at that time because I still in a partial way loved her and my notions had not deepened into the deep convictions they now are. But why remember her here? It was my mother who was my spiritual guide into what lies beyond and the energy that indubitably came from her, benign and sustaining in my moments of misery and despair.

I am sure it is not coincidental that I had just published a novel which dealt with these matters – *Zanoni*. Everything is connected to everything else. My unconscious preparations for my mother's death anticipated by some fifteen months the actual event. My spirit knew something that my rational mind did not. The novel was born of a dream I had, so vivid and disturbing that I had no choice but to begin to write it down in fictional form. Of course, the experienced novelist will always know how to sugar the pill for the ordinary reader and *Zanoni* tells a stirring story. The titular character is the subject of huge speculation – he is supposed to have the elixir of life and there are old men who claim to have seen him decades ago no different physically from what he is now. But in Naples, Zanoni falls in love with the beautiful opera singer, Viola Pisani, they marry, sail to a Greek isle and have a child. When she realises the true mystic nature of her husband, she flees to Paris with her former lover, a young Englishman called Glyndon. But it is 1794 and in order to save the life of his beloved wife, Zanoni relinquishes his immortal powers and dies on the guillotine in her place. Well, it is an effective but trumpery tale, though not trumpery enough for the Inimitable Boz not to borrow its central motif for his *Tale of Two Cities*, a borrowing I am, of course, flattered he made (though some acknowledgement would have been gratifying). Yet the truth is, that my story for all its undoubted excitement and (if I may say) skill was but the superficial, physical vehicle for ideas more profound, which may have been caviar to the general, but have certainly been understood and appreciated by the discerning all over Europe. The ideas were there but it was I who put them into literary form.

How often in the months of grieving and despair that followed my mother's death have they given me comfort! Of course, there has been charlatanry in the world of mediums, exploiting the credulous with cheap tricks borrowed from the world of theatre. Spirit rappings, clairvoyance, astrology I have in my time investigated them all and found them disappointingly unconvincing. But have there not also been deceptions practised in the apparently rational world of science? That does not fundamentally affect my beliefs or my trust in my own instinctive sense of what is and what is going to happen. The great tragedy of my life is that those prophetic instincts failed me at the most critical moment in my life, my decision to marry Rosina. But now I believed, sans politics, sans Rosina, with a decidedly reduced literary workload, the grief and lassitude that overwhelmed me was intended to purge my soul and find the inner peace that had for so long eluded me. I was forty now and my weary spirit looked for renewal, guided by the spirit of my mother.

The tragedy with regard to the supernatural is that there are marvels attested by hundreds and believed by many thousands, but, because philosophers decline to thoroughly probe these marvels, they have been abandoned for the most part to persons who know little or nothing of philosophy or metaphysics, and so remain undervalued and thought of as insoluble. Electricity was, until captured and tamed and made to do the work of man, seen as an impalpable and useless element – a sort of mad demon, frisking in thunderstorms. So perhaps the science of Spiritualism will in the end enable us to establish some satisfactory and meaningful communication with the rarest material element, which we call spirit, and engage it, also, to great human uses, holding it in control and obedience by a knowledge of its own laws.

The investigation has barely begun and if *Zanoni* has inspired at least one brave soul to survive ridicule and disappointment to explore further then my book has not been written in vain. Of my own activities as a member of the Society of Rosicrucians and Grand Patron of the Order, it is inevitably forbidden me to write, even in this intimate memoir. I cannot, will not, believe that my spirit is severed for ever from the spirit of my dear mother, and I will hold on to the moment of illumination I felt at her death bed until I die. I have come a long way from that first encounter with the gypsy girl, where truth and guesswork were so mixed in her predictions, but there is a chain linking these insights and it is a chain I cling to as a support and guard across the dark chasms of life to this very day. I look down into the abyss, but the chain is there.

My brothers attended my mother's funeral and behaved with true manly feeling and filial devotion, but I own that I was always conscious that William and Henry, who had shunned her death bed, came from the world of clubs and hunting and had no inkling of what I had been through during that last week. Nor did I wish to share it because I knew all too well that I would invite ridicule for my weakness and my tears, without even beginning to explain the other intensities I had experienced.

I must record the banalities surrounding my mother's will, although material matters were hardly to the fore for me in the following months. I was now the owner of Knebworth and my name, at my mother's request in her will, a hyphenated Bulwer-Lytton. Predictably, Rosina had no interest in my grief or sense of the grievous damage she had done to my mother's final years. Her only communication was through her lawyers who indicated that, given the recent increase in my income, thanks to my inheritance, surely my wife's small (their words not mine) allowance should be increased.

Given what I have written about my state of mind at this time, I am sure it is no surprise that I refused to oblige.

So Sir Liar finally obtained the object of his life-long exertions, namely the possession of his mother's unentailed property, Knebworth Park, for which he took her maiden name of Lytton, and became Sir Edward Bulwer-Lytton (more accurately Bullying-Liar). The only change this brought for me was to have my pittance paid more irregularly than ever. I also received an insolent notification from the odious Loaden to the effect that it was Sir Edward's desire that I should not assume the name of Lytton, but restrict myself to that of Bulwer. Fortunately, the same post brought me a letter from good Mr. Hyde directed to Lady Bulwer-Lytton by royal assent! However, in this letter he also told me that in order to sue Sir Niggardly for a proper maintenance, proportionate to his present fortune, I would have to return to England as I could not do so outside the jurisdiction of the court. Alas, I did not have the funds for such a purpose and so another year rolled on like a dark cloud, as every year was to me now.

1844–1848

From the Unpublished Correspondence of Emily Elizabeth Bulwer-Lytton

Little Boots loves her Mamma very much xxx
Dear Papa, I love you so much. Little Boots xxx

From the Unpublished Reminiscences of Mary Greene

Teddy, at his father's firm insistence, was sent to Harrow, and though he was often unhappy there, he no longer needed my support on a daily basis. Poor Emily, however, still desperately craved her 'Auntie's' support. Over the years, she had developed a deformity in her shoulder, of which she was acutely conscious, despite the beauty of her countenance, and found it hard to make friends or take part in social activities with other children. Her father wished her to be in every way different from her mother so he did not see her diffidence and submission as in any way a defect, although her misshapen shoulder affected him deeply. Denied all access to her mother, however good the reasons, she hung upon her father's every word and begged for the love and attention he very fleetingly gave her. She longed in every way to make his life easier for him and it is no secret that Sir Edward intended her to become the *chatelaine* of Knebworth when she was old enough. The sad truth was that the social standing and poor morals of the older women with whom Sir Edward chose to associate made them singularly ill-suited to preside at his ancestral home. Prior to assuming this role, Emily was sent abroad, to Germany, in order to improve her knowledge of that language. Although she was without friends or loving support, Emily still had to plead with her father for me to be allowed to accompany her as her own true friend.

From the Memoirs of Rosina, Lady Lytton

Kind friends would, when they could, send me news of my children, though I was cruelly deprived of all sight of them. I continued to write to them and send them gifts I could ill afford. I had no notion whether Miss High-and-Mighty Greene allowed them to read the letters or play with what I had sent and they were strictly forbidden to write to me. All this was heart-breaking but at least the sky lightened a little when news came to me of the beginning of retributive justice on that sanctimonious old snake-in-the-grass.

Emily had been sent to Frankfurt-on-the-Maine by her father in order to study German. Why German, you ask? Sir All Puff had always expressed the highest admiration for German culture, mainly, I suspect, because his books sold well there. Be that as it may, he professed devotion to the works of Goethe, Schiller and the other Teutonic worthies, and the possession of only a schoolboy scrap of knowledge of the language did not stop him from claiming to have read their works entire in the original German. Poor dear Emily was to learn German in order to compensate for his linguistic defects, nay cover his defects, and a future devoted to translating books, pamphlets and articles of the most impenetrable and turgid Teutonic kind was planned for her by her loving father, with every intention of taking all credit for her labours.

I was in Geneva when I learned of Emily's arrival in Frankfurt from a good friend there, who knew the ladylike and accomplished woman with whom my daughter was to stay and study. I have therefore no reason to doubt the truth of the account I received, nor would I wish to, as it is quite delicious. Mary Greene had insisted upon accompanying Emily as her self-proclaimed best friend. Emily's hostess professed herself so horrified by the appearance and vulgarity of the Greene one that she announced that she could not possibly undertake

Miss Lytton's education unless such an appendage was got rid of. Well, the Greene virgin went through her whole repertoire of paroxysms and hysterics at this suggestion. She tried to intimidate poor Emily into writing to her father saying that she would die if separated from her dear old 'Auntie'. She, dear child, apparently only too enchanted at such an unhoped-for opportunity, steadfastly refused to put pen to paper for any such purpose and so the afore named self-proclaimed 'best friend' was required to pack her bags and leave. Hopefully, her days as a parasite are now ended and she will return to the Irish bogland from which she came before I mistakenly made her my friend. Sir Niggardly, I feel sure, must for once have felt similar sentiments. After all, she was costing him money, which he doubtless needed to have free to spend upon his copious mistresses.

On the subject of Sir Niggardly and his ways, it should surely surprise no one that he allowed but £100 a year to Emily's excellent hostess for her education, food and lodging, and yet, when he took Emily with him for six weeks to Baden-Baden (a den of gambling and vulgar intrigue so suited to the needs of an impressionable sixteen-year-old), he actually wanted on their return to deduct those six weeks with him from that magnificent stipend. But then, a simple catalogue of his meannesses would fill six diaries still more capacious than the one I am writing in now and, alas, I have to move on to sadder matters. That book of Fate, so remarked on by Shakespeare, was about to reveal one of its most heart-rending pages.

In 1847, I finally returned to England in a vain (are you surprised?) attempt to renegotiate my settlement. I own to shedding a few tears (but not a great number) over the death of my invalid mother at a flat in Camden High Street, surrounded by a grieving band of disciples, both male and female. The Goddess of Reason was dead, and, though I confess a greater sympathy for her notions of greater freedom for womankind than I once did, I still cannot reconcile myself to her neglect of myself in preference for my sister. So a few tears only, but that is not just heartlessness or indifference. A few months before her death, I had shed a great deal more over a much sadder case, namely the death of my dear daughter at the tender age of nineteen.

Being settled for the moment in modest apartments in East Ham, the best my straitened circumstances could afford, I began to make enquiries about Emily, whose place of residence now she had also returned from Germany (and had doubtless been put to translation work by Sir Ruthless) had always been carefully concealed from me. I inquired among the friends of Sir Liar who were also mine (they still existed in limited quantities) without success but then an accident procured all the information required. Friends of friends (true friends all) discovered by a stroke of luck (the only luck in the whole sad story) that Emily was lying dangerously ill at a small lodging house in Pelham Terrace, Pelham Crescent, Brompton. Demand of Sir Shameless why she was residing there, alone, rather than in the luxury he provided for every one of his countless mistresses. The morning after I received this news, the first I had heard of her illness (typhoid fever was mentioned, also consumption, no matter which her condition was serious), I arrived at Pelham Terrace, accompanied by my old faithful servant, Byrne (who once had been Emily's nurse). I observed at once that this was the style of house which was let out in separate rooms and apartments to people in the humbler sphere of life. My friendly informants urged caution, but I had no doubt what I should do next. I engaged a room at the top of the house for myself and Byrne.

When I first ascended the wretched narrow staircase, and passed by the second-floor back room where Emily was lodged, with only a nurse in attendance, I could only wonder why my sick daughter was in such a sordid place – and what hope there was for her survival.

The time I now spent in the room just above that of my darling can only be imagined by those who have endured such cruel agony. Never in my life, even under the cruellest tyrannies of Sir Bully, have I experienced such anxiety and pain. I fancied that I heard her voice and I knew that she was talking of 'my mother', the one person she desperately needed at this crisis. I wept while the good Byrne did her best to comfort me and then, as has always been the case of necessity in my life, I realised I could not just listen to Emily's cries, I must see her, for her own peace of mind as well as my own.

The landlady was susceptible to bribery and, when approached by Byrne, so was the nurse. After all, she was in the employment of Sir Tightfist so she was being paid a pittance, below even the pitiful wages she usually received.

We waited until after dark before descending the staircase with Byrne holding my hand as if she was again a nursemaid. The door of the bedroom had been left open by the venal nurse and quietly I entered. What I saw left me speechless (I own not often the case). My Emily, wasted by disease, without a friend or relative near her, lay in a room which was almost entirely taken up by the bedstead, which nearly filled the space between the door and the window. I looked for an array of clothes but there were none. She appeared to have no more apparel than the heavily soiled nightdress she was wearing.

Emily was lying insensible, her features changed by fever, and hardly to be recognised in the darkened room, where only the sheen from her golden hair as it reflected in the light of the single candle guided my eyes to the pillow and the sufferer. I stood there, transfixed, gazing on the loved form from which I had been so long separated.

I did not speak, I did not move, but Emily, even in her weakened and feverish state, must have sensed my presence. She opened her eyes, weary beyond her years, and looked towards me. She probably did not know if I was there in reality or in her dreams but a joyful light came into her eyes and I swear a smile went across her parched lips.

'Mamma…'

The single word issued hoarsely from her feverish dying body but she was aware and I do think she really knew I was there.

'My darling…'

I moved slowly towards her, kissed her forehead, then stroked her hair. Always slowly, slowly, because I did not want to frighten her, only to calm her and give her joy. She was nineteen, I had not seen her, let alone touched her, since she was ten. I held back the tears and did my best to smile because I wanted her to cherish this moment, a moment she had waited for so long. My own grief could wait for later.

'Mamma…'

Again that word. I had not imagined those calls for her mother that I had heard in the room above hers. She needed me. She loved me. I kissed her lips this time. Poor darling, the price she had paid because of her unhappy parents. But at least one of them was here to smooth her troubled brow.

I held her close to me and heard her painful breaths, gasping for life. Who knows how long we might have stayed there? But Fate, as always in my experience, is unrelentingly cruel. There was a knock at the door and Byrne thought she heard footsteps on the stairs. Suddenly the nurse (a repulsive creature if ever I saw one, all warts and big bosoms) appeared. She was anxious and urged me to leave because visitors were expected. What choice did I have? I allowed myself to be conducted back to my own miserable room, where I threw myself on my knees and buried my face in the wretched bed in which I was doomed to pass the night.

Except that I could not sleep. Emily's nurse (for a fee) brought us the news that she had been delirious but had spoken of seeing her mother (God be praised!) long after her visitors had left. One of them was my son, who wrote his own self-serving account of this time, which pained me so deeply that I abandoned all wish to ever see him again. But, I now acknowledge, he cared enough for his dear sister to be there with her, unlike his despicable father.

All night I sat on the stairs outside darling Emily's door, sending to the room cooling beverages and any things I had with me which might be of service to my daughter. I did not dare to enter my darling's room again.

But, inevitably, Sir Monstrous had his spies, and my appearance to see my dying daughter was not to be tolerated, even though he made precious little attempt to see her himself. The next morning there was a knock on the door and there were two doctors, Dr. Rouse and Dr. Marshall Hall, who informed me that they were commanded by Sir Edward (her gracious majesty!) to order me to leave the house. Apparently, Emily had become delirious and my presence was both disturbing my daughter and aggravating her disorder. I replied that I had paid for my room for the week and no one could turn me out except the landlady. They declared that Miss Lytton's life was endangered by the very knowledge of her mother's presence.

What can a mother do in these circumstances, which were upsetting beyond measure? Proud woman that I am, I threw myself on my knees in front of the younger and clearly more sensitive of the two doctors, Dr. Rouse, and implored him to let me stay to the end. Dr. Rouse would, I saw, have given way, but he dared not. All he could do was offer his carriage to take us away. I thought of the risk I ran of misrepresentation if I stayed, the implication that I had caused the death of my daughter through over excitement. So I agreed to go, a decision which to this day I deeply regret. But it must be recorded that, very soon after this, Dr. Rouse killed himself. I do not like to think that was because of what had happened in our encounter and Emily's subsequent death. But he was a sensitive and principled man, unlike Dr. Marshall Hall. I recall that I enquired of Dr. Hall which was more important to him – his fame as a physician or my feelings as a mother? 'Oh, my fame as a doctor, to be sure,' he replied, with a horse-laugh.

Despite my limited means, I tried to send in doctors of my own suggestion, doctors who might be sensitive to Emily's needs, rather than those of Sir Selfish. All offers of help were rejected by Dr. Marshall Hall on behalf of his paymaster. Emily died on 29th April 1848. The only consolation – small indeed – was that her last moments, or rather the last few hours, were passed without apparent suffering. Do you need to ask whether I was asked to my darling's funeral? Of course not. Sir Whited Sepulchre, who had allowed her to die in squalid circumstances with only a trumpery nurse in attendance, played the leading man in the funeral, inviting the world to marvel at his deep grief.

As I wrote to the unspeakable Dr. Marshall Hall, Sir Edward Bulwer-Lytton (that incarnate lie of the nineteenth century) has dared to give out that my poor angel child died of 'a natural decay.' I warned him that the primary cause of my poor murdered child's illness was the life of hard labour she led to promote her father's ill-gotten literary reputation as a German scholar (him knowing but a few scattered phrases of that language) coupled with the terrific seclusion and privations of every sort that she endured. Witness her dying without the commonest necessaries of a sick-room about her. Even the wine poured down her throat (alas! too late) had to be sent for from a common public-house! The actual cause of her death, I continued, was Dr. Marshall Hall's gross ignorance, only equalled by the coarse and inhuman brutality of his manner. Dr. Marshall Hall, it probably does not need to be said, went on to have a hugely successful career, ministering to the needs (and schemes) of the very rich. Poor Dr. Rouse, alas, was too honourable to live on in this poisonous world.

I wish sometimes that I had the courage to do what he did. I think it was something to do with razors, but I never fully understood.

Preface to King Arthur; an Epic Poem, 1848–1849

In the more historical view of the position of Arthur, I have, however, represented it such as it really appears to have been, — not as the Sovereign of all Britain, and the conquering invader of Europe (according to the groundless fable of Geoffrey of Monmouth), but as the patriot Prince of South Wales, resisting successfully the invasion of his own native soil, and accomplishing the object of his career in preserving entire the nationality of his Welch countrymen. In thus contracting his sphere of action to the bounds of rational truth, his dignity, both moral and poetic, is obviously enhanced. If presented as the champion of all Britain against the Saxons, his life would have been a notorious and signal failure; but as the preserver of the Cymrian Nationality—of that part of the British population which took refuge in Wales, he has a claim to the epic glory of success.

From an Unpublished Autobiography by Lord Lytton

A biographer of the years after the death of my mother might well name them The Chequered Years. The waves of life were once again vaguely gliding, in the words of that inept but oddly memorable phrase in my early poetry. I had abandoned politics, with no great sense of loss or indeed of achievement. My theatre career has sputtered out after its early promise, despite the continuing success of the plays I had already written. Of course, I continued to write because it was in my blood to write but few of the works of those years count among my best. Indeed, only one work from these years has, for me, any true inspiration, namely, my epic poem, *King Arthur.* When all else in my literary endeavours had lost its savour, I had discovered again my vocation as a poet. The theme of survival of a nation, against the odds here, found powerful expression in a work I considered the grand effort of my literary life.

By delving deep into the Arthurian myths, I re-imagined Arthur as Prince of South Wales, a victor even in defeat, who preserved the values of an ancient English democracy, buried in our age under industrialisation and an effete and self-serving ruling class. In taking my subject from chivalrous romance, I also took the agencies from the Marvellous that it naturally and familiarly affords – the Fairy, the Genius of the Place, the Enchanter, not wholly in the precise and literal spirit which our nursery tales present them, but in the larger significations by which, in their concept of the Supernatural, our fathers often implied the secrets of Nature. For the *cognoscenti,* the Rosicrucian modes of perception inform the poem, but for the world, I hope there is still hope and aspiration in what I wrote, because I had dug deep into my soul to find them.

Others, alas, follow but rarely acknowledge. It would have been generous if the Poet Laureate had acknowledged his debt to me when he started publishing his Arthurian *Idylls of the King* some ten years later, but Alfred Tennyson has never been a generous spirited man. Besides, we had clashed satirically in verse (it's not my place to say who came out best) and he nursed grudges like no other literary man I have ever encountered.

I cannot any longer avoid transferring to paper the pain I experienced at Emily's death, which occurred while I was at work upon my epic. My son, Robert, though he was later to redeem himself, was proving a sad disappointment. I had granted him the public school education which I had denied myself but his trial at Harrow was a complete failure so far as Distinction was concerned. He even failed to take up football, which would have made him fit and healthy like a young Spartan. All he could do was indicate that he was being mocked as 'Poor Lytton' because of the inadequacy of his allowance. Hints there of his mother, which made me even more desolate about what his future would bring him if he had to rely upon his own talents and determination.

But Emily was my delight. Her aptitude for German and her eagerness to help me in my labours were a refreshment to my parched soul in this unhappy time of self-doubt. Of course, there was the sadness of her misshapen shoulder and I had spent considerable sums when she was fifteen sending her to specialists in Neuwied and Canstatt, in the hope that she would return reformed (in every way) from their ministrations. Sadly, they had no success, but she had a most beautiful complexion (the only good inheritance she received from her Carabosse of a mother) and delicate hands worthy of the finest aristocrat. My health and my literary labours meant I did not see her as much as I should, for which I reproach myself bitterly. She was always in my thoughts. I promise that when I was dining with Our Gracious Queen and her Prince Consort, for all the great people and fine surroundings, I thought only of being with Emily.

I am aware that out of guilt I am making apologies because I have left undone those things which I ought to have done, as the prayer book says. It is always my intention to be as honest as I can about my failings, because failings they undoubtedly are. If I held *King Arthur* in one hand and my daughter's health in the other, I hope you know which I would relinquish first. Emily, when she was with me, understood my pain. She stroked my brow and comforted me when I was tempted to give up the struggle of life and lie down and die.

The cruelty is that she lay down and died, not me. She was so young, so gentle, and I will always remember her. It was deeply unfortunate that when she became seriously ill, her worsening condition made it impossible to bring her back to Knebworth. I did my best in the emergency to find somewhere where she would be warm and comfortable with the best nurses that money could buy. Her brother knows how much I loved her and how much I did for her. I even allowed Miss Greene, a woman whose veracity and mental stability I had begun to doubt, to have access to Emily, because I believed it might bring pleasure to my daughter's pallid cheeks.

I cannot blame Miss Greene for what happened but I can, without any doubt or equivocation, blame my wife. Her name sticks in my gullet, so I will try not to use it. Emily had the best care available and she might still have lived, were it not for my wife, who was without doubt the immediate cause of her death. She found a way into the house where Emily lay, using a false name, and then forced her presence upon our daughter. Dr. Marshall Hall, a doctor subsequently of great eminence, requested her to leave because her presence was endangering my daughter's health. She refused. Whether it was her voice which Emily recognised or whether she simply sensed her presence, I cannot be sure to this day, but I still have in my possession a letter from Dr. Hall, which attributes Emily's death to the moral shock of her awareness, in whatever manner, sight or sound, that her hated mother had returned. My darling died the very next day.

After this, there could never ever be any reconciliation with the encumbrance who was still my wife. What she had done was unforgiveable.

The Final Verses From King Arthur, an Epic Poem

There flock the hosts as to a holy ground.
There where the dove at last may fold the wing!
His mission ended, and his labours crown'd,
Fair as in fable stands the Dragon King—
Below the Cross, and by his prophet's side.
With Carduel's knighthood kneeling round his bride.
What gallant deeds in gentle lists were done,
What lutes made joyaunce sweet in jasmine bowers.
Let others tell:—Slow sets the summer sun;
Slow fall the mists, and closing, droop the flowers;
Faint in the gloaming dies the vesper bell,—
And Dream-land sleeps round golden Carduel.

From the Unpublished Correspondence of Emily Elizabeth Bulwer-Lytton

Little Boots loves her Mamma very much xxx
Dear Papa, I love you so much. Little Boots xxx

1851

From Many Sides to a Character, or Not So Bad as We Seem, 1851

DAVID FALLEN's Garret. The scene resembling that of Hogarth's 'Distrest Poet.'

Fallen: (opening the casement) So the morning air breathes fresh! One moment's respite from drudgery. Another line to this poem, my grand bequest to my country! Ah! This description; unfinished; good, good.

> "Methinks we walk in dreams of fairy land
> Where – golden ore – lies mix'd with—"

Enter PADDY.

Paddy: Please, sir, the milkwoman's score!

Fallen: Stay, stay—

> "Lies mixed with – common sand!"

Eh? Milkwoman? She must be paid, or the children – I – I (Fumbling in this pocket, and looking about the table) There's another blanket on the bed; pawn it.

From an Unpublished Autobiography by Lord Lytton

After my daughter's death, I travelled extensively upon the Continent in an attempt to restore myself to a more optimistic and creative frame of mind. But then I have never been a Little Englander and I firmly believe that European culture, in particular Germanic culture as embodied in the immortal

Goethe, has much to teach us. Travelling abroad also gave me some respite from the endless persecutions inflicted upon me by my increasingly deranged, but unfortunately physically healthy, wife. There had been no end to these persecutions, all aimed to be as public and as humiliating to me as if I had been locked in the stocks and she was free to fire whatever missiles she had to hand at my unfortunate person. She went to performances of my plays (and there were plenty of them, I might comment) and encouraged the audiences to boo and hiss, something the *hoi polloi* found deeply amusing and so often obliged her. She sent letters, a score of them every day, to the clubs and hotels where I was well known, addressed in the most insulting terms and containing allegations so vile that I cannot bring myself to transcribe them on to this paper. My son, Robert, endured similar persecution with even less justification. She complained about a 'Press Gang' (unfortunately one of her wittier phrases) which assisted me by denigrating her (appallingly written) literary works and dissuading respectable publishers from publishing them (they needed no dissuasion, believe me). She selected a harmless young music teacher from Wolverhampton and attempted to sue her for alienating my affections (it needed no music teacher to do that, I can assure you). But I must cease. I feel the agitation in my soul rising once again.

Despite these annoyances, when I returned to England in 1850, I had managed to achieve a more sanguine view of the world and my place in it than I had felt for many years. I resumed my activities, political and literary, and I conceived, in totally disinterested terms, a scheme to aid my less successful fellow authors in their hours of need. Of course, it was exactly this unexceptional and totally worthy scheme that Rosina (the name has slipped out) selected to inflict upon me her greatest public humiliation yet. She claimed that she was a put upon and needy author, but little she cared for those who were genuinely in that sad state of affairs.

But I must explain first the scheme and how it came into being. I have known something of the struggles imposed upon an author who has to write for his living, but I am all too aware that I have been one of the fortunate ones. I had always interested myself in the case of Laman Blanchard, the most genial and lovable personality in our literary world. He was born the son of a painter and glazier in Great Yarmouth, published (as we all have) a volume of talented verses, which I reviewed myself very favourably, and then settled into the drudgery any aspiring writer must accept. He never repined, he never wrote less than the best he could in the circumstances, but he never thrived. His struggles grew harder and his health weaker, his wife's still more so. I offered to Blanchard and his family a house I owned in the neighbourhood of London, rent free. But Mrs. Blanchard was too ill to be moved. When she died, her husband was completely prostrated by her death. A few weeks later, he cut his throat and he was found dead on the floor, bathed in blood. He was only forty-one.

My wife, of course, would have had no understanding of this sad case. She would have made one of her clever remarks ('Mr. Blanchard has blanched his last', I might hazard) and gone back to her own self-absorbed world. I know I have my own self-absorbed moments but I do emerge from them to look the cruelties and injustices of the world in the face. This was why Dickens and I embarked upon our ambitious scheme of trying to lighten the hardships of struggling literary men like poor Blanchard. That was how The Guild of Literature and Art was conceived and we now set about raising funds for a venture which, we hoped, would supply authors of the future with that period of rest and freedom from mental anxiety which is necessary to the production of really durable work.

The vulgar always imagine that when two authors of considerable literary and financial success put their heads together to work on a common project, there will be petty jealousies and niggling rivalries. Dickens and I suffered from no such antagonisms. We were equals both in our success and in our generosity towards those who have been less successful. Indeed, a few years later, I was able to persuade Dickens to alter the end of one of his shorter novels, *Great Expectations*, because I believed that the public would wish for an end which would allow for a happy union between Pip and Estella. Dickens, usually so in tune with his (our) public, had planned a bleaker end in which his hero was left blighted and alone, and I knew he was wrong. I argued my case eloquently and he accepted it. Such is the give and take between two writers, secure in what they have achieved and unenvious of the other's achievement.

On this particular occasion, we met at one of our clubs and discussed what might best be done. We agreed that I should write a comedy, which would be produced first in London and then in the provinces, the proceeds being devoted to our cherished scheme. The division of labour proves my point. Dickens adores the theatre, indeed it is his obsession, but he has never had any success with his attempts at dramatic literature. I, on the other hand, given my reticent and private character, have no wish to perform myself but bring a safe pair of hands to the writing of the play.

My play, *Many Sides to a Character, or Not so Bad as We Seem*, was completed early in 1851. Upon seeing the manuscript, Macready, who had just retired from the stage, delivered his professional opinion. He said that a piece like this (he was recalling his success with my comedy, *Money*) would have kept him upon the stage. 'The comedy is a hit, and no mistake. Wilmot is a splendid part.' Lord Wilmot, a young man at the head of the fashionable mode, is the principal character in a piece set in the reign of George the First. Perceived by others as a dissolute, unprincipled rake, Wilmot successfully negotiates the intrigues of the play with stratagems and impersonations to bring everything in the end to the satisfaction of everyone, not least his innocent lady love, whom he finally marries. Other characters have, I hope, their moments and the actors allotted to those parts certainly made their mark, but, of course, there was no doubt who was going to play Wilmot, although, if I am honest, he was already some ten years too old for the careless young man I had created. Dickens could never be denied – except in the ending of *Great Expectations*.

The first performance was planned for May, 1851, at Devonshire House, the elegant Palladian London home of the Dukes of Devonshire. The Queen and the Prince Consort had agreed to attend, along with a large fashionable audience. Which is where, alas, she who should not be named started to interfere. The success of the subsequent performances and the ensuing tour will never erase the humiliations she now chose to heap upon me. Rosina's dangerously radical opinions of our Gracious Queen, whom she regarded as a tight-fisted Jezebel, who had, among other infamies, murdered Lady Flora Hastings (a story for another time) were, through intermediaries, already known to me, but nothing had prepared me for the moment when the Duke of Devonshire showed me the letter he had received.

'Recognise the hand?'

My heart sank. Of course, I did. She had written to the Duke warning him that she intended to enter his house disguised as an orange woman and pelt the Queen with rotten eggs.

The Duke asked, 'Is there any chance of her carrying out her threat?' I had to acknowledge, given her history, that it was not impossible. Dickens received a letter, even longer and more outrageous on the same subject, and condoled with me on a wife who was 'the misfortune of my life'. His own marital difficulties were, at this point, satisfactorily concealed.

Here was a charitable project of undoubted merit and here was a selfish woman threatening to destroy it, not because she cared tuppence for the cause but because she loathed me, and to a lesser extent, Queen Victoria. The Duke had no choice but to employ 'detective police' to patrol Piccadilly and guard against the potential outrage.

My feelings on the day of the performance can be imagined. I had spent my energies in creating something to serve my struggling fellow authors. I was working with a cast filled with the most distinguished authors, painters (Augustus Egg among others) and journalists to fulfil our dream. The august audience included aristocrats, politicians, the cream of our intellectual elite and, above all, Her Gracious Majesty and the Prince Consort. Meanwhile, I waited with churning stomach and forced smile for personal humiliation, my eyes ever watchful for anyone who might be concealing rotten eggs about their person.

In the event, she did not do what she had threatened. She only appeared at the gates of Devonshire House to offer copies of a callow parody of my play, entitled *Even Worse than He Seems*. Nobody who wished me well deigned to take a copy from her hands, though there were those, of course, that did and pronounced it amusing despite its exaggerations.

I had created a gesture of generosity and she turned everything to ashes. If she had not been so foolish, she might even have benefited from the scheme.

1851–1857

From the Uncollected Poetry of Lady Lytton

> Poor ghosts! It was no honest foe,
> In fair and open fight,
> Who dealt ye all the mortal blow
> That swiftly quench'd your light.

From the Memoirs of Rosina, Lady Lytton

Our eyes met and I knew she was part of the conspiracy against me. It was only for a moment before the flunkies hurried her away through the gates and into the house but it was enough. She had seen me and she had seen the leaflets in my hand and the eager hands that took them from me, though everyone tried to look disapproving. They knew I was telling the truth. *Even Worse than He Seems* is only the part of it, the part I can put into print without describing practices the tender-minded barely know exist.

Give me any day the open debaucheries of the Queen's uncle monarchs, George and William, who did not hide away their mistresses and did not offer a hypocritical picture of domestic bliss. Everyone knows that Victoria hounded to death Lady Flora Hastings, just because she was a lady-in-waiting to her detested mother. The Queen and her hirelings spread rumours that the unfortunate unmarried Lady Flora was pregnant. The poor woman was nearly dead from liver cancer before the pack was called off and even then she was not left in peace to die. I do not doubt that Her Gracious Majesty could have given some tips on vicious persecution, false rumours and dishonest plots to Sir Liar, that baronet of her own making.

And she shared another characteristic with Sir Niggardly. You need only to think of that poor madman, John Camden Neild, who, leaving all his poor relations starving, bequeathed one million to our little miser of a Queen, who made a couple of trumpery bequests to the executors, and one to an old servant mentioned in the will, and pocketed the rest. Oh, I lie, she put up a memorial window to this imbecile, though it was as small and cheap as decency allowed. Now, this miser's worthy successor, Victoria, might have paid for the Duke of Wellington's funeral out of this pretty little windfall, without dragging it out of the public. Here, I think, the lesson must have been in reverse, for Sir Skinflint is the *sine qua non* of experts upon how to spend money on himself and deny it to others, particularly his impoverished wife. He was, by this time, already planning his way back into politics, but, it will surprise no one to learn that his much vaunted Radical principles were abandoned because the tide of prosperity and future advancement lay with the Tories. When has it ever been otherwise?

Yet both monarch and lord live in the sanctity of public acclaim, nay, we are even told our nation adores their diminutive monarch, a claim, it has to be said, from the hidden glee in the readers of my pamphlet as they secretly perused it, could never be made for our lanky Sir Liar, who is more generally loathed. I own that on that occasion I felt particularly sorry for the Prince Consort, who looked ill and worn out, as well he might having to serve the insatiable sexual demands of that portly little succubus night after night. Of course, his own preference is for being sodomised by his equerries on a regular basis, a choice you can hardly blame him for in the circumstances. The frightened look *he* gave in my direction was of a man trapped in the coils of a harpy and I remember thinking that he probably would not live that much longer. Maybe he should have taken a leaf from Sir Liar's book, bitten into Victoria's portly jowl and tamed her that way.

I was surprised from my thoughts by a deferential cough by my side. I turned to see one of the Duke's flunkies, who, bending close to my ear, indicated that His Grace would be honoured if I would step inside the gates. Now, I knew nothing to the dishonour of the Duke of Devonshire, save that he admitted this sorry crew into his London residence, in the mistaken belief that it was serving a good cause, rather than the endless egotism and self-regard of the gentlemen involved, who loved to pose as figures of charity. I hesitated for a moment and then, handing the remaining pamphlets to my faithful maid to continue the distribution both to new arrivals and the gathering crowd, I stepped through the gate and was conducted into a secluded corner of the inner courtyard.

But there was no Duke to greet me, only the Insufferable Boz, already wearing the greasepaint he loved so much to daub across his face on every occasion. I turned to leave.

'Lady Lytton, forgive me—'

Did he actually dare to take my hand to detain me? The Insufferable was certainly aiming to be as charming as he could.

'Pray, hear what I have to say.'

Why do people fall for his bogus charm? The man is a dishonest mountebank from top to toe, even when not wearing stage make-up as now. His characters, comic and tragic, play shamelessly to the footlights and the public apparently adores him. I beg to differ.

'Mr. Dickens, I have nothing to say to you.'

'Lady Lytton, of course, of course I understand your sufferings.' The big soulful eyes stared into mine. Well, to be more accurate, they gave the appearance of staring into mine, but the performance was being delivered to the invisible audience he always played to in his head.

'I know that you and my dear friend, Edward, have had your differences. I know there have been wrongs done on both sides and both of you have suffered deeply.'

The Insufferable was at full pelt now, the sincerity oozing from his actor's face. I find it incredible to understand why anybody has ever warmed to this fakery, so I remained silent and, I am afraid, very uncharmed.

'I have an appeal to make to you, Lady Lytton. Not for Edward himself, because I know that the differences between you are probably irreconcilable. But for the worthy cause we are performing in aid of to the best of our humble abilities.'

There was nothing humble about the Insufferable's view of his own histrionic abilities. My thought was that they were all rich so why not just give the Guilt (as I had renamed it) the money it needed and spare us this self-regarding performance by a group of egotists, none of whom would survive five minutes in the real acting profession?

'Many have laboured long and hard for this day. Her Gracious Majesty and the Prince Consort have agreed to be here. We are all here to do something for those who have been less fortunate than ourselves. The needy authors of

England, often talented and sometimes simply unfortunate, cry out for aid these performances we have planned can give.'

There was then what the Insufferable clearly thought was an impressive pause. Should I bite my tongue or say what I thought? Was there ever a choice?

'Mr. Dickens, I am a needy author. My husband earns thousands from his books but is determined to stop my own novels being published, even though it is my only source of income apart from my allowance, which is small and paid irregularly. Will the Guild undertake to support me?'

The Insufferable's impressive pause became an awkward pause. 'You are all in a conspiracy against me,' I continued. 'You hide your own sins by hiding his. Do you think I don't know that you beat your wife and consort with prostitutes? Or that Mr. Wilkie Collins maintains two mistresses in different establishments? Or that Mr. Douglas Jerrold has a liking for small boys? My own husband's vices are perhaps the most wide-ranging but each one of you is steeped in sin and sodomy.'

I must have been one of the few personages alive who managed to reduce the Interminable Boz to silence. Then he started to plead.

'Dear Lady Lytton, please, just for today, forget your differences with your husband. So much hangs upon this event for so many. I am sure, in good time, if it is successful, the Guild will be able to find its way to give some of its funds to your own very worthy cause. We have a fine play and a fine cast and we have all laboured hard and—'

I was already walking away towards the gate. There are times when I think the Insufferable was even more of a humbug than Sir Liar. They were certainly a pretty pair. My pamphlet was read and (I have no doubt) enjoyed but the performance was acclaimed as a success, as were a number of subsequent performances at the Hanover Square Rooms and a tour of the provinces, visiting most of the chief towns in England. Was money raised? Who knows? The lords of literature were too full of taking their bows and congratulating each other on their selflessness to notice.

It will not surprise you to learn that I never heard a single word even in my direst financial circumstances from the short-lived Guilt of Literature and Art. Indeed, there were rumours that they sat in council for four hours in order to decide upon the best plan for effectually crushing me. But this is the lesson I learned. To expose the conspiracy against me, I had to continue to remind the world of the wrongs that have been done me. But those in power from Her Graceless Majesty to Charles Chickens (though in the end they came to roost) then conspired to punish me for telling the truth. And so the cycle continued. No wonder English Society should be the plague spot of cant that it is when we have such a little mass of selfishness and idiocy for a Queen.

I had no choice but to return to the small cottage in the Fulham Road where I was living. I had barely a farthing and all the efforts of myself and my friends to obtain a more adequate allowance had resulted in failure. I should explain again that I had received the magnificent offer of an additional £100 a year if I agreed to give up certain letters in my possession (deeply incriminating to Sir Much Worse Than You Could Possibly Imagine, I need hardly to add). Much as I have suffered in this land, I preferred remaining in it and living down the whole clique to acceding to this additional outrage.

I now spent four months trying to let my cottage and just as ineffectually trying to borrow money. At length, a Good Samaritan on the Stock Exchange, a stranger needless to say, announced that he had heard such a good character of my honesty from my creditors, that he most humanely and generously lent me £1,000 at five per cent. For the next ten years, I was to be paying back £100 a year of the principal, and insuring both my tyrant's and my own life. (I never could decide which I wanted to end quicker.)

With this drain on my already miserable pittance, I knew I could no longer stay in London. My friends, to aid me in economising, asked me to go on visits to them, so I went first to Lady Hotham at Brighton and then to other friends there. But I soon found out that there is nothing as expensive as visiting in great houses. The result was that, after a short trip to Paris with Lady Hotham, I went early in 1853 to bury myself in the little Welsh village of Llangollen.

From the Uncollected Correspondence of Lady Lytton

True Copy. Received through Robert Hodgson, Esq., solicitor, of 52, Broad Street Buildings, Bank of England, London, from that ineffable blackguard, Sir Liar Coward Janus Plagiary Allpuff Edward Bulwer Lytton, the disgraceful swindle of £94 3s. 4d., which he doles out to me, his legal victim, as Out Pauper of those Sodom and Gomorrah sinks of iniquity, the Park Lane and Knebworth Unions.

(Signed) Rosina Bulwer Lytton alas!

From the Memoirs of Rosina, Lady Lytton

When I wrote that I intended to bury myself in Llangollen, I had not intended this to be the literal truth. Wales is less damp and vulgar than Ireland but it is only a question of degree. Still, my hotel was comfortable enough and a view of cattle on the hills and the River Dee bubbling by had something to recommend it after London.

Yet in this Celtic version of Arcadia, an extraordinary attempt was made to kill me. I am aware that there are cultivated and intelligent personages (Mrs. Fanny Trollope springs to mind) who have been persuaded that I am over-fanciful and what I have to tell cannot be trusted. I understand that they cannot believe that I am persecuted in the way I am. Surely the activities of Lawson and Thackeray, caught red-handed by other witnesses, beside myself, should be sufficient proof that I have been the victim of unwarranted attacks – and still am.

But in this particular instance, I understand the incredulity, so let me set down the facts of an incident which occurred within months of my arrival in Llangollen. A vulgar old woman, calling herself Mrs. Pearson, came down to the humble hotel where I was lodged. She scraped an acquaintance with me, and obtruded herself upon me at all hours, at breakfast, dinner, and in my bedroom before I was up of a morning. One day, before I came into the dining-room, she helped me to soup. I found her with her bonnet on, and, before I had time to eat the soup, she pretended she had a sudden summons to London and was off. I had scarcely eaten the soup before I was seized with the most agonising pains and violent retchings. My doctor gave me antidotes and said some attempt had been made to poison me, but the dose had not been sufficient. He is still alive, if ailing, so enquire of him if you who read this do not believe me.

Mrs. P. had scarcely gone when I got letters from London, imploring me to be on my guard, and stating that there was a woman sent from Brighton to Llangollen, who had a carriage always ready on the road in order, if I could be found out walking, to kidnap me and carry me off to a madhouse, as Sir Edward (as these most honourable friends insisted on calling the sodomite baronet) was giving out all over London that I was quite mad. The very idea! How could I possibly imagine that Sir Despicable Beyond What You Could Even Believe would ever wish to do something so cruel to me?

A defeated army retreats and then returns with a new strategy. So was it with Sir Coward and his campaigns, though he had not one small iota of the courage and foresight of the Duke of Wellington. If Sir Bullfrog Littlewit had spent but a fraction of the money he spent over the years on spies, agents and lawyers, on paying me a decent allowance, then we might still have come to some sort of accommodation even at this point. But he, who spent thousands on himself and his mistresses, would grudge me everything, even offering a trumpery hundred pounds a year for letters which would have destroyed him and everything about him.

And then it is I who am supposed to be mad?

I must return to my story. In the summer of 1854 (I believe, though those years of poverty and persecution are left a blur in my battered brain) I finally left the hotel and went into lodgings in a small but nicely furnished house, of which I took the whole except the parlours, which, as the woman only asked twenty-five shillings a week for them, I told her on no account to let to anyone, but if she had an offer to do so, I would pay her for them rather than have any other lodger in the house after all I had suffered. But when I had been there about three weeks, she informed me that she had let her parlours to a lady and gentleman, who had given her two guineas a week for them. I have since learned upon indisputable authority that this couple were always with Sir Liar at Knebworth and Ventnor and elsewhere. Let others be surprised, I was not.

A few evenings after, the evening being sultry, I was obliged to leave my drawing-room door slightly ajar. To my horror, who should come tripping in, with a basket of strawberries, but Mrs. B. (the name was false so why bother to write it?), dressed, or rather undressed, to a pitch that would have alarmed even an art-student! She made me a theatrical speech, in which she introduced herself and her strawberries. I never eat strawberries, I informed her, with enough ice in my voice, I fancy, to preserve any number of strawberries through the hottest week of the year. Nothing daunted, this woman spread her furbelows, and, uninvited, seated herself. Then, seeing her husband creeping up the stairs, she had the crowning impertinence to call him in and introduce him to me, I visibly petrifying the while, and darting into my bedroom, locked the door.

The next day, Our Lady of the Furbelows sent me a note expressing her great sympathy with all I had suffered, and as the cuisine was not particularly good at our lodgings, would I do them the favour of dining with them at the hotel? I sent down a verbal message to say I never dined out. The next day the pair took their departure for London, but the people of the house became suddenly and unbearably insolent, and, although I had taken the rooms for six months certain, said I must leave there immediately as they had let them. Am I insane if I record my belief that Sir Liar's friends, having failed me to poison me in reality, spread verbal poison about my circumstances and reputation which, backed by a substantial quantity of guineas, was believed by the venal establishment with which I had become involved?

I could no longer stay in a place where I had been so outraged and persecuted. This was pleasant because it wanted six weeks to the time I should receive my parish allowance (oh yes, I was still reduced to that), and also to the time when the two months' rent of my cottage was due so I had not a *sou* to hand. It was then that I wrote in distress to a friend, who engaged me rooms in an hotel in Taunton, kept by a Mrs. Clarke. All the wretches at my lodging in Llangollen thought I had gone to London, as I had all my luggage forwarded to a friend in Hyde Park Terrace.

For a time, Sir Vicious and his bloodhounds lost track of me. Or perhaps Sir Self-Important was too busy engendering children on his various mistresses, sodomising Benjamin Disraeli and making interminable sanctimonious speeches in Parliament about any issue that did not involve him looking at his own conduct, to spend every moment of every day tormenting me.

You see? I acknowledge the reality, but that does not mean the persecution was not real. And, recall, he had everything, including my darling children (his only good decision to give Mary Greene her marching orders) and I, for all my efforts, had nothing. Even my writing was rejected by all but the hardiest publishers, who dared to take on the wrath of the Press Gang.

In the end, however, I knew, he would find me. Now Sir Credulous is a man who believes in the supernatural world (and, for all I know, that fairies live in Knebworth Park) and, I have it on good authority, he even consulted so-called spiritual mediums to locate my whereabouts. Perhaps he hoped (certainly wished) to learn that I was already in the other world. And yet still I am supposed to be the mad one, forsooth!

Whether because of supernatural aid or not (most probably not), after I had been a year or more at the Castle Hotel in Taunton, a creature calling herself Miss Henna (I think of her as Miss Hemlock) wrote to request an interview with me. I ignored her request but then she arrived one evening in the pouring rain. She refused to say what her business was and insisted that it was very urgent that she saw me personally.

My good landlady, Mrs. Clarke, told her, without mincing the matter, that she firmly believed her to be one of Sir Edward's spies. She might, therefore, go back and tell him that, after being hunted to death by his infamous emissaries, I saw *no one* not especially recommended to me, but no doubt he would be delighted to hear that I had not been so well for years, and was going abroad in a day or two.

Miss Henna then, by way of establishing her respectability, said she was a governess.

'Oh! most likely,' said Mrs. Clarke, 'I understand most of that vile man's mistresses are, and they afterwards fill the equally honourable office of his spies. Pray, where are you staying in Taunton?'

Miss Henna got very red, stammered very much, and named some doctor living near Trinity Church (two miles from this). 'Indeed!' said Mrs. Clarke, 'but it happens rather unfortunately that there is *no* doctor of law, physic or divinity of *that* name in Taunton, so the sooner you return to your employer the better.' Mrs. Clarke sent a policeman to watch her, and she decamped by the next London train.

I was fortunate that the good Mrs. Clarke, unlike my perfidious landlady in Llangollen, was devoted to my cause, for she had to cope with any number of prying callers and unsolicited offerings from so-called admirers. Everything from apples to plum puddings was left at the house in the hope I might be tempted to take a bite.

Meanwhile, my financial circumstances became ever more desperate and my publishers were either frightened off or forced into bankruptcy because of the abuse I received from *My Grandmother's Gazette*, *The Literary Liar*, *The Assinaeum* and the *No Quarterly*, or whatever that leaden publication is called, all eager to turn black into white and right into wrong at the behest of the Guilt of Literature, that organisation posing as a support for needy authors, except when those needy authors know the truth about its founders.

Soon I owed my dear kind landlady a third quarter of £75 and had no hope of paying her. I had vowed that no earthly power would induce me to borrow another sixpence from any human being, even her, seeing that I had no certainty, or even chance, of being able to repay it.

Sir Liar meanwhile continued to thrive. Prince Albert was visibly failing and I have no doubt he intended to replace him in the lascivious Victoria's bed, though in that he was disappointed by that hulking ghillie, John Brown. His unreadable novels continued to be published to great acclaim from his mutual back-scratching coterie of talentless sycophants, who poured their praise indiscriminately on themselves and on that revoltingly blasphemous book by one of the Brontë harpies, entitled *Wuthering Heights*. Oh, and now he was back as a dyed in the wool Tory, because that was the way the wind was blowing, and there were rumours that he would become Secretary of State for the Colonies. Poor British Empire to be placed in the clutches of a man both avaricious and incompetent! And still never a penny of the money he squandered on his own debauched life ever made its way to me. Indeed, the odious Loaden did everything he could to delay the money I was owed or reduce the amount for some specious reason, requiring expensive lawsuits to challenge it.

I was close to despair. God's hand was so heavy upon me that I could no longer kick against the pricks. Oh, the bitter, bitter curse of being penniless!

In my despair, I poured out my grievances in a pamphlet, entitled *Lady Bulwer Lytton's Appeal to the Justice and Charity of the English Public*. It was printed and published in 1857 by Mr. Isaac Ironside at the Free Press Office, Fargate, Sheffield, because no one nearer London would handle it for fear of reprisals from Sir Allpuff. It was a private pamphlet, so it bypassed the world of booksellers and reviewers he also controlled. I intended it simply as a record of my wrongs, to ease my soul, and to explain my case to those I had begun to fear I had wearied by repeating the details in letters and conversation. The truth was there for all to see. I had been reduced to begging for public charity while Sir Allpuff threw his money to the winds, more accurately his mistresses and he-whores.

From Lady Bulwer Lytton's Appeal to the Justice and Charity of the English Public, 1857

Lady Bulwer Lytton wishes it to be clearly understood that this is a painful and crying appeal to public CHARITY and not to public sympathy; for she is well aware that in a state of society where every vice is not only chartered, but adulated, in men, there is no sympathy for a woman who, passing the conventional Rubicon, presumes to complain, let her outrages be what they may, more especially if she has not made herself friends of the mammon of unrighteousness among men.

From the Memoirs of Rosina, Lady Lytton

Then something remarkable happened. I gave away a few copies to sympathetic friends and advertised its existence in a couple of journals which still remained outside Sir Allpuff's power, indeed heartily hated him. The pamphlet started to sell and on each copy I was soon making a modest profit, but at least a profit mostly mine, once I had paid Mr. Ironside his initial fee, and not subject to the vagaries and prevarications of publishers. And then more requests for copies came. And more. I realised how many people out there in the world hated and despised Sir Liar and all his works and rejoiced in reading the truth about his perfidy. Suddenly, there was a publisher bold enough to publish *The World and His Wife*.

I then conceived the notion of going beyond modest advertisements in small publications, both to earn myself some much needed money and to present my case to a public I believed to be honest and unprejudiced when told the truth.

And then something else happened. Parliament had been in turmoil, Tweedledum followed Tweedledee and vice versa.

The end was that Lord Derby (another sodomite) invited (such a cosy word for such a corrupt arrangement) Sir Liar to join his new formed Ministry as the aforesaid Secretary of State for the Colonies. The acceptance of this office necessitated an election at Hertford. The seat was not contested and the nomination was fixed for June 8th.

Not contested by another politician I mean.

Epilogue: July 1858 and Beyond

From the Somerset County Gazette and West of England Advertiser, July 13ᵗʰ, 1858

One of her chief complaints against her husband was the smallness of the means he allowed her for her support; and certainly if, as is stated, his own income is £10,000, it is a very reasonable one, for the allowance of £8 a year to his wife by a man whose income is £200 would be just in the same proportion; and there are few who would not decry and condemn the injustice which such a payment by a person having £200 would exhibit. Lady Lytton has been severely censured for the bitterness displayed in some of her writings, but perhaps not altogether with justice. Let those who condemn the use of harsh language just learn under what circumstances it has been used; and if they find the author's life has been one of excessive trial and suffering – that she has either been compelled to quit, or has felt it imperatively necessary to flee from, the house of her husband – that from a position of pecuniary ease she has been cast down to a condition of humiliating poverty – that instead of her society being courted by numerous 'friends', she is shunned by most of them as no longer worthy of their regard – that while her husband still moves among the gayest and noblest of society, she remains the occupant of two small rooms in a country hotel – if they make in her cause the allowance which such an accumulation of woes and miseries ought to ensure, they will not fail to be very sparing of censure.

From an Unpublished Autobiography by Lord Lytton

My wife's release from the asylum was, without doubt, the most humiliating episode of my entire life. Dickens, of course, proved correct, and, friend though he was, I could still discern a quiet smirk of satisfaction on his face when I had to capitulate. The provincial papers and the *Daily Telegraph* made much of her 'liberation' and I can only be thankful that *The Times* and other more distinguished publications, which were not in the hands of my enemies, displayed more discretion.

Dubbed by the gutter press 'the Tigress of Taunton', Rosina's intention was now to charge me with unlawful imprisonment. With public opinion prepossessed in her favour, she planned to unfold before a jury the long story of her 'wrongs', to force my unfortunate self to appear and answer her upon all the incidents of my private life and obtain the widest publicity for all her outrageous accusations against me.

It is, no doubt, obvious that this was exactly the course I most desired to avoid. Had she not blighted my life enough with her appearance at the hustings? Fortunately, my son, Robert, at this point displayed a maturity and decisiveness that he had singularly failed to display before, although he was now a hulking twenty-year-old, educated at vast expense and rising in the diplomatic corps (I have dissuaded him from literature, for which he had little talent). He had witnessed the scene at the Hertford election, which was the first occasion he had seen his mother since childhood, although he too had been the object of her persecution, receiving in his various diplomatic posts letters addressed to 'that white-livered little reptile, Robert Lytton.'

Despite this, as his mother's release became inevitable, he heroically offered to take her abroad and try to bring her to a calmer frame of mind. The suggestion was universally well received. Even Rosina agreed a journey abroad with her son would probably have very beneficial results on her state of health. In addition, I agreed to settle her not inconsiderable debts and increase her allowance to £500 a year. In this way, a public scandal, injurious not just to me but to the Government in which I served as the Colonial Secretary, was avoided.

But I must be honest and say that this outcome could only be regarded as satisfactory from a purely pragmatic point of view. My wife had pursued me unrelentingly with accusations, which perhaps contained one grain of truth for every pound of lies. She had made life intolerable, not only for me but for my son and those I was close to. She had killed my mother with the vicious falsehoods incorporated in her fictions (rarely has the word been more accurately employed). To select only the most outrageous libels, I was accused of sodomy with Benjamin Disraeli and adultery with Queen Victoria. Rosina could not even decide which way in her imaginations my sexual propensities lay. How was I supposed to put an end to this stream of abuse, let alone support the woman who generated it?

At the time of her release, I was enjoined to stay silent and dignified by all who knew and respected me and it was excellent advice. But, if I look back on these events now, I can only conclude that my initial perception was right. All the evidence suggests that Rosina was insane. Still is insane, for all I know or care. According to her, I was persecuting her at every turn, from Paris to

Llangollen, with unexpected callers, who were spies in disguise, carrying back messages to me about her adulteries (real or imagined, at this point I do not care – nor did I then) or wishing to break into her residence to discover incriminating documents. Most absurd of all, she believed (or so I have been informed) that I sent elderly women to obscure locations in Wales to poison her soup. If all this is not a definition of insanity, then what is? I continue to believe, reluctantly, that her consignment to an asylum was the kindest decision that I (or the world) could have made, particularly one as humane and well-run as Mr. Hill's establishment.

Where I failed, and where I blame myself, was that I was persuaded by my advisers, legal and medical, to proceed in a high-handed and peremptory manner, whose cruelty I acknowledge. The proper procedures should have been set in place and Rosina's fragile state of mind should have been treated more sympathetically. I should have remembered that I once loved her.

I would like now to write that my life after these events returned to normal, except that I do not believe that my life could ever be described as normal. The gypsy prophecy continued to haunt me, for women were my best friends and my worst enemies, although none of the hostile women ever came within a fraction of a mile of Rosina.

If you wish to learn of my political career, then it is a matter of public record. My time in office was limited and that I cannot regret, because it was time taken away from those things that really matter. Do not misunderstand me, I am proud of what I achieved and the beneficial effect on what I set in motion upon the inhabitants of Australia and Canada, let alone my work in the Greek Islands, where my classical soul met the current reality, survived the shock and set in motion measures to aid the hapless descendants of a great culture. Oh, that I could have been made King of Greece and what I could have achieved! But that is folly. In the long term, my political achievements, in my view, dwindle to nothing.

Of my literary record, I feel more sanguine. After the events I have described in this memoir (entrusted to my son for safe keeping), I continued to labour in the field of both fiction and verse. Nothing has ever changed with the reception of my novels, vilified by venal critics and then imitated by those who escaped uncensored and earned the praise which was rightly my due. In the last work of which I am truly proud, *The Coming Race*, I dared to imagine a world very different from our own, not just like Sir Thomas More's *Utopia*, defined by opposites, but a fully imagined other world with laws of its own.

A young engineer finds his way into a subterranean world occupied by beings who seem to resemble angels. They are called the Vril-ya and they possess the ability, simply through thought, to transmit information, banish pain and put their fellow beings to sleep. The Vril-ya are descendants of an antediluvian civilisation, originally surface dwellers, who fled underground thousands of years previously to escape a massive flood. Chief among the tools of their society is an all-permeating fluid called 'Vril', a latent source of energy that gives them access to an extraordinary force that could be controlled at will to heal, change, and destroy beings and things. In this society, the women are stronger and larger than the men and are always the initiating partners in romantic relationships.

I could continue. It may well be that my vision of an alternative world will inspire others to create alternative worlds, ruled by different rules. But my novel was debased almost as soon as it was written. A vulgarian based in Staffordshire called John Lawson Johnston created a disgusting thick, salty meat extract and decided in honour (so he claimed) of my novel to call it Bovril.

An imagination of other worlds reduced to beef extract. That might, in some way, describe in a nutshell how what I have achieved has been abused. I remain, however, proud and unapologetic about my life's work, although I continue to believe that the world in which we live is but a transitory shadow of worlds beyond. The conventional Christian vision of Paradise (even when it is described by the immortal Dante) means little to me, but my dreams tell me there is something beyond. I am reluctant to describe what I have experienced for fear of the ridicule that has so often been directed at my more personal (and profounder) revelations. But we are tantalisingly close all the time to reaching out towards a spirit world, filled with a calm and a mystery we cannot begin to understand. My mother is there. Emily is there. And in the future, in a timeless world of shadows, we will all be reunited, not in body but in spirit. The otherworldly talk to me, not only in my dreams, but in my books and in my poetry. I cannot wait to be joined to that afterlife, which I only dimly perceive now.

Only one thought troubles me. Will Rosina be there?

No, I must be honest, there is another. If I am remembered after I have slipped away into the other world, will I be remembered more for my quarrels with her than for all the other things, literary, political and personal I have achieved?

From the Somerset County Gazette and West of England Advertiser, July 13th, 1858

Persons who are in a state of madness give indications of their misfortunes at home and abroad. But Lady Lytton, during the three years she was at Taunton, never did aught that we are aware of (and we have taken pains to ascertain the truth) to cause in any one with whom she had communication the slightest suspicion that in her case reason had been dethroned, or that her brain was in any degree affected with lunacy.

From the Memoirs of Rosina, Lady Lytton

I left Mr. Hill's stronghold on Saturday, June 17th, 1858, at 3 p.m. Mr. Hill's little daughter, Mary, cried so violently that I was really grieved to leave her and felt quite selfish in going to be happy. Upon this memorable day, assisted by my good friend, Miss Ryves, who was to accompany us, I had to drive all over London, in quest of ready-made things, and then to go to Farrance's Hotel, and after from Belgrave Square to London Bridge railway station, so that I was really quite worn out when, at eleven at night, I found myself in bed at the Lord Warden Hotel, Dover.

But all my tiredness fell away the next morning at breakfast for there was my dear boy waiting to greet me. He had become so handsome and so grown-up that I burst into tears at the sight of him and could not stop myself from hugging him deeply.

'Dear Mama,' he murmured and I fancy there were tears in his eyes too. 'I am so sorry for what has happened. Perhaps from this day, it will be possible for us all to be happy, or at least at peace.'

I stood back so that I could look into his manly face, all whiskered and bearded, and, yes, he was holding back tears, there could be no doubt. I stroked his cheek. 'My poor, poor boy, how you must have suffered! I pray to God that it may be possible for us to begin anew.'

'Amen to that,' he said in almost a whisper. 'But, I beg you, Mama, let there be no recriminations of any sort. Let us begin a new chapter with a blank page.'

I wholeheartedly agreed, because, as I explained to him, although I had sometimes written things to him, which I knew now to have been hurtful, they came from my deep love and my frustration that I had been forbidden to see him. He nodded in acknowledgement and we sat down to breakfast, although I could barely eat for happiness.

On Monday, the 19th, we crossed to Calais, from whence the party (Robert, Miss Ryves and myself with the servants) proceeded to Paris, and thence to Bordeaux, where we stayed about a month. I was filled with delight to have left the confines of my prison, and indeed the bigger prison that England had sometimes seemed to me, but what truly made the time heavenly was being with my son. We talked and talked about all that had happened, we remembered dear Emily and the not so dear Miss Greene, and I fancy I even managed to say some pleasant things about Robert's father, just to spare his own dear feelings.

Our plans to go on to St. Sebastian and Madrid, however, had to be changed, because poor, dear Robert, my dear Prince Charming, became so ill that his doctor peremptorily forbade his encountering the discomforts of Spanish travelling, and ordered him to the baths of Luchon, in the south of France. I was willing to do anything for my generous boy and so I eagerly agreed to this change of plan.

And, indeed, thank God, Robert's health soon improved. He got up at six, took his bath at half-past, drank the waters, returned to bed and breakfasted at ten. About two, I beat him up a couple of new-laid eggs, with some sherry and hot water. He then walked, rode or drove out with us, and most lovely the rides and drives were. We dined at seven, and to bed at ten, a regimen that agreed with him admirably and soon soothed his anxieties away. It helped that we were in one of the most charming and original nooks I have ever seen, set at the foot of the vine-clad and purple Pyrenees. Luchon itself consisted of a long avenue, about a mile and a half long, of gigantic and umbrageous lime trees, with rows of gay-looking booths of toys, clothes, fruit, confectionery and jewellery, decorated with bright flags and garlands of flowers, which gave it the air of a perpetual fair. At the end of this lime avenue, near our hotel, was an amphitheatre of white Doric columns – this was the Baths. The picturesquely dressed Spanish pedlars, the bells of the muleteers, the constant and really musical cracking of the whips of the mountain guides, the bands playing music, the gaily attired ladies promenading around from morning till night, dressed the place with an eternal holiday look. The fruit – figs, peaches, melons, mountain or wood strawberries, and grapes – were in profusion.

Alas, the *cuisine* was so bad that I often wished to be dining back in Taunton with the good Mrs. Clarke, but I did not really care. Why should I? I was here in Paradise with my adorable boy and he was never tired of repeating that I was now his sole object in life, and, God knows, his every act proved it.

Postscript

From Last Words of a Sensitive Second-Rate Poet by Owen Meredith, 1868

Genius does what it must, and Talent does what it can.

From a Memorandum Written by Edward Robert Lytton Bulwer-Lytton, 1st Earl of Lytton, Knight of the Grand Cross of the Order of the Bath, Grand Commander of the Star of India, Knight Grand Commander of the Order of the Indian Empire, Order of the Companions of Honour

With the best of intentions, I had agreed to accompany my mother to France, following her release from the asylum in July 1858. I obtained leave from my diplomatic duties and offered myself as mediator between my parents on the understanding that there would be an immediate cessation on the part of both of the mutual recriminations which had caused all of us, myself included, public humiliation and private anguish. Chastened by what had happened, they both agreed, but, alas, they were both temperamentally incapable of keeping to that undertaking once we had arrived in France.

For his part, my father wrote to me by almost every post long and bitter recitals of the events which had darkened his life and turned his love into hatred, accompanying them with an insistence that it was my duty to obtain a complete recantation and apology from my mother. I have every reason to believe that he also employed spies to report back to him on how I behaved when seen in public with my mother.

My mother, for her part, poured into my ears daily the story of her grievances in language of the bitterest invective. It is painful to record, but I do believe that she had often been drinking to excess when she did so. She professed a deep affection for me, lamenting all the years we had been apart, and I attempted to believe these assurances of her love, although when she referred repeatedly to the events surrounding the death of my dear sister, Emily, her attitude seemed more that of a vengeful Fury than a grieving mother.

I stood these daily assaults for as long as I could, but in the end I became ill. We moved to a more rural and recuperative environment in the spa town of Luchon where I endeavoured to build up my strength again, in order to cope with my father's missives and my mother's tirades, all the more painful because I was hardly ever out of her company and her travelling companion, Miss Ryves, simply echoed sycophantically everything she claimed. I started to become ill again and my mother's expressions of devotion became still more effusive, writing me little notes after parting at night or to greet me in the morning. What she could not do was abandon her tireless attacks upon the character of my father, which included allegations of the wildest and most incredible kind. My illness increased and I endeavoured to distance myself from her outpourings in order to build my return to health.

The result was, one morning, a violent change in her feelings towards me, the blandishments being suddenly replaced by the wild tones of accusation and hostility I remembered from those much-dreaded missives with my name scrawled across them which I used to be handed at my London Club. The weathercock of her passions veered completely round. I experienced such a torrent of abuse that I was obliged to leave the house in Luchon and take posthorses to Toulouse. Eventually, I made my way to Paris, where my mother subsequently followed me. I made one last attempt to beseech her, for her own good as well as mine, to cease these terrible attacks, which were destroying my physical and mental health, but she was incapable of doing so. There was one last unhappy interview and then we parted, never to meet again. I returned to The Hague to resume my official diplomatic duties and she, I imagine, returned to Taunton to resume the story of her blighted life.

I had done all I could, but there was little thanks from my father, who showed no appreciation of my sacrifice, only blamed me for not having obtained the *mea culpa* from my mother, that he regarded as his due. I have to record that, in my early life, my relations with my father were not of the happiest. He had starved me of money at my public school where I was mocked as 'poor Lytton' and he lectured me constantly upon following a code of sexual morality he had notably failed to observe himself. He crushed my hopes of a literary career with a scathing cynicism, although in later life I was able to obtain some small fame with the poetry I wrote under the pseudonym of 'Owen Meredith'. His decision was that I should become a diplomat and I still cannot entirely let go of the thought that he wanted me to be a diplomat so that I could solve the knotty problems of my parents' marriage, a problem I to this day think far more insoluble than the notoriously complex Schleswig-Holstein question which obsesses diplomatic circles.

But frivolity sits ill in this memorandum. Compared with my father, I acknowledge, I have achieved pitifully little, but then his is a high standard to set for achievement in the worlds of literature, drama and politics. If I compare myself with ordinary mortals, perhaps it is true that I have not achieved quite so little as it sometimes seems to me in my darker moments. My intervention in my parents' marriage, however, as I have indicated, brought me no praise or approval from my father. The year after the incidents I have been describing, while still resident in The Hague, I became engaged to a very dear Dutch girl named Caroline from a highly respectable family. My father objected. He considered the family vulgar and coarse and insisted that Caroline would bring no money and very little else of value to a marriage. He described it as 'a very bad worldly match.' I should have protested but I did not. Still, I did not make a similar mistake when I met my darling Edith. I married her before my father could object, although object he did. Edith was the niece of Lord Clarendon, but, apparently, the family's politics were wrong, and, for this was my father's continuing obsession, they did not possess sufficient money. Estates, he wrote to me, need money and Knebworth consumed all he ever earned and more. Once again, I would be forced back upon my earnings as a diplomat to provide.

My father refused to see us for a year after my marriage. I believe my grandmother did something similar when my father wished to marry my mother. The difference, I am grateful to record, is that Edith and I were very happy in our union, or as happy as any couple is entitled to be. When our first child was born, my father showed little interest, a state of affairs which upset my Edith deeply. On the urgings of his wiser friends, he finally received us at Knebworth and kissed the head of our beloved Edward, named in his honour (and destined to die, alas, at the age of six), but there was still an unforgiving coldness. He could not share in the happiness of others, even his own son's.

The memorandum I am writing, however, has a better conclusion than I might have expected and that is why, perhaps, I am writing it in a more personal style.

In 1866, my father was elevated to the Peerage and finally became Edward George Earle Lytton Bulwer-Lytton, 1st Baron Lytton. This honour had been the summit of his ambition from the earliest days, and, with the attainment of it, the strenuous period of his life came to an end. Put simply, my tormented father gradually became an altogether calmer person in the seven years which remained to him. He would have attributed this to his ever growing understanding of the spiritual powers which lie just outside our consciousness, and, although I beg to differ from him, the change in his spirit as he approached death was observable to all. Edith, who had dreaded visiting him, became a devoted and loving attendant at his deathbed, and our children no longer cowered in fear at the thought of visiting Grandpapa.

He died in great pain but his soul was at peace. I felt I had lost not only a beloved parent but a generous and wise friend. That remained a great comfort to me, although his will presented me with certain problems. I was, of course, the residual legatee, but there were a series of bequests that gave me food for thought, honour bound though I was to fulfil them. They were not insubstantial sums of money (some of them for as much as £5,000), but I had honestly no conception of who Georgina and Gertrude Grant were, nor Arthur and Lucy Lowndes, to name but a selection of the beneficiaries. My father was a very secretive man in many ways and I believe the habit of concealing his extra-marital relationships from my fiercely jealous and, in this case, not unreasonable mother lasted till the end. I have made no attempt to contact personally these people who may, in some way, be related to me by blood.

There was, of course, nothing for my mother. On my own initiative, when I came into the estate, I increased her annual allowance from £500 to £700. It seemed the least I could do, and, if I am honest, the most I wanted to do. I could never forgive her vicious campaign to prove that my father was having an affair with Benjamin Disraeli nor her endless improvidence. If my mother had been granted £40,000 a year, she would have spent it all on annoying others. But still, she was my mother and I could not willingly leave her in need.

From the Diaries of Rosina, Lady Lytton

This has been a memorable day. When I was taking the dogs for a walk, Cheveley (a recent acquisition) tackled a fox and got bitten severely in the ear for his pains. Then, when had I returned home and dressed his wound, I saw in the papers that Sir Liar was dead. Ridiculous tributes to his great gifts and noble soul followed predictably after. I have no doubt that he will be buried in Westminster Abbey among talents (and souls) infinitely greater than his.

But here is something strange. I have always imagined that when I knew for certain that Sir Liar was dead, my heart would feel a great surge of joy. But, oddly, it did not.

***

(Lady Lytton died in 1882, aged eighty. She was living in a modest cottage in Upper Sydenham, surrounded by a motley collection of dogs, creatures she had always preferred to human beings. Unfortunately, her son's diplomatic commitments prevented him from attending the funeral.)

173

Thanks

My warm thanks to my good friends, Gerald Baker, Tim Binding, Peter Bonsall, Christie Dickason and Jenny Sprince, all of whom read various versions of the manuscript and made suggestions which were both helpful and encouraging.

Thanks also to my agent, Valerie Hoskins, who gave advice and support beyond the call of duty.

And finally, thank you to Mark Heines, who got me through.

Sources

The Life of Rosina, Lady Lytton by Louisa Devey (London 1887)

The Letters of the Late Edward Bulwer, Lord Lytton, to His Wife. Edited by Louisa Devey (London 1884)

Unpublished Letters of Lady Bulwer Lytton to A.E. Challon, R.A. Edited by S.M. Ellis (London 1914)

The Life of Edward, First Lord Lytton, by his Grandson, The Earl of Lytton. (Two volumes. London 1913)

Other Works Consulted

A Blighted Life by Rosina Bulwer Lytton (London 1880)

Bulwer Lytton, The Rise and Fall of a Victorian Man of Letters by Leslie Mitchell (London 2003)

The Collected Letters of Rosina Bulwer Lytton. Edited by Marie Mulvey-Roberts with the assistance of Steve Carpenter (Three Volumes, London 2008)

Bulwer and his Wife, A Panorama 1803-1836 by Michael Sadleir (London 1933)

Appeal of One Half of the Human Race, Women, Against the Pretensions of the Other Half, Men... by Anna Wheeler and William Thompson (London 1825. Facsimile edition 1994)

Lady Caroline Lamb by Paul Douglass (London 2004)

The Victorian Novel Before Victoria by Elliot Engel and Margaret F. King (London 1984)

The Dandy by Ellen Moers (London 1960)

Fanny Trollope by Pamela Neville-Sington (London 1997)

You may also enjoy...

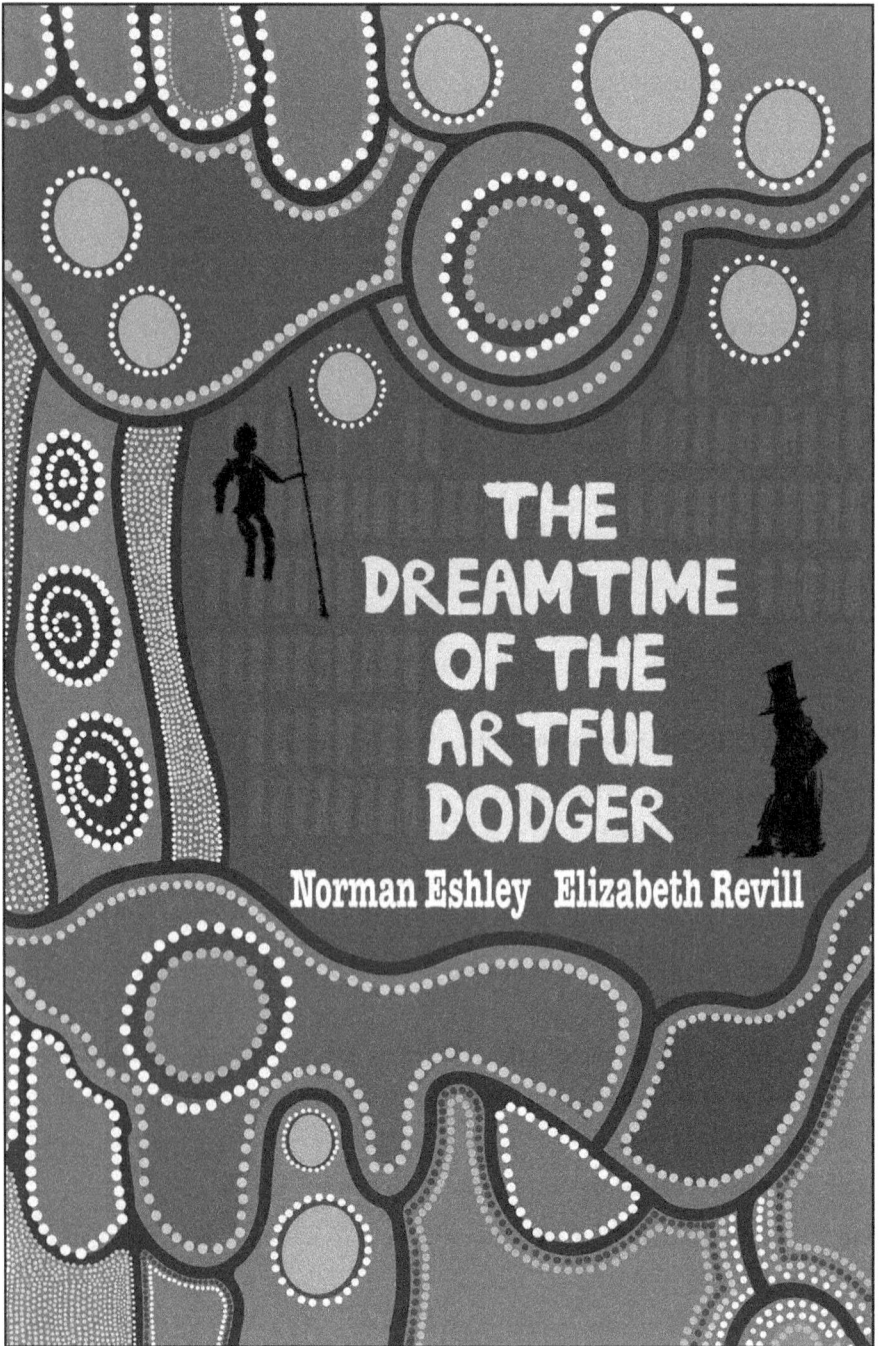

THE DREAMTIME OF THE ARTFUL DODGER

Norman Eshley   Elizabeth Revill

www.ingramcontent.com/pod-product-compliance
Lightning Source LLC
LaVergne TN
LVHW011327080426
835513LV00006B/225